Writing Society through Media

Writing Society through Media

Ethnography of a Hindi Daily

Per Ståhlberg

RAWAT PUBLICATIONS
Jaipur • New Delhi • Bangalore • Hyderabad • Guwahati

ISBN 978-81-316-0472-4

Published by
Prem Rawat for **Rawat Publications**
Satyam Apts, Sector 3, Jawahar Nagar, Jaipur 302 004 (India)
Phone: 0141 265 1748 / 7006 Fax: 0141 265 1748
E-mail: info@rawatbooks.com
Website: www.rawatbooks.com

New Delhi Office
4858/24, Ansari Road, Daryaganj, New Delhi 110 002
Phone: 011 2326 3290

Also at *Bangalore, Hyderabad* and *Guwahati*

Typeset by Rawat Computers, Jaipur
Printed at Chaman Enterprises, New Delhi

Contents

Acknowledgements

The principal characters of this study are all journalists. Without their cooperation this book would not have been possible to write. I am deeply indebted to all those who took me along on their assignments—despite the distraction the company of a foreigner implied in encounters with news sources. I want to give particularly warm thanks to the reporters, sub-editors and other staff of *Dainik Jagran* in Lucknow, who put up with me on a daily basis for a long time—not least to the resident editor Vinod Shukla who allowed me to come and go as I liked in his office. Some journalists were especially generous in sharing both their professional and private time with me: Diviya Prakash Shukla, Sadguru Sharan and Anil Yadav to whom I regard as friends, rather than as 'informants' of my fieldwork.

Outside the community of journalists, there were other people in Lucknow who assisted me in various ways as well as making my stay in the city a very pleasant one. Two of them are booksellers, even though their professional title covers only a small portion of the mission they have taken on. For scholars and intellectuals familiar with Lucknow, the name Ram Advani will come as no surprise. His bookshop in Hazrat Ganj is a truly cosmopolitan meeting place and I am honoured to be among those who have enjoyed his stimulating company. The second bookseller is also the centre of a 'social institution'. I spent many hours with Durga Mishra of *Chetna Kitabghar*, usually together with a number of journalists who had made this bookshop a favourite location to relax in-between assignments. 'Durgadada' is one of the best-informed people about the community of journalists in Lucknow and much of his knowledge he shared with me.

There are also a few people in India but outside Lucknow who have helped and encouraged me at different stages during the work on this project. My friendship with Lalit Kumar Sharma goes back to the time before I started doing my research. He was my first Hindi teacher in 1989 in Mussoorie, I continued to study with him in Shimla in 1995 and during all the stages of my research he made great efforts to assist me with translations from Hindi. I am also grateful to J.S. Yadava, Director, Indian Institute of Mass Communication, New Delhi for allowing me to be affiliated with his prestigious institution, while I was carrying out fieldwork. On frequent visits to New Delhi, the home of Sukhadeo, Vimal and Amit Thorat has always been a welcoming place to return to, and their support has been stimulating.

The Department of Social Anthropology at Stockholm University has been my academic base throughout the work on this study and several friends and colleagues have supported me both with criticism and encouragement. My first supervisor was Stefan Molund (now at the Swedish International Development Cooperation Agency). He was the one who suggested that I should combine my experiences of journalism with anthropology and make a study of Indian news persons. The initial guidance that he gave me in designing this project turned out to be a sound foundation also during later phases of the research. My greatest debt in carrying out and completing this project I owe to Ulf Hannerz, my supervisor for the main part of my time as a postgraduate student. His comments throughout the research have been constructive and encouraging; I always felt that he took a keen interest in my study. Johan Lindquist and Eva-Maria Hardtmann have both read the manuscript carefully and their detailed comments have been invaluable for improving this book. I also want to thank Bengt-Erik Borgström, Peter Frick, Daniel Genberg, Urban Larssen, Christer Norström, Eva Poluha and Mona Rosendahl for reading and giving helpful suggestions at various stages of my writing. Moreover, I would like to express my appreciation to a number of persons with whom over the years I have had frequent conversations on anthropological topics, several of them sharing my interest either in media or in India: Fanny Ambjörnsson, Örjan Bartholdson, Ulf Björklund, Charles Câmara, Gudrun Dahl, Paolo Favero, Anna Gavanas, Peter Green, Anna Hasselström, Sigrun Helmfrid, Hasse Huss, Tova Höjdestrand, Shahram Khosravi, Marie Larsson, Thaïs Machado-Borges, Birgitta Percivall and Helena Wulff. I also wish to thank the administrative staff at the department, particularly Lena Holm, who has been very helpful in handling the economic side of the project.

The research was generously funded by the Swedish International Development Cooperation Agency, the Swedish Institute, the Nordic Institute of Asian Studies, Helge Ax:son-Johnsons stiftelse, Hierta-Retzius stipendiefond, Svenska Sällskapet för Antropologi och Geografi, Wallenbergsstiftelsens Jubileumsfond and the Department of Social Anthropology, Stockholm University. I am grateful to all these institutions.

I also thank my friends Andreas Berg and Joanna Nilsson who have made the cover and Margaret Cornell for editing my English.

My parents Anna-Kerstin and Lars-Eric Ståhlberg as well as my parents-in-law Gunhild and Erhard Hardtmann have been supportive in several ways, particularly in taking care of my two small daughters, born during the study period. Also, my brother Anders and his partner Karin have been helpful at critical moments.

Finally, there are three people to whom simple thanks would be far too insufficient. My wife Eva-Maria Hardtmann has been involved in every stage of this project and knows each aspect of it as well as I do. She has not only been my most supportive critic but also the best companion a man could wish for. Our two new-born daughters, Saga Li and Henny, have also provided me with the liveliness needed to complete the task. To these three females of my life I dedicate this book.

Introduction

When I planned this study in the mid-1990s, the interest in mass media from the discipline of anthropology had just taken off and it was still considered rather unusual to write a PhD thesis on journalism. Since then media studies scholars and anthropologists have grown closer and influence each other to quite some extent. The anthropology of journalism has also emerged as a rather distinct research interest, committed to investigate news as a form of cultural meaning making by studying occupational practices and professionalism among people in the news business. A scholarly engagement with journalism is of course not new but what anthropologists have contributed to media studies in recent time are detailed ethnographic insights from editorial offices and work routines in various social contexts and in different parts of the world. If journalism previously was a rather thoroughly researched occupation in large cities of Western Europe and the United States, we now also have a growing number of comparative studies of news professionals elsewhere, making us better equipped to grasp the diversities and variability in a globally distributed form of media production. I consider this book as part of this scholarship.[1]

As far as I know, this is the first ethnographic study of vernacular journalism in India, conducted in the latter half of the 1990s.[2] I would, however, not have agreed to make a new edition of the book if I didn't think that the study contributes to our understanding of mass media in today's India. My conviction is that this ethnography has something general to say about the transformation of the Indian public sphere during recent decades (Rajagopal, 2009). Furthermore, this edition is in a sense timelier than the original publication. Today, my book about the Lucknow journalists can without difficulty be related to several studies of the Indian mass media, not least to later studies of the Hindi press. I will return to this subject soon, but first I need to clarify a couple of points.

The form of the book is a rather classical anthropological monograph, centred on a particular group of people and with the aim of understanding their everyday reality; thus, this is not primarily a study of newspaper content. In this book that group of people, 'my tribe', happens to be journalists who spend most of their days in an editorial office and on their journalist beats. As a fieldworker I hung around with them during their workdays, and sometimes after work as well; collecting my material primarily by participant observation, or, by rather informal interviews and an alert interest in what they finally wrote in their newspapers. Importantly, though, all I claim to know about 'the Lucknow journalists' is flavoured through my own encounter with them. Like most contemporary anthropologist I try to make this transparent by being present myself on the following pages.

The fact that I am Swedish scholar, not native to North India, does of course denote this study in several ways. Even though I have been a rather regular visitor to North India during the last 25 years, many readers will certainly find themselves more familiar than me, about issues that this book deals with. I do have basic skills in talking and reading Hindi, sufficient to conduct fieldwork and glance through newspaper stories without an interpreter. But, a sensitive analysis of newspaper content had been difficult and was not part of this project. This book is thus concerned with journalists rather than journalism. There are, however, some advantages of not being completely at home, when doing ethnographic fieldwork. As a foreigner, I had the privilege to ask 'foolish' question, and I believe there might also be some insights from details that a native scholar would dismiss as too trivial to write about.

Research on the vernacular Indian press

At the time of my fieldwork, the Hindi-language press had been on a steady growth for almost two decades. Still, however, there was very little academic interest in this radical transformation of the Indian press. Media scholars were more attuned to developments in electronic media and its influence on the political developments in the country. For example, the serialisation of the religious epics Mahabharat and Ramayan on state television in the late 1980s, and its relation to the rise of Hindu nationalism, occupied much of the discussions around Indian mass media.

However, while I was still working with this study, Robin Jeffrey started to publish his work on the growth of "the Indian-language press". First in a series of articles in *Economic and Political Weekly* that dealt with the transformation of the Indian newspaper industry, focusing on one major Indian language at the time. A few years later Jeffrey published his book on "the Indian newspaper revolution" (Jeffrey, 2000), which filled a lacuna in our understanding of the print media in India. This scholarship became the platform from which I built my own study. It made it possible for me to relate my own local ethnography to larger questions about the transformation of the newspaper industry throughout India. I could also make my ambitions with this study more focused. What I try to capture with my ethnography is a new confidence among Lucknow's Hindi-language journalists that previously had perceived themselves in the shadow of their English-language professional peers. In line with an anthropological approach I insist on human agency and try to offer some detailed insights into what people actually do, and how they understand their profession, within a particular media organisation.

Since my book was completed, other scholars have studied similar topics and we now have a growing scholarship on vernacular Indian journalism. To my delight, my own ethnography of the Lucknow journalists has become a recurrent reference, despite that the book has been rather difficult to access until now. Thus, the academic context of this book has expanded in recent years and I should say a few words about how my study relate to later scholarship and at the same time take the chance of giving a brief overview of this literature. The most relevant works dealing with the Hindi-language press are written by Sevanti Ninan (2007), Ursula Rao (2010), Anup Kumar (2011) and Tabarez Ahmed Neyazi (2010, 2011).

Sevanti Ninan's (2007) *Headlines from the Heartland*, follows closely in the steps of Robin Jeffrey and traces the patterns of transformation of the Hindi-language press and what it implies for the society at large. She elaborates for the Hindi-speaking belt on particularly one of the features that Jeffrey has defined as constitutive of the Indian newspaper revolution at large: the localisation of news. Ninan describes how some large Hindi-language newspapers have expanded the market by multi-edition newspapers, giving local news to newly literate readers in villages and small towns; thereby also changing the character of journalism from an elite medium to a mass medium. She builds her study on historical sources, content analyses as well as on interviews with people in the news business – but not on participant observation among news people. Ninan, however, is herself an editor and columnist, and discusses the pros and cons of the growing Hindi-language press in a book that undoubtedly is among the most important contributions to the domestic debate about mass media's role in contemporary Indian society. Even though her book is rather different in style from my own ethnography, we largely agree in our views of the transformed Hindi press. In my opinion our studies complement each other rather well.

Ursula Rao's *News as Culture* (2010) has strong similarities to my own work. Her book is also an ethnographic study of news-making in Northern India. Furthermore, she has incidentally conducted some of her fieldwork among the same journalists in Lucknow that my book deals with (her fieldwork was done a few years after mine, but before I had published anything). However, Ursula Rao has, in contrast to me, done a multi-local fieldwork and visited several other places in the Hindi-speaking belt. She is therefore less focused on journalists and editorial offices in Lucknow. Her study is also broader in the sense that she does not confine her study to the Hindi-language press only and include English-language newspapers too. She compares for example the work cultures of *Times of India* with that of *Dainik Jagran*, and confirms some of the differences that I merely hint at in my study. The main merit of Rao's study is that she more explicitly than others recognises a new attitude within Indian journalism towards political leadership.

Tabarez Ahmned Neyazi's works (2010, 2011) also parallel mine, as he has similarly done a close-up study of one newspaper: *Dainik Bhaskar*. This is the second leading multi-edition Hindi newspaper, with its head office in Bhopal, Madhya Pradesh. Based on his data from both fieldwork and local newspaper stories, Neyazi shows how coverage of specific issues creates awareness and engagement among citizens and, thus, he argues that the day-to-day monitoring of local political issues has deepened the processes of democracy. At the same time, he shows how *Dainik Bhaskar* consciously tries to attract more advertisements by creating an audience for consumer products. Neyazi discusses very insightful both the market strategies and the political implications of this successful newspaper.

The latest addition to the literature on the Hindi press is Anup Kumar's book, *The Making of a Small State* (2011), about the popular social movement that eventually led to the formation of Uttarakhand as a new hill state. This is a study of recent history, which realises the immense importance of the press for political mobilisation. Not long ago, this kind of studies of Indian politics would certainly have made use of news material as sources for information, but probably not regarded journalists as main actors in the political process. Kumar's book makes it clear that the social movement for a breakaway state was not only completely dependent of the local Hindi press, but also that the newspapers embraced the movement in order to get a stronghold in the region. In a study that takes the research on the vernacular press an important step further, he convincingly demonstrates how a local society and the regional press mutually constitute each other.

The emerging scholarship on the vernacular Indian press is remarkably cumulative and consonant. All later scholars rely heavily, like me, on the work of Robin Jeffrey. There are hardly any striking disagreements concerning the reasons behind the growth of the vernacular press, its most characteristic features and the political or social consequences of a transformed newspaper industry. To some extent we all frame our studies within theories of the public sphere and cultural identity. Differences between authors are rather with regard to writing style, focus and methods of research.

Summarising the scholarship on Hindi-language press the unequivocal conclusion is that a strong tradition of Indian journalism – urban-centred, rather elitist and extremely focused on national politics – is definitely changing. Instead, two broad trends stand out: the radically increased 'localisation' and 'commodification' of news. The first implies that a lot of small issues of very local concern find their way into the press. The second trend suggests that the idea of journalism as a political mission has lost out to the market side of publishing. These changes are well documented by all scholars. No scholar of the Hindi press would, however, conclude that the implications of these two trends could be interpreted in a very simple and straightforward sense. 'Localisation' is not always synonymous with trivialisation of news; nor does it unproblematically imply an extension of the democratic potential of journalism. 'Commodification' could of course be understood as a de-politicisation of journalism, but it could also work pretty well together with a new empowerment among previously marginalised groups in society; in the world of news, politics is a commodity and if new political issue attracts readers, few newspapers would shy away.

If we take a step backwards and contemplate the vernacular press in relation to the general transformation in Indian society, the trends of localisation and commodification of news make perfect sense. In this book I claim that the development of the Hindi press was very well tuned to political change on a broad scale during the last three decades. The most obvious point is that the strong relocation of power from Delhi to regional centres that we have witnessed since the 1980s, would hardly have been possible without the emergence of regional public spheres communicating in vernacular languages. More strikingly, the vernacular newspapers have been avant-gardes in a more precise sense: The press was the first industry in India to realise the commercial usefulness of a huge population. In the 1980s, the world of Indian businesses was hypnotised by the growing urban middle class – this was the intended market for household goods and television shows. Newspapers, instead, early saw the potential of a much larger market: all those millions, newly literate with limited economic means outside the large cities. It took some time for advertisers to be convinced, but since the turn of the millennium the vernacular masses have become a prime focus among powerful market-driven media organisations and communication-technology industries. In the new media economy, the large Indian population and its social, economic and political life in a multitude of places, has become of great concern, because here is money to make. But it also means that the public sphere is encompassing a much larger part of the population (Rajagopal, 2009: 15). The vernacular press started this transformation and I hope that my book can contribute with some ethnographic insights into this complex process.

Notes

1. See particularly the volume *The Anthropology of News and Journalism: Global Perspectives*, edited by Elisabeth Bird (2009), and the special edition of the Sage journal *Ethnography,* Vol. 7(1), "Worlds of Journalism", edited by Dominic Boyer and Ulf Hannerz (2006).
2. This book is an Indian edition of a work that previously has been available only from a Swedish university publisher, published as *Lucknow Daily: How a Hindi Newspaper Constructs Society* (Ståhlberg 2002). Apart from this introduction, the title and some minor revisions, the book remains unchanged. The reason for not thoroughly rewriting is that this is an ethnographic study that builds on my impressions from an anthropological fieldwork. As such it aims to capture its subject in a particular place and time.

One

Writing Society

"That's what it's all about". Anil nodded towards the side of the room where a generous lunch was arranged on a long table. Plenty of dishes under silver covers were being kept warm on kerosene burners. We were in a large hall at the Arif Castle Hotel, a quite recently opened establishment of good standard. It was located in a tranquil area of Lucknow, close to the Shah Najaf Imambara, one of the impressive religious monuments that the Persian rulers of Lucknow had built in the nineteenth century.

Suman Motels, a Mumbai-based company in the tourist business, was hosting a press conference. Last year it had opened a country club on the Rai Bareili highway, some 30 kilometres south of Lucknow. The chairman was now visiting the city. He wanted to meet the press, and about 25 journalists from various newspapers in the town had responded to his invitation. The chairman spoke to us in English while we were treated to tea and warm cashew nuts. He talked about the undeveloped tourist potential of Uttar Pradesh and urged the reporters to write more in their papers on this subject. Otherwise, he had nothing new to report on the company and future projects—indeed, a few reporters complained about this.

The press conference was completed in just half an hour and the gathering of newsmen turned their attention to the food. Anil, however, wanted to leave immediately. We headed for the door, passing a company representative who begged us to stay and enjoy the lunch. Continuing to the hotel lobby, another man came running after us, forcing us to accept a gift wrapped up in paper (it turned out to be a flask, worth Rs 109 according to the price tag). A few other reporters who left with us were also treated the same way.

Anil's remark was apt. The sole purpose of this press conference was to soften up the journalists. Obviously, the company was eager to establish good relations with the Lucknow press, hoping that its enterprises would be favourably covered in the news. Readers of regional newspapers were evidently regarded as potential clients of a posh country club and other middle-class leisure facilities.

It was perhaps telling that Anil, along with a number of colleagues, was reluctant to accept the treat, while others readily enjoyed the goodies. For some reporters the event was somewhat unethical, while others saw it as a fringe benefit of their occupation. A few cynical reporters, as well as many critics of the contemporary regional press, might even say that this was in fact what the profession was all about.

But that was not what Anil had meant. The enticing lunch was an odd occurrence for him because he was a crime reporter and this assignment was clearly outside the experience of his usual beat. Earlier in the day we had visited local police stations in different parts of town, trying to get hold of information about how the police were planning to deal with a major political manifestation announced by a regional political party for the following day. Back on the scooter we proceeded on this mission. Riding through the heavy traffic in the central parts of the city, we could also witness how the authorities were preparing road blocks at major crossings. In the vicinity of *Vidhan Sabha* (the State Assembly) the police had dug deep holes in the road and built barricades with huge wooden poles. Lucknow was beginning to look like a town under siege. This subject would be Anil's main contribution to the next day's edition of *Dainik Jagran*.

This book is a study of cultural production in a universally well-known form: it deals with journalists and their work on daily newspapers. The geographical setting is a city in north India, and most of the newspapers referred to are printed in the Hindi language. These dailies belong to a category of mass media that is conceptualised in India as 'the vernacular press'—daily newspapers printed in Indian languages and scripts and distributed within the region where the particular language is spoken. The city of Lucknow, where this study was conducted, is the capital of Uttar Pradesh, the most populous of the states that constitute the Republic of India. Several of the most important newspapers of north India (both English- and Hindi-language) are published here in local editions, and the editorial offices also supply news from this politically vibrant regional centre to editions in other parts of the region.

In this ethnography we shall meet reporters, such as Anil, on their daily beats and follow them as they move around in the city in search of stories to print in the newspaper. We shall also consider what kind of society that is imagined through the efforts of these reporters, and what sorts of ideas are guiding their work. By focusing on an occupation that describes—but is simultaneously inscribed in—contemporary Indian society, I am attempting to discuss a professional practice in relation to processes of cultural globalisation, modernity and political imagination.

Until quite recently, newspapers in English, often more concerned with national issues and generally understood as forming an 'elite press', had a dominant position in India: in terms of circulation, technology and profitability they were usually far ahead of the vernacular press in most regions. But this has changed in a radical way. During the 1980s and 1990s newspapers in Indian languages have grown tremendously, in numbers, in local editions and in circulation (Jeffrey, 2000). They are often financially lucrative and are produced with modern equipment.

This transformation of the Indian mass media is politically and culturally significant. Today, people in India read newspapers as never before. They read them in a language that they understand well; and they may read about topics ranging from events in their own locality to world affairs. Perhaps most significantly, political issues at local and regional levels are intensively covered in the high circulation media. It is no coincidence that politics in India has to a great extent shifted its focus from New Delhi to the regional centres during the same period that the vernacular press has grown in strength (Brass, 1994). One could say that regional politics has found its own public sphere (Ståhlberg, 2002). The growth of the vernacular press has not been unanimously welcomed, however, in the debate concerning the media and democracy in India. While the English-language press in this country has often been seen as a model in the developing world (Hachten, 1993: 59–69), the newspapers printed in languages that more people are able to read have often been looked upon as problematic—politically, professionally and ethically. The Hindi-language press in particular has earned a reputation as overwhelmingly supportive of the Hindu nationalist movement in Indian politics. Regional newspapers have been accused of playing a central role in inflaming Hindu passions and instigating violence between religious communities on a number of occasions—often by inaccurate reporting and printing false rumours. In the Ayodhya dispute over the location of the Babri Masjid mosque at what is claimed to be the birthplace of the Hindu God Ram, which has haunted India since the mid-1980s, the Hindi-language press has been understood to be one of the main culprits.[1] Judging from the headlines and newsclips that are cited, these accusations are not unfounded (Engineer, 1991; Hasan, 1998: 214–15; Nandy et al., 1995: 33–37; Rajagopal, 2001: 151–211). Several of the journalists figuring in this study have reported on incidents connected with Ayodhya, which is situated some 100 kilometres from Lucknow. Few of them would deny that their work had a role to play in the events that evolved. Some even regret their involvement.

The new structure of the Indian newspaper industry and the political significance of the vernacular press form an important background to this study. It is a context that the journalists of Lucknow are well aware of; they know that they work in a sector of the mass media that has recently become commercially successful, politically important and, at the same time, has come under question. I think most of the journalists understood my presence among them with this background in mind. It did not seem strange to them that an academic should take an interest in a form of journalism that had lately become so widely read, but which had such a bad reputation in the English-language elite press and among critics of the mass media. The aim of this study, however, is neither to explain why the vernacular press has grown, nor to expose the alleged misbehaviour of its journalists. My scope is broader. I believe that if we take seriously the claim that the Hindi press has a vital role to play in the political situation of contemporary India, then these newspapers should be treated in a more profound way, rather than just as instruments of manipulation.

The overall point of departure of this study is that the vernacular newspapers, like other forms of mass media, are producing and transmitting culture and ideas. Journalists and other producers of the mass media play a crucial role in handling concepts and meanings that are associated with the transformation of society under modernity (Thompson, 1995). The mass media carry considerable weight in the construction of imaginations, identities and power relations (Dickey, 1997; Appadurai, 1996); they "provide audiences with ways of seeing and interpreting the world, ways that ultimately shape their very existence and participation within a given society" (Spitulnik, 1993: 294). In other words, representations that the media disseminate become part of a base from which people interpret the world and act. Consumers of mass media may imagine their own life and local society in relation to a wider society, other lifestyles, and places far away.

Along with this broad and quite commonly accepted constructivist approach (which, for example, guides most of British cultural studies), the aim of this study is to contribute insights of a more specific nature. First, I think, there is a point in recognising that all mass media are not equal. This is perhaps most obvious when looking at media consumption. The perception of the media is related to particular technologies; it takes different skills to read a book and to watch television. But also, the production of content varies with the form. Radio, television, video, cinema, books, newspapers or magazines are not merely different techniques of producing and disseminating meaning of the same kind: distinctions can be made between the kinds of images that are produced in different forms of mass media. (This recognition is a precondition for seeing relations between mass media forms.) Secondly, similar forms of mass media work in different contexts and have particular histories in various parts of the world, and this will also influence the production of meaning. Thirdly, highly disparate insights may be gained from studies of different parts of the mass communication process. Meanings may appear quite differently depending on whether the focus is put on the reception of mass media, on the 'text' itself or on the production process. As Abu-Lughod (1993) has concluded in her study of television in Egypt, audiences may interpret the media content very differently from the producers' intentions.

Thus, I want to make clear that this is a study of newspaper journalism, as a form of mass media, in a particular place and time. The focus is on the process of production—on the journalists and their work—and my intention is to comprehend this process in a particular historical and social context. My objective is to examine the conditions under which the Lucknow journalists are writing their news. What kind of 'social imaginaries' (Taylor, 2002) are these newspapers constructing and, in practice, how is the news produced? Not least, who are the journalists and what kinds of motivations and professional ideas guide their work?

The anthropology of media

Obviously, this study belongs to the relatively new area of media anthropology. Only recently has anthropology begun to pay attention to those technologies of communication on a large scale that without doubt "in some form or another have touched most societies, and indeed pervade the entire fabric of many" (Spitulnik, 1993: 294). While the discipline was still centred on the idea that 'culture' was the property of people localised in particular, bounded places, it was perhaps not surprising that the mass media were somewhat invisible in monographs, and less the focus of ethnographic research. As Akhil Gupta and James Ferguson remark:

> The mass media violate the notion that places are containers of integrated cultures: the words and images of mass media travel to you rather than you having to travel to them; they are commonly understood to be alienating discourse, not the expression of the consciousness and worldview of a collective 'people' seen as originating authors; and they are mediated by the market, not rooted in place, tradition, or locality. (1997: 9)

Since anthropology has begun to look at connections and influences between people and places, with the local field being studied in its relation to some larger entity, and 'culture' being allowed to travel, it should be evident that mass media practices and representations have a place in ethnographies. Certainly, there have been a number of studies focused on the mass media (for reviews of mass media anthropology see Dickey 1997; Ginsburg, 1994; Spitulnik, 1993). Research on 'indigenous media' (Ginsburg, 1991, 1993; Sullivan, 1993; Turner, 1992) has turned attention to media practice (most often the use of film and video) in the 'traditional' setting of anthropological fieldwork. A growing number of researchers are also doing media ethnography in complex, large-scale societies in various parts of the world. Most attention has been focused on the content and consumption of electronic media, such as television (Abu-Lughod, 1993; Mankekar, 1999), radio (Spitulnik, 1992, 1995), cinema (Dickey, 1993), or videos (Fuglesang, 1994). More rarely has the production side of mass media been studied (notable exceptions are Dornfeld, 1998; Hannerz, 1995, 1998b, 1998c, 2001, 2002, forthcoming; Pedelty, 1995).

Newspaper articles have been used quite often by anthropologists as supplementary information to ethnography that is not particularly concerned with the media (perhaps more often than is usually acknowledged in a discipline that celebrates the method of 'participant observation') (Malkki, 1997). Occasionally newspapers' representations of specific issues have been a subject of study (Wood, 1999). Newspaper journalism has been the focus of interest in a few studies of foreign correspondents' reporting across distances and between cultures (Hannerz, 1995, 1998b, 1998c, 2001, 2002, forthcoming; Pedelty, 1995). Largely, however, the daily press has not been among the major topics of research in the new terrain of anthropology (see, for example, Ginsburg et al., 2002; this recent collection of media anthropology does not include any contribution focused on newspapers). The present study is therefore situated somewhat on the margin of the main trends in media anthropology, both in its focus on local and regional newspapers and in its concern with mass media production.

One of the most important inspirations for the recently awakened anthropological interest in the mass media has been

Benedict Anderson's thesis of 'imagined communities' (1991). Anderson's main argument is that 'print capitalism' made possible a kind of community that had never existed before this historic invention. The technology of printing, and the creation of standardised vernacular languages, provided the means of representing a great number of individuals scattered around a huge geographical area as sharing some essential identity, as being part of an 'imagined community', in other words, a nation. Anderson illustrates the argument with the literary technique of the nineteenth-century 'nationalist' novel in which a social landscape of apparently arbitrary places, peoples and events was painted together presenting a united community. 'Simultaneity' was the device used to connect events which were far apart in a common frame. By the use of the word 'meanwhile' the novel could relate incidents that had nothing in common and individuals that were not aware of each other's existence. Only the omniscient reader was aware of their simultaneous activities.

Anderson's book has become a standard reference work in anthropology, not only in studies concerned specifically with national identities but also in explorations of modernity in general. For anthropologists it has offered a way of combining a traditional disciplinary interest in collective identity formation with an awareness of the complexity of contemporary society. 'Imagined communities' seemed to be a suitable concept for exploring identities that are not formed primarily in the face-to-face encounters of a locality. Much of the new interest in media anthropology is deeply inspired by Anderson in its concern with 'imaginations' of the national order, of national identities and national public cultures—and consequently it focuses on media of primarily national dissemination.

There is, however, a risk in following Anderson's model too closely. When looking at newspapers, particularly of a local or regional kind, his thesis has a number of limitations. Anderson considered the daily newspaper to be an "extreme form of the book" (ibid.: 39), sold on a colossal scale and every day connecting disparate events and places. He did not pay attention to obvious differences between the novel and the newspaper in its significance for thinking about imagined communities. First, the newspaper does not construct one single community; the 'arbitrary' mix of events refers to several categories of 'us' and 'them'. By the simultaneity of publication, a newspaper links disparate stories in time but not necessarily by imagining them as taking place within one community. Second, newspaper stories are not only joined together by the date at the top of the paper (as Anderson argued) but also by being placed into explicit categories of news: 'local', 'national', 'foreign', 'economy', 'politics', 'culture' and so on. The newspaper constructs imaginaries of several different orders and types: of localities, communities, identities, institutions and lifestyles. Third, the newspaper usually describes society in a different frame of organisation from that of the (nationalist) novel (or, for that matter, television serials). Everyday social life, continually evolving, is rarely a subject for newspaper journalism, as is often the case (in a fictional form) in a novel or a soap opera. The newspaper is primarily occupied with the formally organised aspects of society: the state and its administrative functions on various levels, the political process, the market, and institutionalised social activities such as sport and cultural events. Occurrences in less organised social forms—of 'everyday life'—do not usually become news until they depart from the normal: as accidents or crime, for example (that is, when they are dealt with by organised society). Using Hannerz's (1992: 46–52) analytical distinction between four frameworks of cultural processes, one could say that newspapers are primarily devoted to meanings carried in the *state*, *market* and *movement* frameworks. The fourth framework, *form of life*—which involves everyday activities in workplaces, homes and neighbourhoods—becomes news only when it enters into a relation with some of the other forms, for example as commoditised by the market or patronised by the state.[2]

In many senses, the relation between readers of a particular newspaper does not arise from imaginations produced in the media: the social lives of the readers are to a great extent structured by the same institutions and functions, of bureaucracies of the state and the market, in particular. And, this is also the aspect of society that newspapers are much concerned with, more perhaps than other kinds of mass media.

It does not mean that journalism is a 'mirror' of society, that there is nothing constructed in the newspapers. There is an important analogy between Anderson's imagined communities and what is imagined in newspapers. No individual has personal experience and knowledge of more than a fraction of all those institutions and functions of modern society that he or she is so enclosed in and dependent on. Most 'knowledge' of society is composed of mediated images. Through the newspaper you 'learn to know' society, what it consists of, how it works (and does not work), where power is located and what it means for your own social existence. Paraphrasing Anderson, newspapers are producing 'imagined societies' to which readers can relate themselves.

Imagined society

My reformulation of Anderson's thesis comes from experiences gained through studying the mass media, with a focus on the production process. The daily practice of newspaper production influenced my view of the images that were produced. The words that filled the pages of the newspaper were not constructed out of unrelated and arbitrary bits and pieces of reality. The primary agenda of the journalists was not to deal with ambiguous issues of identity or community; they were grappling with society in very concrete ways. I spent most of my time with beat journalists in Lucknow in quite similar looking environments: our days were filled with encounters with officials behind desks in police stations, hospitals, political party headquarters, educational institutions and government department of all kinds. It became obvious that these journalists were occupied above all with formally organised society. These contextually located practices should be part of our theorisation of mass media representations in a more thorough way than most anthropology of the mass media usually acknowledges. Dornfeld has similarly argued for more attention to production in our general understanding of the mass media's role in society:

> We need to rethink producers as particular types of agents, producing media texts within contexts constrained by both culture,

> ideology, and economy, but operating within particular social locations and frameworks, not floating above society, as many approaches to the study of media forms seem to imply. This kind of reorientation would allow us to discuss with greater specificity and clarity the relationship between media forms and practices and the larger public spheres they produce and are situated within. (Dornfeld, 1998: 13)

The Lucknow journalists that I studied were confined in their daily practice to activities in a quite local space. They were most often occupied with events, institutions and people that were reached within a 15-minute scooter ride. Local news (stories of municipal matters) took up a great deal of the space in the newspapers, some of it concerned with issues of interest mainly to residents of particular neighbourhoods. One could say that the reporters were 'experts' on the local society, and as 'beat reporters' were even specialised in a few sectors of that society.

This is a point in my ethnography that deserves to be emphasised. Considering that much interest in the mass media, particularly in anthropology, has been concentrated on the flow of information, images, knowledge and ideas over distances and across borders, a form of mass media that is so concerned with the local seems somewhat deviant. Not least have studies of contemporary India often seen the mass media as prime movers in a development that reorients people's attention from the local to the national (Rudolph, 1992), or even viewed the mass media industry as part of a world-wide development that links India to a global modernity (Appadurai and Breckenridge, 1995).

It needs to be mentioned that vernacular newspapers are certainly not the only mass media that have grown in India. Since 1980, modern mass media and technologies of communication have also entered on a large scale. Recent electronic media like television, video and music cassettes have a massive presence in all urban milieus and play a considerable role in many people's daily lives—without fully displacing older mass media like radio and cinema. Information technologies such as telephone and fax are nowadays widely available in Public Communication Offices (PCOs) which are readily found all over the cities—usually also with facilities for photocopying and sometimes equipped with computers. Internet connections can be found in most district headquarters across Uttar Pradesh, and mobile phone networks have already been established to cover large urban areas.

The vernacular newspapers have to be understood in the context of other media technologies that people in India are using to an increasing extent. In particular, the relationship between newspapers and television has to be considered. Both are today dominant forms of mass media attracting the attention of a huge number of Indians. A remarkable thing is that, in contrast to developments in other parts of the world, both television and newspapers have grown simultaneously during the last two decades (usually newspaper readership declines as television viewing grows). According to a nation-wide survey conducted in 1999 (including both urban and rural populations), 276 million Indians watched television broadcasts at least once a week and 260 million people read a daily newspaper (out of a total population of one billion).[3] Certainly, the overlap between television viewers and newspaper readers is likely to be extensive because the ability to read a paper (literacy) and access to television (economic means) are not unrelated factors.

Where does the growth of local and regional vernacular language newspapers enter into this broad picture of a recent Indian boom in mass media and communication technology? Does this ethnography of journalists producing news about events, localities and people that are often quite familiar to their readers relate at all to debates about modernity and globalisation? Is the growth of regional and local newspapers a trend opposed to the media stream moving in a national, transnational or even deterritorialised direction? Should these journalists be interpreted as providing some kind of resistance to globalisation, fighting successfully to save local concerns from drowning in great world events? At least one anthropologist has argued that in a world where electronic media are transforming relationships between people, "the task of producing locality (as a structure of feeling, a property of social life, and an ideology of situated community) is increasingly a struggle" (Appadurai, 1996: 189). The production of locality is certainly a subject of great importance in the discussion of globalisation and modernity (Appadurai, 1997; Escobar, 2002; Foster, 1991; Gupta and Ferguson, 1997; Giddens, 1990; Hannerz, 1996). According to Giddens, one of the consequences of modernity is, for example, that places become "phantasmagoric: that is to say, locales are thoroughly penetrated by and shaped in terms of social influences quite distant from them. What structures the locale is not simply that which is present on the scene [...]" (1990: 18). Similarly, Gupta and Ferguson dispute any perspective that takes the local as natural and given, without asking how perceptions of the local are formed, discursively and historically:

> The 'native's point of view' on even the most local of happenings may be as much formed by the mass media as by immediate sensory perception, because the mass media may form an integral or, better still, constitutive part of the lived experience of face-to-face communities. (1997: 10)

Local newspapers are in this context particularly interesting because they provide their readers with discursive connections between the local and familiar and all that which lies beyond. Local newspapers are rarely only local in content. They relate to the imaginaries of the electronic media because they write about television serials, movie stars and 'middle-class' metropolitan lifestyles. (Readers of vernacular papers are, of course, also consuming these other forms of mass media.) Like the grand-scale mass media forms, local newspapers also offer a multiplicity of 'possible lives' (Appadurai, 1996: 3). But, if a characteristic of electronic media is the distance between the audience and the 'text', the local newspaper is grounded in the familiar. It offers a link between lived experiences and imaginations of other places and lives. A local newspaper inscribes nearby places, well-known persons and familiar events into a larger context. The local becomes part of a region, a nation and the world. The mundane is not far from the modern.

Mass media, modernity and the middle class

The experience of mass media and public culture in India is undoubtedly a topic that is drawing increasing notice among scholars. Extensive attention has been paid to some forms of media, most notably Indian cinema (for example, Ahmed, 1992; Dickey, 1993; Inden, 1999; Nandy, 1998; Pandian, 1992; Prasad, 1998; Thomas, 1995; Valicha, 1988). Television has also been the focus of a number of studies (for example, Johnson, 2001; Mankekar, 1999; Mitra, 1993; Ninan, 1995; Rajagopal, 1993, 2001; Sonwalkar, 2001). Other forms of media, such as radio (Lelyveld, 1995), cassette recordings (Manuel, 1993), newspapers (Jeffrey, 2000) or information technology in general (Singhal and Rogers, 1989) have attracted more scattered interest. Furthermore, studies of advertising (Fernandez, 2000; Munshi, 1998; Srikandat, 1991; Srivatsan, 1991) are concerned with several mass media technologies.

The main trends in this literature could very well be summarised into what James Carey (1989: 13–23) has labelled as two alternative conceptions of communication: the transmission view and the ritual view. The former is centred on the idea that information and messages are transmitted over distances for certain purposes. It often comes with an undercurrent of technological optimism: "improved communication is invoked by an army of teachers, preachers and columnists as the talisman of all our troubles" (ibid.: 18). Questions arising are about the effects on audiences or about the function of particular communication technologies. The transmission view is present in much writing on India in which the central goal is to understand how the mass media are transforming society in regard to politics, lifestyle or identity. Some might see in the new communication technologies a potential for India "to leapfrog the industrial era in order to become an informational society" (Singhal and Rogers, 1989: 206). Or they might celebrate particular technologies in their potential for greater 'democratic participation' at the same time as dangers of new forms of commercialism, factionalism and religious chauvinism are recognised (Manuel, 1993). Others understand social change in village India as a result of extensive television watching (Johnson, 2001), or regard recent political developments as tightly dependent on the mass media; it is held, for example, that certain television serials have completely changed the complexion of Indian politics (Rajagopal, 2001).

The ritual view, on the other hand, is not concerned primarily with processes of transferring information but with the representation of shared beliefs. This view recognises the common roots of terms such as 'community', 'communion' and 'communication'. The archetypal case of communication, according to this view, would be "the sacred ceremony that draws people together in fellowship and commonality" (Carey, 1989: 18). The ritual view is prevalent among those who look at media as manifesting cultural and social processes in society. This is a conception often found in studies of the Indian cinema where popular films are seen as reflecting Indian society and politics (Ahmed, 1992; Sardar, 1998), or, simply, that "[t]he popular film *is* low-brow, modernising India in all its complexity, sophistry, naivité and vulgarity [...]" (Nandy, 1998: 7). Likewise, Purnima Mankekar's study of television and its relation to middle-class subjectivity falls chiefly within this view (1999). The ritual view is the perspective I find myself most comfortable with, even though I believe it is unnecessary to evade all conceptualisations of the mass media in terms of transmission and effect. I agree with the intentions, in a recent volume on audio-visual media in India, to comprehend the media "not only as a mode of communication or technology of dissemination, but also as a network connecting a range of activities of sense-making, including the constitution of community and the construction of social order" (Brosius and Butcher, 1999: 6–7).

Whatever their views on communication, several scholars are stressing the rapidity with which new mass media technologies have advanced and thoroughly penetrated Indian society. At least three different studies have used the strongest possible word to denote the changes in various fields of communication: a 'revolution' is believed to have taken place.[4] This radical transformation within Indian society is usually comprehended together with another rapid expansion: the rise of the 'middle class' and the prospect of many for a 'modern' lifestyle. The omnipresence of new mass media technologies indicates that Indians are now 'consuming modernity' (Breckenridge, 1995) in forms that are found all over the contemporary world. This modernity is manifest in commodities possessed primarily by the middle class: the television and video recorder are among those items that are 'compulsory' in a middle-class family and desired by those who struggle to enter middle-class life (cf. Appadurai and Breckenridge, 1995; Varma, 1998: 109; Rajagopal, 2001: 123).[5] It is quite logical that the growth of vernacular newspapers is rarely noticed in this context. A newspaper is not a good symbol of middle-class modernity; it is inexpensive and accessible to almost everyone (not much to aspire to) and, furthermore, is not thought of as something 'new' or technologically fascinating.

There is, however, all reason to contemplate the vernacular press in relation to the 'middle class'. Newspapers are not situated outside the contemporary forms of Indian modernity. They are produced primarily for the middle class, and by people of the middle class. Moreover, a focus on the vernacular press does add some understanding of these notions; it highlights the historical depth and some of the ambivalence inherent in the ideas of 'modernity' and 'middle-class' life. A brief historical background of the Indian middle class should clarify my point.

Modernity has a history also outside Europe and North America, and neither modernity nor the middle class are new to India: they are not exclusively tied to the very latest phenomena of the metropolitan cities—such as cable television, internet cafés or pizza restaurants. In India, as well as in many other places, modernity is often a legacy from colonial times—still visible, for example, in the bureaucracy, the education system, city plans, the railway network and not least in the popularity of a game like cricket (Appadurai, 1996; Cohn, 1997; Dirks, 2001). Among these institutions of colonial modernity are also the newspapers, still surviving as the English-language elite press.

The Indian middle class was also born during the colonial period, intentionally created as a privileged class between the British and the great mass of subjects.[6] It was transformed during the struggle for independence, into an elite with a particular mission on behalf of 'the nation' (Varma, 1998). Through independence and up to the 1970s, this class was rather small, although not undifferentiated. It consisted mainly of people in government service, qualified professionals and business entrepreneurs. Most of them were upper caste and well-to-do economically. They were well educated and virtually all of them spoke and wrote English. But, the unifying and distinguishing feature of the Indian middle class was, according to Varma:

> A certain commonality of approach and thinking, an attitude towards the nation and society, a sense of idealism and high-minded purpose transcending purely individual concerns. In short, an ideological framework to which it owed allegiance. (1998: 27)

The middle class started to change its outlook already in the 1960s. As a result of a series of political events and developments it lost much of its 'innocence' and became more interested in its own well-being (Varma, 1998: Ch. 3). While certain sectors of the economy grew, the middle classes were able to consolidate its economic position and new categories were aspiring to middle-class status—in numbers, however, disproportionate to the expansion of the economy as a whole (ibid.: 108). At least until the early 1990s, the rise of the middle class was less a matter of real economic improvement for more people than it was a shift in the government's economic policy and its attitude towards the wealthier classes of society. From independence up to the early 1980s, the official policy of economic development had been directed towards the eradication of poverty, and the middle class was supposed to act in solidarity with this cause. Economic development was planned through heavy industry, and the consumption of 'luxury' goods was discouraged; the import of foreign items was severely restricted.

Rajiv Gandhi's appearance on the political scene signalled a change in attitude (Mankekar, 1999: 75; Varma, 1998: 113). The eldest son of Indira Gandhi was a 'modern man', a pilot by profession and with a taste for the latest of technologies. The same year (1981), as he was elected to parliament, India started to produce colour televisions as part of a government plan; broadcasts in colour were commenced the following year to coincide with the Asian Games held in New Delhi. This was a spectacular event of which Rajiv Gandhi himself was in charge, designed to show the world "what India is capable of doing when we really mean business" (Sonia Gandhi, quoted in Varma, 1998: 113). Just as the Asian Games became a success internationally, the whole idea seemed to appeal to the middle class of the host country. Rajiv was a leader who recognised the middle class as a political constituency of growing significance—and consumption as an economic force. As Prime Minister he took the first steps in 1985 to relax the state-controlled economy, measures that in the following decade would bring India into the era of economic liberalisation, more fully introduced in 1991 by the Narasimha Rao government and masterminded by the Finance Minister, Manmohan Singh (Khilnani, 1997: 95–106). Now, India was supposed to become a player in the world economy, and the prospect of its success was very much a matter of trust in the middle class and its ability to consume. This was certainly a role that stood in sharp contrast to the middle-class image of an earlier period. To put it bluntly, the well-being of the nation now relied more on a frivolous spender than on a self-sacrificing intellectual.

Television had an essential part to play in this project. When television was first introduced in India (it was launched in Delhi in 1959), it was perceived as an instrument for development and social change.[7] Programmes were produced by the state television on educational topics such as health and agriculture and the intended audiences were schoolchildren and adults who needed to be nurtured with 'scientific values' (Mankekar, 1999: 57–58). In order to reach these audiences television sets were installed in schools and community viewing centres, in cities as well as in rural areas. But during the 1980s the target audience of *Doordarshan* (the state-run television) shifted over to the urban middle class. Programmes were produced in order to attract an audience that would satisfy sponsors and advertisers, rather than to promote development. Entertainment serials were introduced in 1984 with the *Hum Log* (We the People), which was a tremendous success—and it established Maggi noodles, a main advertiser, as an essential part of the Indian cuisine. A whole range of other serials followed, the majority of them explicitly intended for the urban middle class. Subsequently, the sale of television sets increased steadily.[8] But those who could never afford to buy this new commodity also tried to keep up. Crowds of people outside tea stalls and small shops equipped with a TV set became a common scene on Sunday mornings, when the most popular serials were broadcast. Purnima Mankekar has described ethnographically how viewers in south Delhi felt profound identification with the characters in these serials and their predicaments. She argues that the middle class was constituted as a 'viewing family':

> Indeed, in its portrayal of 'modern' middle-class lifestyles and its encouragement of consumerist desires, television seems to have played a crucial role in the cultural *constitution* of these middle classes as a powerful historic bloc. (1999: 9)

To repeat, the rise of the middle class should only in part be understood as a demographic expansion. Certainly, people with economic means to live a 'decent life' were becoming more numerous (a common figure is that the Indian middle class amounts to 100 million people). In practice, though, to become 'middle class' is still a desire for a life which is very remote from most people. According to the 2001 census, only 16 per cent of Indians have access to electricity, safe drinking water and a toilet.[9] The 'average Indian' has a long way to go before obtaining the fruits of being 'middle class'.

If the television set has become an icon of the new middle-class modernity, the English-language newspaper was (and still is) a sacred concern of the old middle class. Newspapers are one of few strongholds of an 'idealistic and high-minded' middle-class attitude (this characteristic will be described more fully in Chapter Six). Newspaper publishing is also one of the businesses that have been exempted in the liberalised economy; foreign ownership of newspapers is still not allowed in India. The vernacular newspapers, though, encapsulate both images of the middle class. With the commercial aspect of publishing as a prime consideration, these newspapers need advertisers, and advertisers, in turn, want to be assured of a readership with the means—and the desire—to consume. Therefore, like television, the vernacular newspapers both target and construct the new middle class. At the same time, these newspapers are part of the same 'field of cultural production' (Bourdieu, 1993) as the English-language press. They are measured on a scale where the latter sets the norm. Editors and journalists on vernacular newspapers want to be as 'professional' as their English-language colleagues. The journalists I have studied in Lucknow do regard themselves as 'middle-class' professionals, but they are torn between two images of what that identity implies. The Hindi-language newspapers are largely staffed by people with a background from outside those groups that were previously recognised as middle class, but they claim the same status as colleagues working on English-language newspapers. The vernacular press is an ambivalent mass media form; it is associated both with an intellectual middle-class ideal and with the middle-class consumerism of later decades.

The vernacular newspapers have to be considered in relation to television's representation of society in yet another sense. I have already made the point that these newspapers are producing localities of various order, while television is often described in its role of constructing a 'national' community. Several observers have also understood *Doordarshan*, the state-run television, as the prime producer of a new pan-Indian national culture. In particular, two successful entertainment serials, broadcast to a national audience, have been seen as immensely important. Both of them were based on popular Hindu epics that were formerly known in local versions all over the country, characterised by great regional variations. Through television they were dispersed in unified form. *Ramayan* was started in January 1987 and ran every Sunday morning until August 1989, when it was succeeded by the *Mahabharat* serial in ninety-four episodes. Many scholars have argued that these entertainment serials played a key role in the construction and diffusion of a national Hindu consciousness. The televised religious epics went hand in hand with the Hindu nationalist agenda of defining the 'nation' as 'Hindu' (Mankekar, 1999; Mitra, 1993; Rajagopal, 1993, 2001; Rudolph, 1992; van der Veer, 1994). Few observers would claim, however, that there is a simple causal linkage between television and 'communal' violence (cf. Mankekar, 1999: 165; Farmer, 1996: 102). Even though the serialisation of *Ramayan* (which is about the life of Ram, the Hindu God-king) coincided with an escalation of the Ayodhya movement, it would be difficult to argue that television directly instigated particular outbreaks of violence. There is a complementary character in the criticisms that have been levelled against different forms of mass media. National television is said to promote a uniform Hindu identity, while the vernacular press and, to some extent, cassette recordings (Manuel, 1993; Rudolph, 1992) are accused of directly provoking violence between religious communities.

Lucknow: field and beat

I conducted most of my fieldwork in one single city—Lucknow (the capital of Uttar Pradesh).[10] Rather than making use of recently discussed options to redefine 'the field' (Gupta and Ferguson, 1997), the methods I used were relatively conventional: participant observation and interviews with journalists working on a number of newspapers in Lucknow.[11] One, not too far-fetched, alternative would have been to do 'multi-sited fieldwork' (Marcus, 1995) in several places in the region. Most of the newspapers I was interested in are published in a number of local editions and I could have chosen to study the production of, for example, *Dainik Jagran* in a dozen cities in Uttar Pradesh. This method would probably have highlighted the organisational aspects of the business and shown more of how the editions are linked to each other and to the head office in Kanpur. What I hope to have gained by localising my fieldwork to one place is a deeper understanding both of the everyday practice and of the professional ideas of these journalists. By following a limited number of journalists attached to one place during an extended period I got to know these people and their 'beat'; multi-sited fieldwork would necessarily have relied on more superficial interviews.

My choice of Lucknow as a site for my fieldwork was to some extent strategic (cf. Marcus, 1995 on strategically situated single-sited fieldwork). In this city I had access to a number of the most important regional dailies of north India that were published with local editions. It was also a place with some history of newspaper publishing and where English-language publications were still part of the mass media scene. Furthermore, as a state capital, I expected Lucknow to be a location where I could follow political reporting more intensively than in other places in Uttar Pradesh.

However, I want to emphasise that in the context of this study the journalists should be understood as particular kinds of professionals rather than as residents of a particular city. A feature of this profession is that not many journalists are devoted to one newspaper and one place throughout their career. Relatively few of them were natives of Lucknow and most of them had worked in several other places, or, if they were new to the profession, they would most certainly move on to other cities in the future. To the degree that one could talk of a Lucknow community of journalists, it was a very unstable group of people. They were Hindi-language journalists rather than Lucknow journalists.

But many people I came to know in Lucknow would be deeply disappointed with me if I claimed that for the purpose of this study the city of Lucknow is interchangeable with any other place in north India. Even quite temporary residents are eager to point out that Lucknow is special. And, of course, they are right. Not least, in relation to the point I have made earlier, it does matter where the journalists work because their work is to a great extent concerned with activities confined to particular localities. It makes sense to say something in this introduction about the city where I conducted most of my fieldwork.

Lucknow: The city of the Nawabs

Lucknow is situated on the Gangetic plain in northern India, 400 kilometres south-east of New Delhi—the national capital. Lucknow is spread out on both sides of the Gomati river, which flows through the city from north-west to south-east. The historical parts of the town and the main city centre are on the south side of the river; the recent extensions of residential and commercial areas are mainly on the north side. Even though the town is built on flat land, the cityscape is far from monotonous. Dense and crowded *bazaars* like the Chowk (the oldest part of town) and Aminabad contrast effectively with open and calm places on the south bank of the river with their historical monuments and large parks. The congested traffic of Vidhan Sabha Marg, a main thoroughfare where the State Assembly and a large complex of administrative buildings are located, adjoins to the south a tranquil part of town with plenty of lush greenery. The latter is the former colonial cantonment, the Mall

Avenue, where ministers and senior civil servants today inhabit huge bungalows with generous gardens.

As far as population is concerned, Lucknow comes in the second rung of Indian cities, far below metropolises like Mumbai, New Delhi and Kolkata.[12] According to the 2001 census, Lucknow had a population of 2,207,340 in the city and 3,681,416 in the whole urban area.[13] This makes it twelfth in size among Indian cities. Notwithstanding the capital city, Lucknow is not even the largest town in Uttar Pradesh, but second after Kanpur, some 60 kilometres to the south. Kanpur is also more important as an industrial and commercial centre, with large-scale production of textiles, leather goods and military equipment (Molund, 1988), and with a stock exchange. Lucknow is not renowned as a place of thriving business, except perhaps for the manufacture of and trade in handicrafts—in particular the *chickan* embroidery industry (Wilkinson-Weber, 1999).

Lucknow is also overshadowed by several other cities and places in the region as a centre of cultural and historical renown. Visitors to this part of the world are usually heading for Agra, Varanasi and Delhi; the monuments of Lucknow are rarely counted among the main attractions of north India. The competition is, however, rather unfair. Lucknow does have a fascinating history and the city has plenty of architectural structures that bear witness to this. There is also a certain nostalgia for the Lucknow of bygone days among the inhabitants as well as among many habitual visitors. The city is often praised for its special ethos of cultural refinement and its cosmopolitan lifestyle. This particular *Lakhnavi* culture was shaped, it is commonly believed, during a brief historical period when Lucknow was the capital city of Awadh[14] and ruled by a Shia Muslim dynasty of Persian origin. The period of splendour and sophistication in Lucknow coincided with the decline and disintegration of the Mughal empire during the late eighteenth and nineteenth centuries. The first Persian ruler of Awadh was a provincial governor, appointed by the emperor in Delhi. His successors climbed to viceregal status and obtained the title of *Nawab*; the historical period of this dynastic rule has also become known as Nawabi Awadh. Even though the Nawabs ruled quite autonomously of the Mughals, it was not until 1819 that one of them proclaimed independence for Awadh. The independence from one empire was, however, at the mercy of a new power—the British. During the Nawabi period, Lucknow blossomed as a cultural centre but politically it was heavily dependent on the East India Company, which through its appointed agent, the Resident, intervened in most affairs of the state (Fisher, 1997).

One of the more famous of the Nawabs was Asaf-ud-Daula, who moved the capital of Awadh (then still a province) from Faizabad to Lucknow in 1775. He also became known as a patron of the arts and architecture as he built several of the city's most impressive monuments. His successors followed in his footsteps and for eight decades, as the centre of Nawabi rule, the image of Lucknow was created. The Nawabs raised buildings in stucco and gilt along the Gomati river, in a style characterised by unorthodox borrowing from virtually anywhere in the world. The historical buildings—palaces, gateways, towers, tombs and religious monuments—of Lucknow are not only hybrids of Muslim and Hindu architecture but also contain distinguishable influences from Turkey, Greece, Italy and even China. The most well-known and distinctive buildings in Lucknow are the *imambaras*, large ceremonial halls used during the Shia festival of *Mohurram*, with their adjoining mosques and minarets. Especially impressive is the Bara Imambara, built by Nawab Asaf-ud-Daula, and once said to have had the largest vaulted hall in the world. The strangest building in Lucknow was, however, designed by a Frenchman, resident in Lucknow at the end of the eighteenth century as adviser to the Nawab court. La Martinière, built as a combined tomb and residence and now housing a famous school, really looks like a gothic wedding cake in brick.

The extravagant expenditure of the Nawab court drew a large number of artisans to Lucknow, and the generous patronage of music, literature and dance also made the city an important cultural centre of the time. Urdu literary life, in particular, bloomed under the Nawabs. Many writers and scholars made Lucknow their home when the Moghul regime in Delhi was fading, and important contributions to the development of Urdu as a literary language were made during this period of the city's history (Naim and Petievich, 1997). The Nawabs also seem to have been fascinated by foreign things and quite a few Europeans enjoyed the privileges of being attached to the Awadh court; they were employed, for example, as engineers, physicians, hairdressers, horticulturists, artists and saddle-makers (Pemble, 1977: 29). In addition, Lucknow also built a reputation as a centre of Muslim scholarship of both Sunni (dating from before the arrivals of the Nawabs) and Shia tradition. Altogether, the short period of Nawabi rule has left an image of a particular *Lakhnavi* culture, described by some commentators as decadent but praised by most people of Lucknow as refined and with a spirit of tolerance and understanding. This *Lakhnavi* ethos is frequently evoked in order to explain why Lucknow in the post-independence period has escaped much of the communal violence that has afflicted many other Indian cities.[15]

The Nawabi era came to an end in 1856 when the British annexed Awadh and shipped off the last Nawab, Wajid Ali Shah, to a pathetic existence in Calcutta (on the pretext of mismanaging of the state affairs). Only a year later the great rebellion of 1857 (the 'Indian Mutiny' in colonial history) broke out and Lucknow became one of the most important strongholds of the rebel troops. The city was under siege for 140 days, during which many Europeans took refuge in the Residency (the building where the British agent resided). This story has been thoroughly documented (Pemble, 1977) and the heavily damaged Residency today attracts a small but steady stream of tourists interested in the history of British India.

During my fieldwork among the journalists, the historical Lucknow, for the most part, formed a background of rather limited significance. When I followed the reporters on their beat I often passed by these monuments but I rarely stopped. Some names from history were mentioned frequently in the editorial offices, but merely to identify places of contemporary importance. Begum Hazrat Mahal, for example, was the wife of the last Nawab; she remained in Lucknow during the rebellion and fought against the British. Today, Begum Hazrat Mahal is better known as the name of a centrally located park where large political rallies take place. Most Hindi-language journalists have some basic idea of historical Lucknow but it would not be correct to say that the city's image from bygone days forms an essential part of their professional worldview.

The more recent political history of the city, however, had a more prominent role in the editorial offices. That history could be said to start in the first decades of the twentieth century when Lucknow re-emerged as a political centre (of Congress politics in general and of Muslim political activism in particular) and eventually was given back its status as a state capital (Robinson, 1997).[16] The contemporary reputation of Lucknow owes much to the basic fact that the capital of Uttar Pradesh matters politically at an all-India level. Since independence, Lucknow has produced a large part of the political elite of the country: eight Prime Ministers have been elected from Uttar Pradesh. For journalists, Lucknow represents political power, and they are often very knowledgeable about north Indian politics and politicians of the more recent decades. Few of them would, however, describe contemporary Indian politicians in flattering terms. If the Nawab rulers were culturally sophisticated but politically impotent, today's rulers in Lucknow sometimes appear as an inversion of that image.

Outline of the study

The structure of the book is as follows. There are seven chapters in all, including the present one. Chapter Two, *The Present and the Past of Indian Journalism*, relates the Lucknow newspapers to the larger context of Indian journalism. The chapter has two parts. The first describes the recent successes of vernacular newspapers, particularly with regard to technological innovations and political dimensions. In the second part, I present and discuss some relevant themes in the history of journalism in India.

Chapter Three, *The Cartography of News*, is a presentation of the product—the newspaper. I give a general account of how the Lucknow newspapers look, from the layout and disposition of the pages to the kind of news that one expects to find in the different sections. In more detail I describe *Dainik Jagran*, page by page. I conclude by reflecting on how society is imagined in the Lucknow newspapers.

Chapter Four, *On the Beat*, is concerned with the process of production, the work the journalists do. It describes the organisation and work routines in the editorial department of *Dainik Jagran*, and provides ethnography from the beat reporters' everyday activities. Locations that the reporters visit, and sources that they encounter are major subjects of this chapter—in particular, the journalists' relationship with the state bureaucracies. I also deal with the somewhat delicate issue of the private 'benefits' of being a reporter.

Chapter Five, *The Journalists*, is about the producers of news. The aim is to portray the people who work in the editorial offices and to discuss subjects such as gender, caste, religion, education and family background. Furthermore, I shall look at the occupational careers of the journalists and see how the newspapers recruit their staffs. The chapter is not confined to employees of *Dainik Jagran* only but refers more broadly to newsmen in Lucknow. In particular I discuss differences between Hindi- and English-language journalists.

Chapter Six, *Professionals for the People*, presents crucial ideas that the Lucknow journalists hold about their occupation. It is concerned particularly with the journalists' notion of their profession as a critical one in a democratic society. Focusing on a specific ethnographic case, it discusses the tense relations between the Hindi- and the English-language press and how this relates to professional ideals. I argue that, despite the hostility, journalists of the two languages basically agree on a bifurcated professional image: the English-language press has 'credibility' and Hindi journalism is 'close to the people'. The latter part of the chapter deals with how the journalists appreciate some predicaments of working in 'the public arena'.

In the concluding chapter, *Global Modernity Spelt in Hindi*, I shall try to relate the ethnography of the previous chapters to a macro-anthropological perspective, discussing how the Hindi press can be understood in terms of modernity and cultural globalisation. I argue that there is an important dynamic between journalism as a universal form of cultural production and the increased density of local representations that the Hindi press offers. From this perspective I touch on the question of how the vernacular press in India relates to the political imaginaries of Hindu nationalism.

Some notes on presentation

Journalists are public people. They write in a newspaper every day and they are usually pleased to see their bylines in print. For this reason, I have not followed the usual practice in anthropology of refraining from using proper names in ethnographical accounts. Most journalists appear with their proper names. Also, the names of newspapers and locations in Lucknow are the real ones. There are exceptions to this rule. Sometimes I have found it unnecessary to expose people who figure in the text and have kept them anonymous, or in a few rare cases I have changed a name—the latter practice when I have feared that my writing could get someone into trouble.

It should be noted that most of the utterances attributed to particular people in this text are reconstructed from my fieldnotes. A few quotations, however, are transcripts from taped interviews, slightly edited but kept as close as possible to original formulations. All translations of newspaper articles and other materials in Hindi are made in collaboration by me and my former Hindi teacher in Shimla, Lalit Kumar Sharma.

One feature of 'vernacularisation' in India is that Hindi words have entered into written English in a striking way (just as many English words have long been integrated with Hindi). The English-language newspapers sometimes carry headlines completely in Hindi—something which is irritating to many English-language purists and quite unthinkable not long ago. In this book I follow the informal practice adopted by the English-language media in India (as well as by most scholars of recent years), when writing Hindi words and sentences in the Roman script. This practice is not always strict. The names of newspapers appearing frequently on these pages are, for example, spelled as they usually appear in the Roman script—*Dainik Jagran* rather than the more consistent *dainik jaagran*.

A main background to this book is that the Indian mass media scene has changed rapidly during the last few decades. This is a tendency that is still continuing, not least with regard to the newspapers in Lucknow: owners, staff, circulation, technology or reputations—all may change, not much is stable. New publications are launched and others may disappear. My ethnography is about the world of Lucknow journalism from the mid to the late 1990s. For an 'insider', much of it will probably appear as history when this book is published. To emphasise this impermanence, I have for the most part used the past tense when writing ethnography. Sometimes, though, when I discuss less temporal features of the Hindi press, writing in the past tense would appear as an anachronism, and I have changed to the present.

Notes

1. The Ram Janmabhumi (the birthplace of Ram) movement was aimed at destroying a mosque in the town of Ayodhya and replacing it with a Hindu temple. The sixteenth-century mosque, Babri Masjid, was claimed to stand on the ruins of a temple believed to mark the birthplace of the God-king Ram. The campaign grew during the mid-1980s and increased the tensions between Hindus and Muslims, causing much violence. On 6 December 1992, when the mosque was finally destroyed, riots broke out across India, leaving thousands of people dead or wounded.
2. One could go on listing differences between the novel and the newspaper and what implication the form of a mass medium has for the construction of 'imaginaries'. Looking at the consumption side in the mass media process it is, for example, important how a mass medium is used. A newspaper is obviously read in a different way from a novel, probably by most people far less carefully.
3. *National Readership Survey 1999*, referred in *Frontline*, vol. 16, issue 20, 1999.
4. Singhal and Rogers (1989) have described a general trend in the growth of electronic communication as 'India's Information Revolution'; Peter Manuel (1993) has focused on the less high technology-based 'Cassette Revolution' (the immense popularity since the late 1970s of the tape recorder and the booming market for music cassettes); and Robin Jeffrey (2000) has recently described the transformation of print media in terms of a 'Newspaper Revolution'.
5. Other commodities that signify modernity and middle-class life in India are, for example, the refrigerator, the air conditioner, the scooter and the car.
6. The British intention of creating this class is usually summarised in Lord Macaulay's famous Minute on Indian Education from 1835:

'We must at present do our best to form a class who may be interpreters between us and the millions we govern; a class of persons, Indian in blood and colour, but English in taste, in opinions, in morals, and in intellect' (Varma, 1998:2).

7. The government was also concerned with the role of newspapers in its development policy. It tried to promote a rural press.
8. The sale went from 5 million in 1985 to 35 million in 1990 (Mankekar, 1999: 6).
9. www.censusindia.net
10. My fieldwork in Lucknow was divided into two parts. During the first period, from December 1995 until May 1996, I was engaged with participant observations mainly on one newspaper, *Dainik Jagran*. The second part, from December 1997 until February 1998, was more focused on interviews. I conducted about 60 loosely structured interviews (most of them taped, from half an hour to two hours) with journalists of various newspapers in the city. Before my fieldwork I was also exposed to Indian mass media (television, film, magazines and newspapers) during extended periods (altogether one and a half years) of Hindi studies in New Delhi, Mussoorie and Shimla.
11. Less conventional is perhaps the extent to which I have used printed matter—the newspapers—for the purpose of writing ethnography.
12. During the 1990s some well-known Indian cities changed their colonial names to vernacular ones: Bombay became Mumbai, Madras changed to Chennai and Calcutta was renamed as Kolkata. I have used the new official names when writing ethnography (even though Calcutta was renamed after my fieldwork) but retained the old names when relating to history. For a discussion on this type of 'vernacularisation', with a focus on Bombay, see Hansen (2001).
13. www.censusindia.net
14. The Anglicised form of the name is Oudh.
15. The last major Hindu-Muslim riot in Lucknow took place in 1924. The city escaped violence even during partition in 1947 and throughout the Ayodhya conflict in the 1990s. Ashutosh Varshney has recently explained this by the high level of integrated associational life that exists between the communities in Lucknow (2002).
16. Allahabad had been the capital since 1877 when Awadh merged with the North-Western Provinces to form the United Provinces. In 1921 a decision was taken in the Legislative Council to build a new council house in Lucknow and to move the secretariat from Allahabad. Formally, however, Lucknow was not recognised as the capital until 1947 (Reeves, 1997: 213).

Two

The Present and the Past of Indian Journalism

In Chapter One, I argued that the vernacular press has to be understood in relation to the Indian middle class and its expectations and experiences of modernity, particularly with regard to the consumption of other forms of mass media. The aim of this chapter is to provide a context that is more immediately related to newspaper journalism. Nevertheless, it is a context that is not always readily available in my field material but to some degree is compiled from broader readings on Indian society and history. In order to understand what the Lucknow journalists are doing, one has to look outside the everyday practice of the profession. The aim of the first half of the chapter is to situate the Lucknow journalists in the contemporary newspaper world in India. I shall describe the structure of the newspaper business and the state of journalism in the country today. However, to understand certain concepts and features of contemporary journalism, it is necessary to look back on how the profession has evolved over the decades. In the second half of this chapter, therefore, I shall dwell somewhat on the history of Indian journalism. With both these aims, I shall pay particular attention to newspapers and journalism in Lucknow and Uttar Pradesh.

The newspaper revolution

During the first part of my fieldwork, in 1995–96, there were six Hindi-, three English- and two Urdu-language morning papers published from Lucknow. The newspaper with the largest local circulation was the Hindi-language *Dainik Jagran*, which sold around 65,000 copies of its Lucknow edition every day.[1] Its main Hindi-language competitors were *Aaj*, *Rashtriya Sahara* and *Swatantra Bharat;* two other papers with considerably smaller circulations were *Navjivan* and *Swatantra Chetna*. In addition to these, a rival of the local Hindi papers was *Amar Ujala*, which had an office with several journalists in Lucknow but was edited and printed in nearby Kanpur (but delivered to subscribers in Lucknow simultaneously with the local papers). The *Times of India* and the *Pioneer* were competing for the English-language readers, while the *National Herald* was merely struggling for survival. *Quami Awạz* was the leading Urdu paper. I was told repeatedly during my fieldwork that the city was oversupplied with newspapers. There was neither sufficient readership nor advertising revenue for so many publications.[2] A widespread opinion was that at least a couple of the newspapers were bound to close down soon. But, when I returned to Lucknow in December 1997 for the second part of my fieldwork, all of these newspapers were still being published. Furthermore, in the newspaper vendor's list of locally produced newspapers, I found three new titles to choose from. The Delhi-based publishing house of the *Hindustan Times* had launched both its English- and Hindi-language editions from a newly constructed editorial building in central Lucknow. And, a newcomer in the Hindi-language market, *Kuber Times*, had chosen Lucknow as one of three places (the other two being New Delhi and Mumbai) from which to publish. In practice, a newspaper reader in Lucknow now had nine Hindi-language morning papers to choose from. For English-language readers, four locally produced newspapers were available, and if they could wait until the afternoon it was of course also possible to subscribe to a newspaper from New Delhi or Kolkata (which bureaucrats not native to Lucknow often preferred).

Altogether, it was certainly an impressive number of publications to which readers had access in an urban region of something over 3.5 million people.[3] Admittedly, as a politically important state capital, Lucknow did have more newspapers than most Indian cities of equal size. But, the multitude of publications found here is nevertheless a clear sign of a phenomenon that is characteristic of urban India in general: in all towns of any size many newspapers are published. This has not always been the case. A newspaper vendor in Lucknow, and most other Indian cities, had much less to offer in the early 1970s (only two Hindi-language newspapers were published locally: *Navjivan* and *Swatantra Bharat*). The increase in the number of newspapers is part of a transformation that Robin Jeffrey has called 'India's Newspaper Revolution' (2001). This 'revolution' forms the immediately most relevant context for my study and can be summarised as follows. Both the number of newspapers published and the total circulation of dailies in India have increased tremendously since the late 1970s; vernacular newspapers with a regional circulation have been much more successful than English-language newspapers with a 'national' profile; editions and printing centres of newspapers have multiplied, thereby expanding the readership to smaller cities and rural areas. One implication of this structural transformation is that the focus of journalism has changed: from an almost exclusive interest in national politics towards localised events closer to the readers. Not least, journalists working outside the metropolitan-centred, English-language elite press have been infused with a new self-confidence. My account of the contemporary newspaper business in India resembles rather closely the 'revolution' that Jeffrey has described, although I shall often expand on his arguments, particularly in regard to the situation of newspaper publishing in Uttar Pradesh.

First, some terms often used in the context of the Indian newspaper industry need to be clarified. When the Indian press is discussed by the public, or is the subject of surveys, newspapers are often categorised in two different ways: by language usage or by geographical dispersion. According to the first model, the Indian daily press consists of two categories—the English and the vernacular (also commonly called 'the language press'). The other model differentiates between 'national' and 'regional' (sometimes also 'local') newspapers. Both ways of categorising have hierarchical connotations. The English-language press has a higher status than the vernacular, and 'national' papers are perceived as more serious than 'regional'.[4] And even though some Hindi dailies have ambitions to be 'national newspapers', the terms 'vernacular press' and 'regional press' are often used synonymously. An English-language paper always seems to be perceived as more 'national' than a Hindi paper, despite the fact that the latter may have ambitions to cover issues at an all-India level—and may even have a far wider circulation. This is an image that is certainly very irritating to many editors of vernacular newspapers; some would even say insulting (cf. Rajagopal, 2001: 163).

To give a general description of the vernacular press is an awkward task because we are talking about newspapers published in at least twelve different languages, written with nine different scripts. Even though a Hindi speaker can probably make out something from newspapers in language regions close by, such as Bengali or Gujarati, the linguistic differences are in most cases not small variations. Newspapers in south Indian languages and scripts are incomprehensible to someone from northern parts of the country. Moreover, language borders do to a great extent also coincide with regional or administrative borders.[5] The mass media in vernacular languages are, therefore, not only separated in linguistic terms, they are also dealing with different political situations in their respective states. More generally, the large regional differences in India do leave their mark in the media: what is public knowledge in one part of India—political personalities, topics, scandals, disasters, cultural events—is not exactly the same in other regions. Not least, journalism in various parts of the country has not developed at the same pace, and the papers are all conflated with their regional cultural and intellectual environments (Jeffrey, 1993, 1997a, 1997b, 1997c, 1997d). These differences are also part of the occupational identity among journalists. For example, Hindi journalists sometimes show an admiration for journalists working in Bengali (West Bengal) and Malayalam (Kerala). The Bengali press is envied because it is believed to be more respected; it forms part of the intellectual milieu of Kolkata. The press in Kerala, on the other hand, is looked upon as a model in a market-oriented sense; it took steps to increase circulation early on. In many aspects, south Indian newspapers, particularly those of Kerala, initiated the newspaper revolution.

Properly speaking, the changes in the newspaper world in India have been a matter of rapid transformation rather than the instant upheaval that the word 'revolution' might imply. Jeffrey describes a time span from 1976 up to the late 1990s during which newspapers in India have grown tremendously both in numbers and in total circulation. In 1996 there were five times as many newspapers published as in 1976 (2001: 48) and the total daily circulation of all newspapers had increased more than four times during the same period (ibid.: 1).[6] Taking population growth into account, there would have been more than 80 Indians for each newspaper copy in 1976 but only 20 in 1996 (ibid.). Moreover, adding to the availability of news in practical terms, the great winners in the newspaper boom were daily papers printed in vernacular languages. The English-language newspapers also grew, but much more modestly, and their share of the market diminished sharply. This dramatic change in the structure of the newspaper business can be illustrated by a comparison between the developments in circulation of the Hindi-language and English-language newspapers. Newspapers printed in English, a language understood only by some 3 per cent of all Indians, had a circulation throughout most of the 1970s that well exceeded those printed in Hindi, the largest of all the Indian languages, spoken by over 40 per cent of the population. In 1979 the Hindi-language newspapers for the first time passed the English-language newspapers in terms of daily circulation. By that year the Hindi-language newspapers sold 3 million copies a day, the newspapers in English somewhat fewer. During the 1980s, however, the gap widened for every year that passed. By 1992 the English-language newspapers had a circulation of 3.9 million but the Hindi newspapers had grown to 11.2 million copies a day. The circulation of the Hindi newspapers was now almost three times than that of the English newspapers (Jeffrey, 1997b: 78; 2000: 46).

Robin Jeffrey tries to explain why and how this 'revolution' came about and points to a number of circumstances working together. Two of these form the basis of his interpretation. First, the number of Indians able to read and write has increased, and therefore also that of potential newspaper readers. Second, improved technology to produce and distribute newspapers in Indian scripts has become available. These factors alone, he claims, do not explain the newspaper revolution. More importantly, he states, "[newspapers] grew because entrepreneurs detected a growing hunger for information among ever-widening sections of India's people, who were potential consumers as well as newspaper readers. A race began to reach this audience" (Jeffrey, 2001: 48).[7] Basically, I agree with Jeffrey's analysis and I also structure some of my discussion around factors that he has identified. I would, however, look less deterministically at a number of issues. My aim is not to explain *why*, or *how*, newspapers have grown, but to provide a context and outline a background to the ethnographic material I shall present in the following chapters of this book. Here I first briefly discuss the impact of the growth in literacy, the new technology and the ownership structure of the vernacular press. I then pay somewhat more attention to the political context in which newspaper reading has grown.

Literacy, technology and ownership

The development of primary education has not been a priority area in independent India. More efforts have been directed towards higher education. Thus, while India has "one of the world's largest reservoirs of trained and skilled manpower," it simultaneously has the largest number of out-of-school children (Varma, 1998: 55–56). Because of this the rate of literacy has been low, which, of course, can be interpreted as a constraining factor for newspaper circulation in a society. But even a moderate growth in literacy in the huge Indian population produces a great mass of people able to read. In 1971 there were 162 million literate people in India, while in 1991 the figure was 352 million (Jeffrey, 2001: 29). And, the literacy rate has continued to grow during the 1990s. In the 2001 census it is claimed that 65.38 per cent of the population are now literate compared with 51.63 per cent in 1991.[8] It would be easy to see the increase in literacy as the single most important factor behind the increased sale of newspapers. If the literate population almost doubled between 1971 and 1991, this factor alone could very well be a good part of the reason why circulation figures went up by 2.7 times over the same period (ibid.: 47). Literacy is also the factor that most journalists and editors mention when they want to explain the recent success of the vernacular press. But, the circulation of newspapers has grown not only proportionately to the growth of literacy, but at a higher rate. Furthermore, even in relation to the literacy rate in the 1970s, newspaper sales were very low (in Jeffrey's estimate, the circulation of newspapers was 9 million among 160 million literate Indians). Literacy figures show primarily that the potential for the newspaper business in India to expand has been, and continues to be, huge. With regard to Uttar Pradesh, it should be added, the recent growth in literacy means the ability to read and write in Hindi. While several other states in India have promoted education in several languages, the policy in Uttar Pradesh has strongly favoured one language at the expense of other widely spoken regional languages, primarily Urdu (Hasan, 1998: 181).

Three technical developments arrived in India roughly simultaneously and made way for the possibilities to, print newspapers in Indian languages cheaper, faster, in greater numbers and more attractively; furthermore, technology also allowed for their more effective distribution. The new technologies were the offset press, computer typesetting and the computer modem. The same technologies have transformed newspaper production in most parts of the world, but their importance in India has particular characteristics. The offset press, which transfers text and images chemically and photographically, was introduced in the industrialised world after the Second World War. It succeeded a printing technology that basically had worked in the same way since Gutenberg's first experiments with printing: text composed of metal types was pressed against sheets of paper. The offset press was able to work much more efficiently and rapidly. Its introduction in India was, however, delayed. One reason was that the import of printing machinery was for a long period restricted (and was anyhow expensive) and that Indian companies did not start to manufacture offset presses until 1975. The main reason, however, was that offset technology was of limited value in India so long as another problem remained unsolved: that of composing text (setting types) for printing in Indian languages. All Indian scripts, except Urdu, are in principle strictly phonetical; every sound is represented by a unique symbol. Thus Indian scripts work with a great number of symbols, while scripts based on the Roman alphabet can manage with only a few, because every letter can sound in many different ways. "A printer's case for an English font might consist of eighty compartments, made up of twenty-six upper-case and twenty-six lower-case letters, numerals from 0 to 9 and some punctuation marks. For an Indian language, a printer's case for a single font thus had to consist of a minimum of 300 or 400 compartments" (Jeffrey, 2001: 35). With the old technology it was difficult to make type-casting machines work with such a great number of different characters, and it was expensive to manufacture the variety of fonts needed to make an attractive-looking newspaper. Most Indian-language newspapers had access only to a small number of fonts, which, for example, limited the possibilities to make headlines of different size. Newspapers looked rather dull.

Composing on the computer screen made all the difference. Equipped with software that could handle the complications with Indian scripts, it was possible to compose text with all the variations that characterised print in Roman script, and almost as fast. With the computer it was possible to produce text that could be printed out and pasted on a page, then photographed and made into a plate to be printed on an offset machine. Furthermore, the new production process saved a lot of work, and the computer equipment required relatively moderate investment.

New technology has also been useful in handling another problem that has constrained the Indian newspaper business: the circumstance that many potential readers live in small towns and villages, far from the places where newspapers are produced. The demography and infrastructure of India are not ideal for newspaper distribution. Even though India has plenty of big cities, it is still primarily a rural country. According to the 2001 census, 73 per cent of the population live in areas classified as rural. Including smaller and medium-sized towns and cities, an overwhelming majority of people live outside the big cities.[9] If the production of newspapers is centralised to a few metropolises, it means that newspapers have to be loaded on trucks or trains and transported great distances to reach readers. When roads are bad and trains slow, it takes time to transport newspapers outside the place of publication or its vicinity. Not long ago, a literate person living in a medium-sized town of Uttar Pradesh simply had no chance to read a fresh newspaper before he went off to work because it had to be transported to him from one of the few large cities that were producing newspapers—perhaps a half day's journey away. A daily paper ages by the hour and if it is not available for readers until the afternoon (or, worse, the next day) it is already old and has lost much of its attraction.

This problem has now to some extent been solved, not because roads have become much better and trains faster but because newspaper production has been decentralised. Newspapers are printed closer to their readers. Electronic communication has been an important new technology in this development. When newspapers are composed with computers, news stories and even edited pages can easily be sent to distant places by computer modem. With these technologies it has become possible to print a newspaper simultaneously from various places in editions that look similar and have a lot of content in common, but that also include local material. Previously, to set up a local edition of a newspaper was an expensive venture because it meant that the full cycle of production had to be handled in the new place. Today, it is a relatively cheap affair to launch a new edition, or a printing centre, of an already existing newspaper.

Most of the big regional newspapers today are produced and printed from multiple places, thus reducing the distance that papers have to be transported. Several of the Hindi-language papers are printed from more than ten places. This means that if you take the train from Lucknow to Agra (or Varanasi, Meerut, Allahabad) and on the same day visit a newspaper vendor, you will find several papers with the same name as in Lucknow. But they will have a somewhat different content, because other local editorial offices produce them. Many of the top stories are printed in all editions and several stories go into more than one, but in most cases only the editorial pages are identical everywhere. On the one hand, some north Indian regional newspapers are huge media organisations with a total circulation that exceeds half a million copies a day. On the other hand, these figures are divided among many local, distinct editions with more modest circulation. A big regional paper could, in a sense, be considered as a number of local cooperating newspapers within the same organisation. This decentralisation of production is continuing at an amazing rate. *Dainik Jagran*, which in 1998 had ten editions and was printed from 13 centres, claimed in 2001 to have 15 editions printed from 18 places.[10]

One aspect of the newspaper revolution seems to have been that owners of vernacular newspapers launched a hunt for readers to raise their circulation by marketing their publications in a way that had not characterised the Indian press before. The business of publishing newspapers in Indian languages went from being a trade of rather modest economic expectations, and often conducted with the aura of a political mission, to becoming a more unblushingly capitalist enterprise (Jeffrey, 2001: 105). This development has to be explained in connection with the structure of ownership of the Indian press.

Just as in other parts of the world, politicians and intellectuals in India do not regard the mass media as simply any kind of business. The mass media have a political influence on their audiences; it does matter who the owners are. Since independence fear of monopoly capitalism has been a frequent theme in the debate concerning Indian democracy and the issue has been investigated in a number of reports by government and union bodies (ibid.: 106). The cause of this fear, however, has primarily been the concentration of ownership of the English-language press in which a few newspaper chains dominate; in particular, the strength of the two media groups that publish the *Times of India* and the *Indian Express* has been a sign of this concentration. As long as the English-language newspapers were seen as the most important news media in the country, the fear of monopoly was not unfounded. With the growth of vernacular newspapers the debate has fallen silent; it would be difficult to fear ownership concentration with regard to the multitude of newspapers that are published in vernacular languages. Instead, the ownership debate during the last decade has been focused on whether or not foreign investors should be allowed to buy shares in Indian newspaper industry. The fear is that foreign owners would use the political power of newspaper publication and try to influence opinions in the country.[11]

Newspapers in Indian languages are mainly family-controlled enterprises (Jeffrey, 2001: 112). They are either privately owned or registered as public companies but with shares restricted to a small circle of relatives. With rare exceptions the publishing companies are not listed on the stock exchange. One reason for the relative diversity of ownership in the vernacular press is the difficulty of running newspapers in more than one language. There have been attempts, not least from the big English-language publishing houses, to launch editions in several languages. Sometimes this has succeeded, but in many cases it has proved difficult. The diversity of languages is in itself a barrier to all-India concentration of ownership.

Within each language region the diversity of ownership is, of course, not as striking as it appears at the national level. Nevertheless, it is difficult to talk about concentration of newspaper ownership in any of the big languages. Even though, in some states, a few newspapers are leading the market (such as *Malayala Manorama* and *Matrabhumi* in Kerala or *Eenadu* and *Vaarta* in Andhra Pradesh), they have not killed off all competition. In many small and medium-sized towns all over India a great selection of local dailies are available at the news-stand, and they are usually published by competing proprietors. This situation may not last long. Perhaps the multitude of newspapers is just a temporary stage; many entrepreneurs joined the race when the potential of profit in newspaper publishing was recognised. But, the growth in readership cannot continue forever. With increasing competition a few successful dailies may grow at the expense of the diversity. Small and medium-sized family-owned newspapers will experience difficulties in facing the challenge from large commercial media enterprises. As I have already noted, this was a development that the journalists in Lucknow, particularly the resident editors, expected to happen. Still, despite the fact that some dailies were struggling for survival, new ventures were launched in the late 1990s.

Is it only because of the chance of making economic profits that new entrepreneurs are turning to newspaper publishing and established proprietors are expanding with more editions? To take the Lucknow newspapers as an example, the commercial logic behind certain ventures is not immediately obvious. Some resident editors admitted that they had small hope of running the newspaper edition at a profit, at least in the short run. The reason for launching a new newspaper, or for continuing to publish an edition of questionable success, is sometimes found outside purely economic motives. Even though the business appears more market-oriented than it was in the 1970s, the connection between politics and newspaper publishing still has not been lost. The political motive for running a newspaper, however, is not necessarily in the idealistic sense of furthering a cause. From the point of view of a newspaper proprietor, Lucknow is a good place to publish an edition, because the city has great political significance as a state capital. The turbulent political situation during the last few decades has accentuated this. The political changes that India has gone through have been particularly evident in Uttar Pradesh: the decline of Congress(I), the rise of Hindu nationalism and the great importance of regional parties and low-caste movements. And, because journalism in India is strongly focused on politics, a base in Lucknow is essential for every media organisation that is active in the northern part of the country.

Another point, concerning the relationship between newspaper proprietors and politicians, is often raised in the public debate on the media. It is argued that the real purpose behind some newspapers is to further the owner's interest in other commercial activities. The newspaper may be run at an economic loss (and without due journalistic care) because the gain is the political strength that comes from ownership of a newspaper—and which could be utilised in dealing with the government and with politicians. This accusation is primarily aimed at those new media enterprises that have been started by successful companies with no previous experience in the mass media. Among the Lucknow newspapers it is *Rashtriya Sahara* and *Kuber* that represent this type of organisation. The former was previously known primarily as the name of an aviation company and the latter had its successes in finance and housing. There are also cases where companies outside the media have bought established newspapers. Sometimes it seems that industrialists have turned to newspaper publishing not because they were attracted to the chance of *making* large profits, but because they *had already made* fortunes that they wanted to invest wisely in a political and strategic sense (cf. Jeffrey, 2001: 116). This logic also works the other way round; old newspaper owners have expanded their commercial activities to areas outside the media. The owners of *Dainik Jagran*, for example, whose original interest was only in newspapers, are today involved with business in sugar, textiles and electronics.[12]

The criticism that successful industrial companies are launching unsound newspaper projects only to obtain a base for political influence is not altogether coherent. After all, the Hindi-language press is generally a commercially lucrative business, and it is not particularly strange that some editions are run at a loss for some years, but are expected to generate profits in the future. Furthermore, for some of the new owners, the Hindi-language newspaper is part of a broader interest in the mass media; simultaneously they are launching projects in the electronic media. All this is a trend that seems likely to continue. Kuber is not the last industrial group to suddenly launch a Hindi-language daily. For example, in early 1998, a south Indian group of companies advertised in north Indian papers that they wanted 'hundreds of professionals', the reason being that they wanted to launch a new Hindi-language newspaper that would be published from several centres. This group of companies, called Sanghi, described itself as "a 2000 crore conglomerate with multi-dimensional, multi-locational interests that include textile processing, zip fasteners, rigid pvc, plantations along with its presence in a vernacular daily with the launching of *Vaartha*—the Telugu national daily".[13]

Newspapers, politics and pleasure

Why do an increasing number of people *want* to buy and read newspapers? Because they feel a need of becoming better informed, particularly about politics, is the answer that Jeffrey suggests (2001: 30). He claims that political excitement and engagement go hand in hand with newspaper consumption, and that the political situation since the late 1970s has evolved in such a way that it has provoked popular interest and involvement. This is, of course, something that is very hard to 'prove' and some of Jeffrey's examples are not wholly convincing.[14] But, without doubt, "the newspaper revolution" coincides with an exciting period in Indian politics. "[T]he crucial decade of the 1980s [...], observers of Indian politics should agree, profoundly altered the contours of politics in modern India" (Hasan, 1998: 5). It started with the end of the 'emergency' that Indira Gandhi proclaimed in June 1975 and which lasted for 22 months. Already before the emergency, newspaper publishing was constrained by government control of newsprint imports and restrictions on the size of newspapers. When the emergency was imposed newspapers were immediately censored and could not print anything that was interpreted as criticism of the government (Mankekar, 1978). Rumours circulating about government abuses, for example in connection with the family planning programme, could never be confirmed or denied with the help of the press.

It was when the emergency was revoked and Indira Gandhi was defeated in the subsequent election in 1977 that newspaper circulation started to rise rapidly (Jeffrey, 2001: 39). Obviously, people were eager to get information about what had happened. The years to come continued to offer a political situation well suited to the newspaper market. If the first decades after Indian independence had been relatively stable and politics predictable, with the Congress party in a secure and dominating position, now politics was in turmoil (Brass, 1994). The Congress party was on a route of decay, new parties and leaders were emerging on the scene and politics was becoming more competitive. At least two features of this development were particularly connected with the mass media. One was the rise of a Hindu nationalism, with political leaders who showed skill in mobilising large masses of people. They needed events and issues to focus on, and they were in need of mass media that could effectively disseminate their ideas and messages. One of the most important issues that they aired was the campaign aiming at the removal of the Babri Masjid in Ayodhya. The whole campaign involved several events that became big news all over the country but were particularly on the agenda in Uttar Pradesh where Ayodhya is situated. It certainly affected the circulation of newspapers, according to most editors I talked to.

Another feature of political developments following the emergency has been the regionalisation of Indian politics. "The decline of the highly centralised Congress party has resulted in a decentering of politics and has shifted its locale from New Delhi to the states", Hasan (1998: 4) writes. A multitude of new parties has come to prominence on a regional base. Thus, every state in India has its gallery of parties and leaders and a political stage with its own particularities. State politics during this period has become a complicated intrigue of alliances between parties and leaders, involving the defection of politicians from one party to another and the formation of new constellations in state assemblies. The parallel regionalisations of the mass media and politics are strikingly well adapted to one another. Each regional press has its own political events to make sense of and state-level political leaders have access to a media that make their actions public.

In Uttar Pradesh, which formerly was a Congress stronghold, the party has virtually been wiped out since the 1980s. When the Congress started to decline, the political space was first occupied by two forces, Hindu nationalism and socialism—today represented by the BJP (Bharatiya Janata Party) and the SP (Samajwadi Party).[15] While these two parties are strongly opposed on most issues, on one point they have worked in the same direction. They have both had a policy of promoting the Hindi language. The SP has done this with political slogans confronting the English-speaking elite (*angrezi hatao—eliminate* English), the BJP by evoking the religious connotation of Hindi as a language of the Hindus as against the Urdu of the Muslims. In any case, the political ground for the Hindi-language papers to thrive has been favourable. Zoya Hasan has noted that the Hindi literati of the state have become a key instrument in both a cultural and political resurgence: "Hindi and Hindi newspapers have become the vehicle through which new cultural symbols are forged and disseminated" (1998: 187).

It would be tempting to conclude that people read newspapers because they want to be in touch with politics, that they want to form their opinions on issues of common concern and take part in a democratic society. Such a conclusion evokes an almost idealised vision of the healthy relationship between the mass media and popular political participation, quite in tune with Habermas' original idea of the 'bourgeois public sphere' (Habermas, 1989). The newspapers which are the focus of this study are, however, without doubt commercial enterprises (this goes for the English-language newspapers as well, even though they are less successful in commercial terms than the vernacular papers). They sell news for consumption and if they devote a lot of effort to political reporting it is because they regard politics as a commodity in popular demand. To the extent that politics forms part of a public knowledge—some of it shared among people within a region, some shared all over the country—it is not necessarily because the subject is 'serious'. Indian politics does have qualities that may very well compete with Hindi movies or television serials for public attention: excitement, colourful characters and fascinating intrigues (which are, of course, aspects of politics that are not unique to India). In this sense, one should not, in my mind, view political news as something completely different from other kinds of news material.

People in India might have turned to newspapers, after Indira Gandhi's emergency, because they had built up an 'immense curiosity' and were "eagerly searching for news about what had happened around them" (Jeffrey, 2001: 38). The journalists, on the other hand, had had some new experiences during the months of censorship. They had learnt to write stories that did not directly concern politics. News of the government was restricted to uncritical reports on various development programmes and cultural affairs. It was, however, quite safe to write about lower levels of the Indian administration and expose mismanagement, because criticism of the bureaucracy was not interpreted as being against Indira Gandhi and her regime (which took strong measures to check the bureaucracy). This was clearly an incentive to localise news, to deal with particular issues in specified departments of the bureaucratic administration. It was also part of a conscious mass media strategy from the Indira Gandhi government, which instructed its television and radio officials to name and identify people and places in order to evoke interest and credibility (Jeffrey, 2001: 103). This trend has become strong in the newspapers ever since. The localisation of news has also extended to subjects other than the bureaucracy. Everything of local concern—from petty crime stories to wholesale prices in the small town vegetable market—has been brought into the newspapers. This is a logical outcome when journalists far away from the big cities write in newspapers. It is also an important aspect of the newspaper revolution. It is not hard to imagine that newspapers might have been of limited concern to many people, when they were produced in the metropolises for an elite readership concerned with national politics. The localisation of the content in the newspaper goes hand in hand with the decentralisation of its production.

Another type of writing that newspapers turned to 'by force of circumstances', during the emergency, was 'feature' stories, that is, non-political 'light' reading on film, lifestyle and other aspects of popular culture. "Before the emergency, there was no concept of a feature in the daily newspapers, we started to do it to replace political news. After some time the response from readers was good. It became part and parcel of a newspaper", said a Lucknow journalist, who started his career in the early 1970s and has held many senior positions in several of the most important Hindi-language newspapers of Uttar Pradesh. A newspaper that has been particularly successful in exploiting this genre of writing, and probably has been a model for others, is *Punjab Kesari*, published in Punjab and since the late 1980s one of India's largest selling Hindi dailies (Jeffrey, 2001: 95–96). During the emergency it started to print its front and back pages every day as a colourful magazine, devoid of any material that usually counted as news. The news reporting started on page three. This seems to have been a formula that readers liked, because, unlike most other newspapers, *Punjab Kesari* did well during the emergency. When censorship was abolished *Punjab Kesari* went back to its traditional style, removed the magazine and introduced news on the front page again—and the readership declined. The management came to the conclusion that the idea of selling a newspaper with a features magazine on the front page had not been so bad after all. The re-introduction of the magazine started a rapid climb in circulation figures for *Punjab Kesari* during the 1980s (ibid.).

The tendency of newspapers to emphasise content outside the political reporting is also supported in my ethnography. Not to the extent that any Lucknow newspaper was yet printing feature stories on the front page or treating political news as secondary to other kinds of content; political coverage undoubtedly remains the backbone of Indian journalism. But most efforts to succeed in the competition for readers did not aim at improving the political news. It was with other kinds of content that editors in leading positions tried to attract readers and raise their circulation. Local news and feature stories in particular were believed to have great potential. Consequently, if people turned to newspapers out of political engagement and searched for political news, other kinds of reading at least did not turn them away.

History of Indian journalism

A popular saying in the journalist profession (in many parts of the world, I believe) has it that "nothing is as old as yesterday's newspaper". I think it is easy to cherish a similar feeling when looking at the history of an occupation that is so conflated with the contemporary. But, even though I insist that *Dainik Jagran* and other vernacular Indian newspapers ought primarily to be understood as phenomena of the present time, it would be a mistake to dismiss the historical perspective as redundant. Not everything in the world of journalism is the outcome of the recent 'revolution'. The history of Indian journalism reveals that certain concepts and ideas in today's media world have obvious backgrounds in the past two centuries. Characteristics of the journalist profession that one would think of as being particular to present-day political and cultural circumstances sometimes have amazing parallels in history. And, of course, the journalistic sense of devotion to the contemporary is an ancient feeling.

The history of journalism is manifestly present in some of the press institutions in Lucknow. A few newspapers have a particular status, almost as icons of journalism, although their contemporary situation is not always impressive. This is particularly true of the *Pioneer* and the *National Herald*, the two English-language dailies that once were important 'national' newspapers based in Lucknow. They are deeply associated with the journalism of the city, and acclaimed for their brilliance during earlier decades, rather than for recent successes. Both of them draw their reputation from famous people who have worked on them; during their days of glory they had editors and journalists who left their mark in the history of Indian journalism, as well as in the memory of Lucknow scribes. The Hindi-daily *Aaj* is less synonymous with Lucknow journalism (its head office being located in Varanasi) but it has a celebrated history in Uttar Pradesh as one of the most important vernacular newspapers that formed part of the nationalist movement.

The Press Club in China Bazaar and the journalists union, the Indian Federation of Working Journalists (IFWJ) (with an office in the Press Club) are two other press institutions in Lucknow that had a more vital role before the newspaper revolution. During my fieldwork the board of the Press Club, for example, still consisted primarily of journalists associated with newspapers that were prominent thirty years ago and there were very few representatives from the big Hindi dailies. And, the IFWJ was in practice not much involved in the everyday local reality of the working journalist. But its national chairman was a well-known figure among the Lucknow journalists, because he lived in the city—in one of the colonial bungalows in the vicinity of Mall Avenue, alongside the political elite of the state. The IFWJ was more visible in the national arena in situations when the government needed to identify a journalist representative to negotiate with (for instance, for Wage Board purposes or on Press Council issues). Its position was definitely stronger in the era when newspapers were more regulated by the government.

Chronology of Indian newspaper history[16]

The first newspapers in India appeared in the 1780s. They were published in English and targeted at the European communities of traders, merchants and administrators living in the big colonial cities: Calcutta, Madras and Bombay. They were rather thin publications, with usually a few pages of local news and gossip relating to the community of their audience, but also containing extracts from newspapers in Britain. The circulation of these eighteenth-century newspapers seldom exceeded 200 copies. The early papers, however, were not always trivial and politically marginal. It was often individuals outside the colonial administration who started these papers, and they were not obliged to show loyalty towards the East India Company. The man usually honoured as the pioneer of Indian journalism, James Hicky with his *Bengal Gazette* published in Calcutta, almost instantly became highly controversial for the manner in which his paper attacked the government and the Governor-General, Warren Hastings. Hicky was accused of using vulgar and malicious language and he was eventually charged and sent to prison. A number of other editors during the early period were deported from India because of their criticism of the government. This seems to have been one of the reasons that Indian editors began to be recruited by newspapers: Indians could not be deported.

Indian-owned newspapers arrived on the scene in the second decade of the nineteenth century. Individuals associated with, or inspired by, the social reform movement that occurred during this period usually started them. This movement was particularly lively in Calcutta, home of the *Brahmo Samaj* and its founder Rammohun Roy. It is not surprising that the first ventures into Indian-owned papers were in the colonial capital. Rammohun Roy and his associates published extensively: books, tracts and pamphlets, but also several weeklies and magazines that survived for shorter or longer periods. The first short-lived weekly was printed in English and had the same name as James Hicky's original newspaper, the *Bengal Gazette*. It was succeeded by a Bengali weekly, the *Samboud Kaumudi*, which seems to have attracted considerable attention. Soon, Rammohun Roy also launched a Persian weekly, the *Mirat ul Ukhbar*. The purpose of these papers was to educate Indian people about Western science and ideas, and to propagate reforms of social and religious practice in Hindu society. Religion was much in focus as a controversial subject in the early vernacular press; the newspapers published by Rammohun Roy and his followers were opposed both by organs of more orthodox Hindu opinions and by Christian missionaries who also published papers in Indian languages. The early vernacular newspapers were, however, not exclusively concerned with religious and social enlightenment. They also contained local news reporting, foreign news, shipping intelligence and market prices; criticism of the government and ventilation of public grievances were also printed (Natarajan, 1962: 46–47).

The first vernacular and Indian-owned newspapers in Calcutta certainly had their critics, not least among the government authorities, but the English newspapers of the time were not necessarily antagonistic. Calcutta in the early nineteenth century was a city of amazing cultural creativity. It was the time of the Bengal Renaissance, which in large part was the fruit of the encounter between European and Bengal culture (Hannerz, 1992: 182–92). A contemporary of Rammohun Roy was James Silk Buckingham, editor of one of the main English newspapers of the city, the *Calcutta Chronicle*. Buckingham seems to have been a remarkable personality who came to Calcutta in 1818, following extensive travelling in Asian countries. He had a keen interest in local culture (his other fields of concern ranged from air-balloons to English literature and fossil mammoths) and was sympathetic to his counterparts in the vernacular press:

> The pleasure with which we regard the effusions of the Native Press, does not arise from the intrinsic value of these productions of its infancy; but as an earnest of what it may produce when it has attained maturity. We therefore regard with pity those attempts that have been made to treat it with contempt by supercilious remarks on the ideas of one and the puerile criticism on the style of the other. The languages of the East are surely fit for nobler purposes than being conned over in schools and colleges and stored up in Lexicons. (James Silk Buckingham, quoted in Natarajan, 1962: 43)

The foremost historian of the Indian press, S. Natarajan, regards Buckingham as the first great inspirer of journalism in the country. Rammohun Roy was evidently greatly influenced by his editorship and between the two men there appears to have been considerable affinity and mutual respect (ibid.: 45). (Buckingham was, however deported from India after only five years in Calcutta.) On the whole, there was no great rift between the British-owned and the Indian press during the first half of the nineteenth century. The two coexisted side by side on more or less equal terms, both at times working under severe restrictions regarding the printing of comments on government activities (the Adam Regulations, 1823–35).

The important event that inserted a wedge between British and Indian-owned newspapers was the revolt of 1856–57. Before this eruption the press in India had not posed any real danger to the colonial regime. "None of the Indians conducting newspapers ... was anxious to see the British leave the country. The important group influenced by Rammohun Roy in fact felt that British contacts and English institutions were necessary for the regeneration of the people" (ibid.: 49). The 1857 revolt emphasised the division of society in British India, all relations between colonial masters and Indian subjects were informed by deep mistrust. Also, after this event, the press was perceived as being made up of "two distinct entities—one Indian and one Anglo-Indian [British-owned] press—sharing a common history, purpose, and ethos, but separated by some as yet ill-defined politicised communal loyalty" (Israel, 1994: 4). The British press began to act as defenders of the colonial regime, often displaying a degree of racism, and the Indian-owned press was set on the course that would eventually make many of the newspapers vocal supporters of the nationalist struggle.

In the early period all newspapers in India had been quite strictly regionally circulated. But, the introduction of new means of transportation and communication in the middle of the nineteenth century—the railway and the telegraph—opened up the possibility for newspapers to be spread over wider geographical areas. Furthermore, the English-reading public had grown with the British policy of cherishing a Western-educated class of Indians in-between the colonial masters and the masses (Varma, 1998). The British East India Company for a long period continued with the practice introduced by the Muslim rulers of using Persian as the official language. During the first half of the nineteenth century

English replaced Persian as the language of the bureaucracy and became the most important second language of the Indian elite (King, 1994: 53). In the second half of the century a number of English-language newspapers, both British- and Indian-owned, became recognised as 'national' papers, read in different parts of the country even though they were still rooted in one of the regions around the urban centres—Calcutta, Madras, Bombay or in the north, Allahabad. Some newspapers of this time are still in existence today as respected centenarians of the Indian press (the *Times of India*, the *Statesman*, the *Pioneer* and the *Hindu,* for example). A press was born that wrote on events and politics in an all-India context and was read by an elite audience, consisting of two opposing groups. The British-owned press became an influential voice of colonial interests in India, often indirectly supported by the government through purchase and advertisements. The Indian-owned elite press, on the other hand, became the voice of the nationalist struggle and was often managed and edited by men who were leading figures in the movement. When the Indian National Congress was formed in Bombay 1885, one-third of the seventy delegates who attended were associated with Indian newspapers of the time (Natarajan, 1962: 126). It was after 1885 that newspapers started to carry editorial pages dealing with political issues (ibid.: 118).

Yet, the Indian-language press developed slowly. It was fairly strong only in Bengal and Bombay until the latter part of the nineteenth century. There was, however, in many regions, a hand-written 'manuscript press' which sometimes had a wider readership than printed newspapers; in 1850 the Nawab of Awadh is estimated to have employed 65 news writers on a monthly salary. The manuscript press was, according to Natarajan, an irresponsible and careless press that "carried the most fantastic rumours" (ibid.: 86). When printing equipment became cheaper it began to decline and to be replaced by printed papers in vernacular languages. The *Amrita Bazaar Patrika*, founded as a weekly in 1868, became a powerful newspaper published in Calcutta but with an impact far beyond Bengal. Its strongly critical stand against the government was probably one of the main reasons behind the introduction of the Oriental Language Press Act in 1878, which gave the authorities legal means to control the vernacular newspapers. The *Amrita Bazaar Patrika*, however, quickly escaped this threat by converting itself into an English-language newspaper; the law was repealed after only three years.

Until the turn of the century almost every significant development of the press in India originated in Calcutta. At that time, the initiative was to some extent shared with Bombay. Bal Gangadhar Tilak and his followers in Maharashtra learnt from the Brahmo Samaj reformers in Bengal how to use the press to influence public opinion on religious issues. But Tilak also used this lesson the other way round: in the two papers that he started in Bombay, one in English and another in Marathi, he used religious sentiments and Hindu symbols to attract political support from large sections of Hindus in Maharashtra. He was successful to such an extent that his glorification of a mythical Hindu past, in particular the historical ruler Shivaji, with little relevance outside Maharashtra, became popular even in faraway Bengal. Other nationalist leaders and newspapermen soon followed Tilak's example. Madan Mohan Malviya did the same thing in newspapers that he launched in northern India: the *Leader* and *Abhuduya*. Muslim leaders, such as Mohammed Ali in his *Camrade*, used their newspapers to propagate pan-Islamic identity (Varadarajan, 1999: 176). The marriage between religious populism and the press was definitely established.

In the early twentieth century the British-owned press was a rather homogeneous English-language elite press with a 'national' journalistic profile—often technically advanced, financially sound and, above all, politically hegemonic in its loyalty to the regime and closeness to the bureaucracy. The Indian-owned newspapers made a striking contrast: they were highly heterogeneous and segmented on many levels. There were newspapers in English as well as in a multitude of vernacular languages, regionally circulated with varying professional competence and produced within a range of different technical and financial conditions. In most cases the Indian newspapers neglected the commercial side; they were idealistic enterprises concentrating on developing and distributing ideas.

And, there were many opinions. "Every Indian newspaper came into being to express a point of view, and with the spread of education and the development of representative institutions there were many points of view claiming to be heard" (Natarajan, 1962: 171). Furthermore, points of view were ventilated from, and on behalf of, different interests within Indian society.

The development of the Indian-owned press could at several points be seen as a parallel to the emergence of the 'bourgeois press' in Western Europe, as described in Habermas' treatise on the 'public sphere' (1989). Just as in Europe, the Indian newspapers emerged as an arena between state and civil society where public opinion could be formed. In India, the press began to grow during a period when the legitimacy of a colonial regime was being questioned. The formation of a sphere of critical discourse was part of a slow transition from colonialism to independence, just as Habermas considered it to be part of the transition from absolutist to more democratic forms of government in Europe. The history of newspapers in India also confirms the close relation between 'print-capitalism' and nationalism that Benedict Anderson (1991) has pointed out. It is not possible to narrate the history of the Indian press apart from the history of the national movement.

The Indian example, however, diverged at some crucial points from the models that Habermas and Anderson have outlined. The 'public sphere' in Europe was in principle an open arena in which differences of status between participants should be of no importance; and the nation always seemed to be imagined as quite homogeneous.[17] In India, the emergence of newspapers never produced a single public sphere open to all, nor did the newspapers help much to imagine the nation in a unified way (Varadarajan, 1999). The policy of the colonial power of treating India as a society divided by caste and religion, and to use these divisions as a base for the representation of the subjects, was on the whole mirrored by the Indian elite. To be recognised as a legitimate voice one could not claim to speak on behalf of the whole country. "Most Indian newspapers in the latter part of the nineteenth century had internalised the colonial political culture to such an extent that even when colonialism was challenged or excoriated, it was often from a 'Hindu' or 'Muslim' point of view" (ibid.: 174). The image of India, during the early stages of the national movement, was a collection of communities rather than a unified entity; India consisted of Hindus plus Muslims plus Sikhs plus Christians and so on (Pandey, 1990). There were also journals that formed opinion from the bases of a particular caste identity, such as the *Kayashta Samachar* (Carrol, 1973).

For the greater part of the nineteenth century the vernacular press in northern India mostly consisted of journals devoted to literature, religion and science. They were primarily written in Nagari (the script used in Sanskrit) or Persian and sometimes they carried both scripts. Hindi and Urdu had not yet crystallised as separate languages associated with particular communities. But this was exactly what happened in the latter part of the century. Hindi written in the Nagari script and Urdu in Persian script were promoted by opposing religious interests and reshaped to form distinct languages (King, 1994; Lelyveld, 1993). Hindi was 'purified' by the use of many Sanskrit words, and Urdu by the use of an extensive Persian and Arabian vocabulary. They became languages of conflicting religious communities. One of the proponents of Hindi was the writer Bhartendu Harishchandra, who entered the field of journalism and started a number of publications from 1867 onwards. Being the main literary figure of the time in north India, his efforts are usually counted as the main impetus towards some growth of Hindi-language journalism, still, however, mainly in the form of literary journals. Incidentally, according to Natarajan (1962: 104), the first daily news that could be read in Hindi was in a newspaper published from London. The *Hindustan* (1884) was printed in three languages simultaneously: Hindi, Urdu and English.

It was not until the second decade of the twentieth century that Hindi dailies with a significant circulation started to appear. Again, it was from Calcutta that the impulse came with the *Bharat Mitra*, which became the most successful Hindi-language daily of the time. When the rich Benares merchant Shiva Prasad Gupta launched the daily *Aaj* in 1920, in the proper Hindi-speaking area, he managed to recruit three journalists from the renowned Bengali newspaper. Shiva Prasad Gupta had high ambitions for his new publication. He supported the goal of independence for India, saw the need for a newspaper in Hindi and wanted to establish *Aaj* as a national institution. The newspaper was supposed to educate in the nationalist spirit and was aimed at a broad readership and sold for a low price (ibid.: 192). With the *Aaj,* the Hindi-language press finally gained momentum and overtook the Urdu newspapers, which until then had been more important. Nevertheless, Hindi journalism was mainly found in weekly or monthly journals. Parthasarathy (1995: 189) mentions that in 1924 there were 102 Hindi newspapers, but only four of them were dailies.

The *Aaj* remained the leading Hindi daily up to independence, when several of the English-language dailies launched Hindi editions that became successful. The *Hindustan,* published from the *Hindustan Times* group, came already in 1936, whereas the *Pioneer* and the *National Herald* both started publishing their Hindi editions—*Swatantra Bharat* and *Navjivan* respectively—in the year of independence, 1947. In 1950 the *Times of India* introduced *Nav Bharat Times,* which for a long period was the most widely read Hindi paper. The owner of the *Indian Express*, however, failed with *Jansatta*, 1952–54 (but it was successfully revived in 1983). The big English-language publishing houses possessed several advantages that enabled them to colonise the Hindi-language market: good technology, a working system of distribution, advertising revenues from their main edition and, not least, credibility from their English-language elite papers (Jeffrey, 1997b: 77). Hindi newspapers outside the English-language press establishments remained few. According to one Hindi editor, the English press was "sabotaging the development of the Hindi press" (ibid.). Besides *Aaj,* until the 'newspaper revolution' began the most important were *Amar Ujala* (established in 1940), *Dainik Jagran* (1947) and *Punjab Kesari* (1965).

In Natarajan's opinion, journalism in India went into a sad decline after independence (1962: 297). A journalism that during the struggle for freedom had been associated with a heroic mission had lost much of its purpose. The occupation was badly paid and hardly attractive to young people with ambition. Journalism could not compete with new career possibilities—in government offices, industry and commerce—that had opened up when the British left the country. This was also the period when newspaper publishing began to be transformed from an idealistic into a commercial enterprise. The new proprietors were businessmen who took an interest in the financial side of journalism, which had often previously been neglected. This did, of course, nurture the awareness that the sales of a newspaper had something to do with what was printed on its pages. The newspapers started to explore 'populism' and Natarajan points out in particular one side of this development, which he calls 'sensationalism'. This is a word commonly used by media critics today, in the depiction of the regional and vernacular press. For example, when the newspapers exaggerated casualties in the violence during the Ayodhya conflict, it was commented upon as 'sensationalism'. Already, in the 1940s, though newspapers were denounced as 'sensational' in the particular meaning that the expression is currently used.

> [S]ensationalism in the context of Indian journalistic controversy means distorting communal and political differences and latterly presenting reports with little supporting evidence. (ibid.: 284)

Natarajan refers to an editor-proprietor in Bengal who had remarked that "[e]ven the newsboys refuse to touch my paper if my rivals report a larger number of deaths than I do" (ibid.) and allegedly got results in sales with a policy of prominently exposing riots and disturbances in his pages.

The decades after independence were also a period of enlarged institutionalisation of the relationship between the state and the press. Both the government and a number of critical voices within the press increasingly expressed the need to review the role of newspapers. In 1952 a government commission was appointed to look into the condition of the press. Among its participants were representatives of editors and working journalists through the respective organisations that were newly formed. The work of the Press Commission resulted in the setting up of bodies like a Registrar of Newspapers to keep track of all regular publications, a Press Council to promote the development of "a healthy and responsible press" (ibid.: 298) and a Wage Board to fix minimum wages for journalists.

Lucknow as a place of newspaper publication

Lucknow had been an important place of publishing in the late nineteenth century, particularly with regard to Urdu literature and Urdu newspapers (Naim and Petievich, 1997; Narain, 1998).[18] The contemporary significance of Lucknow as a city of many newspapers is, however, not very ancient. The *Pioneer* and the *National Herald* both established their head offices in Lucknow in the 1930s. This was the decade when Lucknow had in practice regained its role as the provincial capital and consequently became more attractive as a publishing centre for newspapers. For half a century Allahabad had been the premier city of the region and was far ahead in newspaper publishing; in the 1920s there were five newspapers published in Allahabad but only one in Lucknow (Pant-Joshi, 1991: 242). For more than three decades the *Pioneer* and the *National Herald* remained prominent institutions in the life of Lucknow, with an influence beyond the state of Uttar Pradesh. In addition to their English-language flagships, they also published vernacular editions. Gradually, these publishing houses have lost their leading positions. While the *Pioneer* is still a newspaper with some vitality, and with an edition also in New Delhi, the *National Herald* is barely surviving with a minuscule circulation. Since the *Times of India* launched its Lucknow edition, it has evolved as the leading English-language paper of the city.

The biographies of the *Pioneer* and the *National Herald* capture some important features of the history of India journalism. The *Pioneer*, whose history is much longer than its presence in Lucknow, represents the colonial inheritance in the press. It was started in Allahabad in 1865, and is one of the most evident examples of a British-owned newspaper that in colonial times had clear loyalties to the government and close ties to officials. Natarajan claims that the paper was launched as an answer to a persistent demand from officials for a government newspaper to meet the criticisms from the Indian press. The *Pioneer* seems instantly to have filled this position and obtained privileged access to advance information about government policies (Natarajan, 1962: 84–85). Another historian of Indian journalism asserts that a few decades later the *Pioneer* was leading the British-owned press in their attack against the Congress party (Parthasarathy, 1995: 83). In 1933 it moved its head office and production to Lucknow (without missing a single edition, the folklore has it). In the same year it became the first of the great British-owned newspapers to be taken over by Indian proprietors; the first owners were members of the landed aristocracy in Lucknow (the *taluqdars*). On the eve of independence, the publishing house also started a Hindi-language edition, perhaps in order to wash away some of the colonial dust. The Hindi newspaper was appropriately named *Swatantra Bharat* (Independent India). The former closeness to the colonial regime has not completely discredited the history of the paper. Few of the contemporary employees would fail to mention that two famous British Nobel laureates have contributed to the reputation of the *Pioneer*. Rudyard Kipling was a member of the staff in 1887 and Winston Churchill covered the British war in Afghanistan at the end of the same century for the paper. When the *Pioneer* is celebrated as 'A Milestone of Lucknow Journalism', however, it is mostly the post-independence period that is emphasised—and particularly the editorship of one man, S.N. Ghosh, who became the first Indian editor of the *Pioneer* and stayed with the paper for more than three decades.[19]

Jawaharlal Nehru, the man who became India's first Prime Minister, launched the *National Herald* in 1938 for the reason that the Congress party had no support from any of the major newspapers in the United Provinces (as Uttar Pradesh was then called) (Israel, 1994: 23; Natarajan, 1962: 233).[20] By doing so he was not only following a tradition among leaders of the nationalist movement but also in the steps of his father, Motilal Nehru, who in 1891 had established the *Independent* in Allahabad, which would, he declared, "think aloud for India" (Israel, 1994: 1). Chalapathi Rau, often mentioned in journalist hagiographies as one of the great editors of India, was appointed to the *National Herald* in 1946 and held the post of editor for 30 years; during much of that time he had a powerful rival in S.N. Ghosh of the *Pioneer*. In the 1960s and 1970s, the

Herald was certainly one of the most powerful newspapers in India. Even though its circulation was never high, its influence came through patronage from the highest political circles. Chalapathi Rau became known not only for his abilities as an editor but also for his deep loyalty to Jawaharlal Nehru (and later to Indira Gandhi whose husband, Feroze Gandhi, was also managing director of the newspaper in the 1940s and 1950s). The prime commitment of the *National Herald*, together with its editions in Hindi and Urdu, was to expose and popularise the ideology of Nehru (Parthasarathy, 1995: 270). In a sense the *Herald* had the same privileged role in relation to the Nehru government as the *Pioneer* once had to the colonial regime.

Chalapathi Rau was closely associated with the development of several press institutions during the decades after independence. He was instrumental in forming the Indian Federation of Working Journalists (of which he was the first president) and he was a member of the first Press Commission. In the global arena he represented Indian journalism in several international organisations and participated (on some occasions accompanying Jawaharlal Nehru) in a number of conferences around the world.

The times when the *National Herald* mattered are, however, gone. The newspaper remained so close to Congress (I) that it was perhaps inevitable that it would also accompany the party in its decline. When I visited the editorial office in February 1998 the paper was still being published, but its English and Hindi editions amounted to no more than a few hundred copies each, and they looked like roughly printed leaflets with news-agency briefs (the Urdu edition, though, fared somewhat better). It was amazing, however, that it was published at all. The staff had not been paid for 13 months and the whole atmosphere was one of bitterness and dejection. The journalists had appealed to Sonia Gandhi, who personally had a stake in the newspaper, to do something—but without success. Loudly, the journalists cited the BJP leader Atal Bihari Vajpayee who had recently commented that if the Congress was not able to run its three newspapers, how could it possibly claim to run a country? It was strange to think that this dilapidated newspaper office had once been part of the sphere of national political power in India and with established links to international media policy makers.

Chalapathi Rau, who cherished a visionary attitude towards journalism, predicted that "[t]he future of the Indian press means essentially the future of the Indian language press" (1968: 8). But of the extent to which the vernacular press would come to grow he could have had no idea, least of all in the heart of his own region. Just one decade before it all started to happen, he wrote:

> In the Hindi-speaking areas, the position [of the vernacular press] is depressing. The language used is still stilted and, while there are several large towns, there is no metropolitan city which could have been fertile ground for a few large newspapers. Delhi, still enormously growing, is the only place with big Hindi-language dailies. (ibid.: 143)

Today, the widest circulated newspapers of northern India are printed in Hindi and they are mostly published and circulated outside Delhi, in a large number of medium-sized towns. Much has changed in journalism since the heyday of both the *Pioneer* and the *National Herald*. One character from history, however, seems to continue: the leading newspaper of Lucknow still has a special connection with the political power in India. The relationship between *Dainik Jagran* and the BJP government is perhaps identical neither with the relationship that the *Pioneer* once had with the colonial government, nor with that the *National Herald* had with the Congress. The intimacy, however, can hardly be denied when the chief editor is also a member of parliament of the party in power.

Notes

1. All information on the circulation of newspapers in India is known to be notoriously unreliable. I therefore avoid giving precise figures. It is an open secret in the newspaper world that it is possible to manipulate even auditing by the Audit Bureau of Circulation (ABC).

2. One has to take into consideration that Lucknow is a political and administrative rather than a commercial centre. Advertising is therefore limited.
3. The total number registered as literate in the 2001 census was 1,514,827. Several resident editors I talked to calculated a figure of roughly 200,000 for the total number of copies that could be sold in Lucknow.
4. The status hierarchy is not only a diffuse perception among newspeople. It is manifest, for example, in advertising revenues. An English-language newspaper may charge more for advertising space than a Hindi-language paper, even though the circulations of the papers are the same.
5. The Indian states are in principle constructed along language borders. Hindi, is the official language of eight north Indian states.
6. For figures on the number of newspapers published Jeffrey refers to the Registrar of Newspapers for India, which had records of 875 in 1976 and 4,453 in 1995. The figures on circulation refer to Press in India, an annual report from the Ministry of Information which calculates a growth from 9.3 million to 40.2 million copies per day from 1976 to 1996.
7. One might note that Jeffrey's argument, interestingly enough, seems to be an inversion of the usual transmission view of communication: people's will to participate in politics has changed the structure of the mass media, rather than the other way round.
8. www.censusindia.net
9. The 2001 census found 27 Indian cities with a population of more than one million. Those cities had a total population of 73 million. Thus, 954 million Indians lived in smaller places (www.censusindia.net).
10. www.jagran.com
11. See, for example, Nireekshak, 2000 and Kang, 2001.
12. Media critics have, for example questioned the owner/editor of *Dainik Jagran* in connection with the establishment of a sugar mill. (*Vidura*, 1995: 12–14)
13. See for example, *Dainik Jagran*, Lucknow, 24 December 1997.
14. It is, for example, difficult to point to Kerala, with its turbulent political situation and high voting turnout, as an example of the close correlation between political expectations and newspaper reading, because this state also has the highest literacy rate in India. Likewise, the fast growth rate of newspapers in poor states like Uttar Pradesh, Orissa, Andhra Pradesh and Karnataka only shows that

literacy is probably more important than economic growth in raising newspaper circulation (Jeffrey, 2001: 32).

15. During the 1990s a third party, BSP (Bahujan Samaj Party) representing Dalit interests, carved out a sizeable niche in UP politics.
16. When no other source is referred to, this section draws on Natarajan's (1962) influential work on the history of the press in India.
17. How open the European public sphere was in practice has been questioned. See, for example, Fraser, 1992.
18. In particular, the printing business started by Munshi Nawal Kishore in 1858 produced a large number of books and journals in Urdu, Persian, Hindi and Sanskrit.
19. A young journalist that I encountered showed me a paper with this title that he had written for a diploma degree in journalism.
20. In Madras the *Indian Express* was established in the same period and for similar reasons (Israel, 1994: 94).

Three

The Cartography of News

A good place to get an impression of what the Lucknow dailies look like is in the arcade in front of Indian Coffee House at the busy intersection of Mahatma Gandhi Marg and Ashok Marg. Here, one can find a couple of Lucknow's best-supplied vendors of magazines, posters and newspapers, the first two of which dominate the scene. As one enters the arcade, it is the colourful pictures of movie stars, gods and small babies, pinned up on the wall, attracting attention. By a long table people are crowding round to make a choice among (or just have a look at) a multitude of glossy magazines devoted to films, sport, lifestyles or current news. The daily newspapers lie in rows on the pavement, conveniently close to the vendor himself where he sits and collects rupees for his goods; the newspapers may be less prominently displayed, but are probably the category of printed matter that sells best. In one row lie the papers from other regions, arriving on the afternoon trains from New Delhi or Kolkata, while another row consists of the locally produced newspapers. In both cases the papers are arranged overlapping each other so that only the mastheads are possible to read, except for the one on top. A customer does not usually make his choice of reading matter from what the different newspapers have on their headlines on a particular day. He just approaches the vendor, identifies the paper that he wants from the mastheads in the row, picks it up and hands over the money. We shall soon take a look at some of that reading, but first a few words about my approach to newspapers in this chapter.

In many senses the primary components of a newspaper are the individual stories. Each story is written as a single complete piece of text, and a newspaper contains numerous such stories every day that can be read and analysed as distinct pieces of journalistic work. For the reporter the story is the natural unit in which to conceptualise his or her work. Most of the daily routines in an editorial office are aimed at producing a sufficient number of completed and separate stories to print in the next edition of the paper. What attract the reader's conscious attention are also individual stories that deal with topics that interest him or her. It is obvious that a great deal of research on journalism focuses on the stories and closely analyses pieces of text. But if one is interested in journalism as a cultural product, there is all the more reason to invoke the old saying that one may risk not to seeing the wood for the trees. That it is essential to pay attention to the form of a mass medium, and not only the content, was one of Marshall McLuhan's [1994 (1964)] insights that is worth taking seriously. James Carey is of the opinion that "the most important descriptions and explanations of journalism are lost when they are sliced into daily fragments, thin issues of reality, disconnected from a narrative framework" (1986: 158). The very mix and display of news items on the pages of a daily newspaper can tell one something about journalism that would never appear from hundreds of news clippings of individual stories. Journalism in a society cannot be reduced to the actual content of stories that readers are inhaling as pure information. A daily newspaper is a physical product of ink and paper that can be looked at, touched and even smelled. And most people consume it in a quite randomly selective way: glossing it over, reading a few lines here and there, their attention perhaps caught by a few stories. (In a sense, consuming a newspaper is not unlike watching television with a remote control.)

Thus, this chapter, which aims at giving a picture of how Lucknow newspapers look when they reach their readers, has the character more of browsing than of close reading. I shall pay attention to the disposition of the pages, the kinds of sections that are found in the newspapers and how the stories are categorised. Particular stories will be cited and referred to in order to offer a flavour of the content in the papers, but will not be the focus of textual analysis. Mainly I want to present a picture of what the Lucknow newspapers' 'panorama of facts and persons' (Carey, 1986: 163) looks like.

But one could start by stepping even further back from analysing the content to reflect more broadly about journalism and newspapers in an urban Indian milieu. Already, the fact that a daily mass-spread newspaper exists distinguishes a society from one without such a paper. Even an illiterate person will know that there is information available about events that he or she has not seen; one can always inquire from people who have read the news. The newspaper often acts as an authority even among non-readers. A verbal rumour can circulate embedded in "the newspaper says that ...". Journalism as an institution is also present in a society in a way that goes beyond its actual task. The newspapers of Lucknow are an integral part of the city whether one reads them or not. All cities have their icons that are important for the urban identity of their inhabitants. Lucknow has its university, government departments, law courts, hospitals, historical buildings and all the other institutions that are so familiar to its citizens; the established newspapers are clearly among them. King George Medical College, Vidhan Sabha, Charbagh and the *Pioneer* might be very diverse as institutions—a hospital, the State Assembly, a railway station and a newspaper—but they are all important points of reference for a Lucknowite. This is most obvious in a geographical sense. To describe "where I am going" or "where that shop is located", these sites are used more frequently than street names (the name of a newspaper is also the name of an editorial building, which in most cases is a centrally located and well known place). But these institutions also work as emblems of a city's identity: this is what we have in Lucknow (not all cities have an Eiffel Tower, a Buckingham Palace or a Manhattan skyline, but they always have something).

So, how were the newspapers of Lucknow visible in urban life, during my stay in the town? First, of course, no other icons could compete with the presence of the mass media institutions right in the homes of so many city inhabitants every day; roughly 200,000 households in the city were getting a (or several) newspapers every morning, delivered on the doorstep between six and eight o'clock. Moving around in the city, especially in the morning, you could see people reading papers in teashops or just at the roadside. Along the main streets and thoroughfares there were plenty of billboards and hoardings advertising the town's different newspapers with slogans like 'Number One in U.P.', 'The Leader in Lucknow', 'The Fastest Growing Paper in Lucknow' or 'Not Just a Newspaper, Also a Friend'. And, again, the editorial buildings themselves were leaving their imprint on the city. The 'Fleet Street' of Lucknow was situated in the eastern part of downtown, in *Sikander Bagh*, where one could find five of the city's newspaper buildings within a few minute's walking distance of each other. In this part of the town the journalists almost dominated the scene, moving in and out of the editorial buildings, coming and going on scooters. Wherever you saw small groups of men chatting in teashops or at street corners in this area, many of them were probably reporters taking a break between assignments. Even in the middle of the night when the rest of the city was dark and quiet, there would always be some activity and a few cheap restaurants still open serving kebabs and omelettes to journalists on duty. Also in other parts of town reporters were quite easy to spot, as they almost always moved around on scooters with a 'Press' sign on the rear mudguard. In certain places there would be a greater chance of finding them, such as around the State Secretariat, outside police stations and at the headquarters of political parties. In the evenings there was always a crowd of 'Press' scooters outside a beautiful pink historical building in the area called China Bazaar, the location of the Lucknow Press Club.

However, the Lucknow newspapers were not present on the urban scene in one of the ways that the press permeates city life in Europe and North America, that is, as newspaper logos and news in bold letters displayed on placards outside retailers on each and every corner. Morning newspapers all over India are mainly circulated by monthly subscription and news vendors are few. Someone who is not familiar with the town can walk up and down the street for hours looking for a shop to buy a newspaper. The only area of Lucknow where you can find them in some numbers is in *Hazrat Ganj*, the up-market shopping area. On the other hand, there are retailers with impressive selections of reading matters, such as the vendor outside the Coffee House mentioned at the beginning of this chapter.

The outsider who, in 1998, took a look at the local morning papers on display on the ground would easily have discerned a considerable resemblance, despite the fact that the English, Hindi and Urdu newspapers use distinct alphabets. All newspapers were printed in the same broad-sheet format (390 × 540 mm) and page layouts were based on eight columns. Pages were edited quite compactly with many articles, a lot of text and few pictures or illustrations. Headlines or pictures rarely exceeded three columns. The newspapers were almost identical in the number of pages they contained, normally 16 (excluding supplements). None of the papers were glued or stitched, the pages easily fell apart as you read them. But, of course, to anyone familiar with the Lucknow press, the newspapers did not look exactly the same. Fonts, styles, policies for headlines, use of lines and colours, disposition of the pages were a little different in all the papers. Furthermore, the quality of the paper made them look somewhat different. It was easy to distinguish the *Pioneer* with its pale white paper from *Dainik Jagran,* using a dimmer shade of white, or the *Times of India* that was a little greyish.[1] One has to say that the news vendor in Lucknow had a variety of fairly attractive and well-produced local newspapers to offer a customer. It might need to be pointed out that most of the newspapers found here were not some kind of primitive Third World version of newspapers. Generally, the days of barely legible news, printed with lead-type technology on the cheapest quality of paper, are gone. All the major newspapers are printed with at least the first and last page in colour. This was not the case two years earlier when only a couple of the Hindi-language papers were printed in colour. The English-language press in particular had been hesitant to depart from the ideal model of a 'serious' paper that prescribed black-and-white. But, due to competition, even these papers were forced to convert to a more popular appearance. Nevertheless, according to a European model of journalism, one has to conclude that overall the Lucknow newspapers appeared visually as constrained and serious; screaming black headlines and seductive pictures did not characterise this press.

What distinguished the different newspapers was, however, the price. Most Hindi-language papers in 1998 were priced at three rupees a copy. The newly started *Kuber Times* had rapidly succeeded in capturing a substantial part of the market by charging only two rupees. Paradoxically, the English-language newspapers, which presumably had the wealthiest readers, were the cheapest to buy. In order to compete with the increasingly well-produced vernacular papers they had already in the mid-1990s cut their price to one and a half rupees a copy.[2]

News sections

The Lucknow dailies followed more or less the universal model of classifying news stories.[3] On top of each page one would find a banner that referred either to a geographical category (the more common) or to a subject. The geographical categories that were frequently found in the banners referred to Lucknow, Uttar Pradesh, India and the world.[4] One can note that this model of geographical classification, which all of the newspapers used, is formally hierarchical, in the sense that the larger categories encompass the lower, like Russian dolls: Lucknow is part of Uttar Pradesh, which is part of India, which is part of the world. The exception is possibly a banner found in most of the Hindi-language papers (but in none of the English) that referred to administrative districts close to Lucknow (*zila*, *aspas*). But this category could also be interpreted as part of the hierarchy; these pages presented news from a rural vicinity, subordinate to Lucknow.[5]

The Lucknow dailies were also uniform with regard to the banners referring to subjects. All newspapers had particular pages for 'economy', 'sports', 'editorial' and 'features' and there were no great differences between them in the amount of space these subjects were given. Most carried two pages on the economy and one or two on sports (on both these subjects the Hindi press tended to have a little less material than the English press). All papers had one editorial page, and half of them used the opposite page for columns of an analytical character (op. ed.). In all newspapers, the last page, always in colour, was used for features material. It is notable that universally common subjects such as 'politics' and 'culture' were not used as banners at the top of pages in any of the Lucknow dailies. In the case of 'politics', this was hardly because news on this subject was missing in the newspapers. Rather, I would say, political news predominated on several pages to such an extent that it was useless as a category. The absence of a page on 'culture', on the other hand, did reflect north Indian newspapers' weak preoccupation with 'high' culture, such as literature, art or classical music and dance; material on popular culture like films, popular music and television was placed on the features pages.

Returning to the geographical categories used, it is easy to detect a difference between the English- and the Hindi-language newspapers. The latter newspapers all had around five pages with a banner that announced 'local news', while the English-language papers were content with two pages. 'National news' was on average given two pages in the English-language papers, and one or two pages were used for 'international' news. The Hindi papers often had one page in common for both 'national' and 'international' coverage. The patterns of geographical categories used at the top of the pages seemed to confirm a general image of both the English and Hindi presses: the English-language newspapers appeared to pay more attention to news of 'national' concern and the Hindi newspapers seemed more 'local'. But these patterns did not exactly mirror the quantity of news ascribed to different geographical levels. For example, all the Hindi-language papers—but none of those in English—carried several pages with a banner announcing 'various', on which news from state and national level was placed. We shall see that there are more reasons to qualify a commonly held impression that the Hindi-language newspapers were extremely 'local' in their concern.

I want to emphasise that geographical location—'place'—is a matter of great importance in journalism universally. For reporters all over the world, 'where?' is a question that should be answered preferably already in the first paragraph of an article (together with what? who? why? and how?). Likewise, the way journalism uses and juxtaposes the numerous places and geographical categories that appear every day on the pages is an important subject if one wants to understand the newspaper as a cultural product. This is a feature of journalism that makes it essential in the perspective of modernity. The consumer of mass media has an opportunity to extend his or her geographical horizon, to transgress the face-to-face context and build a notion of his/her place in the world. This should have some bearing on people's sense of belonging. To a great extent, the tools for imagining who and where you are, are constituted through the representation of space in the mass media (Anderson, 1991; Thompson, 1995: 31–45).

An analysis of how the Lucknow newspapers shaped the world cannot, of course, be confined to a glance at the banners used at the top of the pages. But already this superficial level of geographical categorisation shows some notable tendencies. One is that the predominant geographical categories were 'nation' and 'local'. The Hindi-language papers most clearly profiled themselves as 'local' by categorising a third of all their pages under this banner. The attempts of the English-language press to appear as 'national' were less obvious if one compares the space that was allotted to this category of stories. One interesting feature was that neither the Hindi- nor the English-language newspapers were emphasising the 'region', or any geographical category between 'nation' and 'local', in their terminology. There were generally only one page under the banner referring to Uttar Pradesh in all of the newspapers; the largest Hindi daily (*Dainik Jagran*) had even discarded this page altogether in 1998.

It may be pointed out once again that Lucknow is the capital of an Indian state with a territory larger than Great Britain and with a population exceeding that of Germany and Great Britain combined. Both in popular speech and demographically, Uttar Pradesh is usually divided into a number of regions such as East, Central and West, Uttarkhand is now a separate state and Bundelkhand. None of the newspapers were using these, or similar categories to structure news from the state or to situate Lucknow in a defined region. One might, for example, have expected that the newspapers in Lucknow would have emphasised the historical region of Awadh which in other contexts plays a great role in the cultural identity of the city. But they did not. One could conclude that, at this level, the 'regional press' did not appear very regional at all. The Lucknow newspapers, at least, did not bother much about constructing their own region.

This is not to say that the state of Uttar Pradesh was invisible in the news. 'Lucknow', as the name of the state capital, was often used as a metonym for the whole of Uttar Pradesh, in the same way as Washington, London or New Delhi often refer to the political power in the United States, Great Britain or India. In particular, news stories from state government departments (situated in the capital) that obviously concern all of Uttar Pradesh were often placed on the Lucknow pages. And despite the fact that generally only one page in the newspapers was headed with a 'State' or 'U.P.' banner, the front page of all the newspapers always gave a lot of prominence to state politics.

A closer look at the front pages will reveal that, among the main stories, the dominance of news ascribed to 'New Delhi' and 'Lucknow' was overwhelming. Of all the articles printed on the first page in eight of the Lucknow dailies during the last week in December 1997, 32 per cent had 'Lucknow' and 34 per cent 'New Delhi' in the date line.[6] If one counts only the three most important (conspicuously placed) news stories each day, the tendency is even clearer: 35 per cent were from Lucknow and 51 per cent from New Delhi. Interestingly, if one looks only at the front pages, the Hindi-language press did not appear more local than the English-language press. *Dainik Jagran*, which was the newspaper that devoted most space inside the paper to 'local' news, focused more on 'New Delhi' on the front page: out of the 18 most important news stories of the week, 'Lucknow' got only three while 11 referred to 'New Delhi'.

Among the front-page news that did not carry 'New Delhi' or 'Lucknow' in the date line it was difficult to see a pattern. There were places of both great and small significance, from all over India and abroad, represented. One could not discern any clear tendency to favour news from other places in Uttar Pradesh. It was also significant that Indian metropolises such as Mumbai, Bangalore, Chennai and Kolkata did not have any prominent place on the Lucknow newspapers' front pages: out of a total of 794 stories in the sample only 28 referred to any of these places (the majority to the financial centre of Mumbai). In the same sample there were 20 foreign news stories.

The newspapers' major preoccupation with Lucknow and New Delhi had a close connection with subjects that were considered newsworthy. The high frequency of these place names at the beginning of front-page news did not imply that these cities were reported as urban places from a variety of aspects. To repeat, both 'New Delhi' and 'Lucknow' were often used as metonyms. In the world of newspapers 'New Delhi' represents national concerns that are decided and organised from the national capital, while 'Lucknow' represents the same for Uttar Pradesh. These cities are interesting to the media because they are where the government departments and political institutions are located. From this it follows that for a newspaper to have 'a national perspective' is not a question of covering events from different places all over the country, but rather of reporting issues concerning the central government.

Politics

Browsing through the headlines on the front page of a Lucknow daily on an ordinary day revealed one obvious characteristic of Indian newspapers: they seem to be 'obsessed with politics' (Yadava, 1991). Of course, all over the world, journalists pay a lot of attention to politics. But, in India, journalism and political coverage are almost synonymous. Most of the major headlines on the front page would contain the name or acronym of a political party, or the name of a politician. The few pictures would most likely show politicians, either as portraits or in typical poses: speaking on a podium, greeting the masses, inaugurating some 'function' or sitting on the floor at some meeting—always wearing the uniform of an Indian politician, the 'kurta-pajama' (if it was not a rare woman or a Muslim). And 'politics' is usually narrated in the sense of referring to the party political game rather than to political issues or social problems of a fundamental or ideological character.[7]

News on politics is probably the 'commodity' that to a great extent sells the newspapers. The political game has a general interest and is not something exclusive to a well-educated elite. Politics could actually be considered part of popular culture, in much the same way as cricket or movies from the dream factory in Mumbai (*Bollywood* in colloquial speech). When moving around in Indian society, you can hardly avoid hearing, over and over again, the hit song from the latest film; but it is also unlikely that you will fail to be reminded of the political game. Political personalities like Atal Bihari Vajpayee, Sonia Gandhi and Kanshi Ram, or subjects such as 'communalism', 'reservations' and corruption, are prominent in what Appadurai and Breckenridge (1995) have called the 'public culture' of Indian modernity.[8] They are commodities of political-cultural consumption. Most political issues that become public knowledge and topics that become the focus of public speculation are bound to come from the mass media.[9]

In general, Indian newspapers do not have any official political bias. (The exception in Lucknow was the *National Herald* with its sister publications in Hindi and Urdu, which were owned by a trust close to the Congress(I) party.) Nevertheless, every Lucknow newspaper had a reputation of loyalty towards a particular party, and that reputation was generally pretty consistent.[10] In practice, the newspapers in Lucknow were known to be friendly towards either the Bharatiya Janata Party (BJP) or the Samajwadi Party (SP). The third of the main political parties in Uttar Pradesh—Bahujan Samaj Party (BSP)—seemed to have no friends among the press. This party, supported mainly by Scheduled Castes (SCs) and Muslims, had also been in major conflicts with the press on several occasions.[11] The recent success of this party should seriously qualify the importance of the mass media in the political process: obviously, it is possible to perform well in elections without a sympathetic press.

The basis for the political reputation of a newspaper was not always that the editorial page had an obvious political angle or that preferences shone through in the political coverage. More often, when the issue came up in my discussions both with journalists and with other citizens in Lucknow, it was the personal political image of the owner, chief editor or resident editor that was referred to. In the case of *Dainik Jagran*, the reputation was obvious because its chief editor/owner Narendra Mohan (residing in Kanpur) was a member of *Rajya Sabha* (the

Upper House of Indian Parliament) for the BJP. Otherwise, my impression was that the Lucknow editions were perceived in their local political context, making the resident editor a crucial figure in determining the reputation of the newspaper. A case to illustrate this was the *Times of India,* which had recently appointed a new resident editor during the second part of my field study in early 1998. This man was moved from the same position on another edition of the same paper—in Patna, the capital of Bihar, where he had ended up in trouble because he had run the edition in strong opposition to the powerful Chief Minister, Laloo Prasad Yadav. This was a well-known fact among journalists in Lucknow. But from the line that the resident editor had taken in the political context of a neighbouring state it was difficult to tell where his sympathies and antipathies would lie in Lucknow. So, the *Times of India* was in fact the only one of the main Lucknow newspapers that had a political leaning that was a little uncertain.

On the front page

The first page of a Lucknow newspaper contained a great number of stories and quite a lot of reading. It was definitely much more than a place to announce what was to be found inside the paper. Even though front pages were used as shop-windows to capture attention with the 'best' stories of the day, they were not dominated by a few conspicuous headlines intended to sell the paper. On the contrary, the first pages of the Lucknow dailies demonstrated a relatively low contrast between the top stories and news of less importance. Sometimes one story was displayed much more prominently than the rest—given more space, a picture and a bigger sized headline—but more often three or four main articles had about equal space and headline size. The more important story was placed, however, higher up on the page. The multitude of stories of different lengths that were fitted into the front page made its visual appearance rather cramped and messy. None of these dailies would have won a prize in an international newspaper design contest. Some stories were concluded on the front page but most of them continued inside the paper. None of the newspapers had adopted the model of printing summaries on the first page and displaying the full stories on inside pages. Advertising space was usually modest on the front pages and, apart from a one-column square on each side of the head logo, was confined to the lower portion of the page.

Even though political news was in abundance, the front pages did, of course, contain other material. Crime stories often found their way to the front page, as did sports news and, in most papers, the weather forecast. Occasionally, some event would beat all the politics and capture a prominent place in the newspapers; it might be a major train accident, a fire in an urban area or a local 'girl of the year' contest. On some days of the year it was obligatory to break into the flow of hard political news and top the front page with an appropriately respectful colour photograph; for example, on religious holidays such as Diwali, Id or Christmas, on Republic Day or on the anniversaries of the deaths of important national leaders. The point is, however, that the Lucknow newspapers on their front pages appeared rather strict and serious. One could see no evidence of an editorial staff that routinely dug for stories with a sensationalist twist to provide a prominent display. And, one only had to turn a few pages and glance through the brief police items to see that there was no lack of material with potential to exploit. In this respect, there was no obvious difference between the English press and the Hindi press. The English-language newspapers might have been a little more reluctant than some Hindi-language newspapers to diverge from its 'serious' approach, but quite contrary to what one often heard from intellectual media critics (and, I have to admit, contrary to what I initially thought), the Hindi press did not routinely indulge in cheap sensationalism.[12] I would like to illustrate this with how the newspapers in Lucknow treated one particularly gory story. At the same time, I shall attempt to portray how this press appreciated different kinds of stories with regard to 'news value'.

A moderately sensational crime

On 4 February 1996, which was a Sunday, the Hussein Ganj police station in central Lucknow informed press reporters who paid them a visit on their daily beat that a man had been found murdered near Vidhayak Niwas. This was a centrally located residential area known to house many members of the State Legislative Assembly and other VIPs. The body of a young male had been found wrapped in a jute bag; it had signs of injuries and bloodstains—and it was headless. The story was published in most editions of the newspapers the following day but none of them had used it as a main article to top the front page. In *Dainik Jagran* the story appeared as a short one-column item on the lower part of the front page. The headline, which was of the smallest size used in the paper, simply read 'Headless Corpse Found Close to Vidhayak Nivas'.[13] Another Hindi daily, *Rashtriya Sahara*, had printed the story as a four-column piece at the bottom of the front page, and given it a more prominent display with a rather big headline and illustrating it with a map of the location where the body was found.[14] In other newspapers, however, it was treated as a routine affair, not big enough to be a story on its own but forming part of the crime report that day (on a local page), together with some cases of suicide and a few arrests for disturbing the peace and illegal gambling. This was how the English-language papers, the *Times of India* and the *Pioneer,* handled it.

In the newspapers the following day, some more information had been added to the story. As several reporters wrote, the police had "achieved a major breakthrough" in the investigation by identifying the place where the man was killed. It was established that the crime had been committed on the seventh floor in one of the smart multi-storied buildings, in a flat belonging to a former member of the State Legislative Assembly, a politician of the Hindu nationalist party—the BJP. *Dainik Jagran* carried the story in a red frame on top of the front page ('Murder was committed in former BJP-legislator's apartment'). The murder competed for attention with several stories that received the same or a better display, for example, a ban on private practice by government-employed doctors, a violent conflict between the staff and police at Lucknow airport and an administrative officers' conference held in the city. Also, *Rashtriya Sahara* continued to run the story on the front page. In this paper it was placed on a roughly equal footing with a government proposal of new quotas for government jobs, a foreign affairs story concerning Pakistan and the ban on government doctors' private practice. The English-language press still had not found the murder important enough to deserve a place on the front page. The *Times of India* made it a top story on its city page ('Man was killed at BJP MLA's house') and the *Pioneer* had apparently missed, or neglected, the new development of the case altogether, as it was not to be found anywhere in the paper.[15] One might add that all four of the newspapers mentioned had the same opinion about which news event that day was the most suitable to illustrate with a picture on the front page; a three-column photograph of senior officers sitting around tables in a big hall everywhere illustrated the administrative officers' conference.

On the third consecutive day in the life of the murder story, it made the front page in all of the Lucknow newspapers. The new turn in the case was the police statement that they had evidence of the murder being a case of ritual sacrifice. Bloodstains under a picture of the Goddess Kali, known in Hindu mythology for her blood-lust, were found in the flat where the murder was committed, together with various paraphernalia said to be used in such rituals. According to the newspapers, the former member of the Legislative Assembly was suspected of having committed the ritual murder in order to improve his election prospects. But not even this development made the case an unquestionable top story on all the front pages. Surprisingly, it was only the *Times of India* that made it the biggest story of the day, running it over five columns just below the masthead with the sensational headline 'Man sacrificed to brighten poll prospects'. *Rashtriya Sahara* had it as one of three main stories on the upper half of the front page but was more careful with the headline: 'The police are considering "human sacrifice" behind the headless corps found at OCR' (in small letters) and 'Former BJP legislative suspected' (as the main headline).[16] *The Pioneer*, whose editorial office was located just across the street from where the murder was committed, made it only a one-column story on the lower half of the page, also giving it a headline that expressed some doubt about the facts ('Human sacrifice at MLA's house, claim police'). *Dainik Jagran* was even more hesitant towards the claims of the police. It made it a rather small story at the bottom of the page and gave it the neutral headline 'The murder case in the former MLA's flat has become more mysterious'.[17]

Which were the stories that on 7 February successfully competed for attention with a presumed politically motivated human sacrifice in a VIP quarter of the city? First, there were some new ingredients in an old dispute between the states of Tamil Nadu and Karnataka about the use of water resources from the Cauvery river. This was the top news on the front page in both *Dainik Jagran* and *Rashtriya Sahara*. Second, the president of one of the main opposition parties had issued a statement on the question of who was to be the chairman of an alliance between some opposition parties—a main news item in most papers. Third, high priority was generally given to stories on how the recent fall of the rupee had effected the market for consumer goods. All of these were so-called 'national news'; on this particular day there was not much local stuff that could compete with the murder. The exception was a photograph on several of the front pages, showing the Australian national hockey team arriving at Lucknow airport for a tournament that was to take place in the city.

Dainik Jagran page by page

In order to present a more coherent picture of what a north Indian newspaper may look like, I shall briefly glance through the pages of *Dainik Jagran* to see what kind of news we can find and how it is presented. It is important to remember that any description of a newspaper is confined to a particular time. The newspapers are constantly making small changes to their layout, and their journalistic profiles are also gradually undergoing changes. I have chosen to describe how *Dainik Jagran* looked in the winter of 1997–98, which was during the second period that I followed the press in Lucknow.

The front page of *Dainik Jagran* was, in comparison with other newspapers of the city, the one most densely packed with stories. During one week in December 1997, it contained on average 23 articles or news items per day. This could be compared with the *Times of India* which during the same week had only had half as many items on its front page. Usually, the

Dainik Jagran's front page had three or four lengthy articles with somewhat bolder and bigger headlines than other articles, what could be called the main stories. A few stories, a little less prominently displayed, could be described as secondary front-page stories. But what made *Dainik Jagran*'s front page so dense with news was all the brief items that filled up the space. The smallest of these were put together in the column on the left-hand side of the page, often framed and under the vignette 'brief news'(*sanksipt*). Somewhat longer news briefs were often kept together in the fourth column of the page, but could also be scattered anywhere on the page.

Appearing daily on the front page was also a short list of contents to be found inside the paper. Another daily vignette was 'temperatures' (*tapman*), giving the highest and lowest degrees Celsius for the previous 24 hours. Directly under this information the address for the Internet edition of *Dainik Jagran* was printed. Almost always there would be a three-column colour photograph on the upper half of the page (and sometimes also a smaller one somewhere else), which was usually an illustration to one of the main articles.

Dainik Jagran also used coloured lines in its front-page layout: under the head logo there was a thick blue line and at the lower half of the page there was a second multicoloured line marking out the articles on the bottom. The latter line had some symbolic significance as it had borrowed its colours—green and orange with a white space in-between—from the Indian flag.

To put some flesh on the skeleton just outlined we could take a glance at the front page on one particular day. Quite at random I chose the 24 December 1997 issue. The Lucknow subscribers of *Dainik Jagran* who picked up their morning paper on this Wednesday did not encounter anything extraordinary (particularly not that people in many parts of the world were celebrating Christmas eve on this very day). The three-column colour photograph that might be the first eye-catcher on the page showed a group of politicians, with the Congress President Sitaram Kesri easily identifiable, in a not very exciting situation; the men were obviously in a room holding a meeting, sitting on the floor covered with a white cloth. It was a visual illustration of politics that every newspaper reader in India was very familiar with; this type of photograph appeared almost every week in the papers. The photograph accompanied one of the main stories, which was about the resignation of a prominent member, a former minister, from the Congress party; a small portrait of the resigned politician was added on to the big picture. Another story, in the upper left-hand corner of the page, was about a judgment of the Mumbai High Court concerning certain directives issued by the Election Commission in connection with the approaching parliamentary election. These two articles were clearly placed at the top of the page to stand out as the main stories of the day. A third article, on the lower half of the page, could possibly be counted among the main stories. It was a report of a political mass meeting organised by BJP and some of its allied parties, close to the Uttar Pradesh city of Mathura. On this particular day, all three of the main stories were obviously political news and at least the first two could be said to be of 'national' concern. Both of them were also taken from news agencies. The one about the BJP meeting was more of an all-Uttar Pradesh concern and was written by one of the Lucknow staff reporters who had been sent on this assignment.

Among the second rung of articles, those in between the main stories and the brief news items, I counted seven articles on this day. In this category staff reporters in Lucknow had produced most of the material. A couple of articles dealt with the higher echelons of state politics and government; the Chief Minister as well as the Governor were, as almost every day, cited on some questions. A number of minor front-page stories were about the work in state government departments or municipal departments; on this day the Electricity Board, the Public Works Department and the Forest Department were topical. All of these secondary stories were, just as the main stories, also continued inside the paper.

In the category of longer news briefs (10–20 lines)[18] there were nine stories, most of them were non-local and taken from news agencies. For example, a nuclear plant in Rajasthan had set a record in energy production; in the northern parts of the country more than 20 people had died due to the cold winter;

in Mumbai it had been announced that fees for Internet connections would be reduced by 33 per cent; and in Faridabad a whole family had been killed when the roof of their house collapsed. There was one foreign news story among the longer news briefs, reporting some change of judges in the Pakistan High Court.

Under the vignette *sanksipt* (brief news) in the column on the far left-hand side of the page there were on this particular day eight brief items (3–7 lines). All of them consisted of domestic but non-local stories, about New Delhi politics or various minor events across the country. Four of them were reports on 'extremist' activities in Kashmir and in the north-east of the country.

The main front-page advertisement on this Wednesday announced in letters bolder than any of the headlines, that this would be the last eight days to get a 'Whirlpool' fridge or washing machine for 7,990 rupees. The other two advertisements on the page, one on each side of the masthead, were for 'T.T.' underwear and 'Mr Kleen' dishwash powder. Alongside the masthead *Dainik Jagran* also did some self-promotion by proclaiming that it was indeed the most widely read Hindi-language daily in India.

Local

If we turn the first page of an issue of *Dainik Jagran*, the local news (*sthaniya*) starts and continues over five or six pages stuffed with stories of various size and character. The local pages are not organised thematically but contain a mixture of everything—big and small issues. One will generally find a lot of stories reporting on, or scrutinising, government departments and authorities. Other stories simply report miscellaneous events that have taken place in the city. Frequently these 'events news' are about meetings that have been held in any of the city auditoriums by some political, cultural, commercial or social organisation (what in India go by the name of 'functions'). These pages also contain regular vignettes on specific matters, such as local information on events, trade union news, letters from readers and columns of a trivial (such as 'gossip' from the corridors of power) as well as a serious nature. There were also quite a lot of advertisements on the local pages. These were mostly for consumer goods, local shops or cinema theatres; but there was also plenty of space paid for by the government, such as advertising for positions, calls for tenders and announcements of changes in public services. An interesting characteristic was that quite a few of the commercial advertisements were published in English or a mixture of English and Hindi together. Another fact to be noticed was the very few classified advertisements—there as well as elsewhere in the paper—except for the day when the advertisements for matrimonial candidates were published.

The editorial staff in Lucknow naturally produced most of the journalistic material for the local pages. Each proper article began with a byline of some kind. Only a few, however, had the name of a staff reporter in the byline. This privilege was reserved for stories that were considered exclusive to the paper. More common were anonymous bylines like 'Jagran reporter' (*Jagran samvaddata*) or 'Jagran office' (*Jagran karyalya*) or 'news source' (*samvad sutr)*, revealing only if it was a staff reporter, several reporters together or a stringer who had written the article. A dateline opened the articles, with the name of the place where the story was compiled (on the local pages it was of course mostly 'Lucknow', or occasionally the name of a place adjoining the city) and the day of the week when the story was written. Another feature that had to do with the layout (and which went for other sections of the paper as well) was that all the stories were set fully in plain text. No sub-headlines were used to break up the stories into shorter sections and bold letters were not used in the opening paragraphs. Sometimes, however, important sentences from an article were duplicated in bigger letters and set within frames.

What did a reader in Lucknow expect to find when he opened the local pages of *Dainik Jagran*? Above all, he would daily encounter numerous articles concerned with local branches the Indian bureaucracies or public institutions, such as State government departments, municipal authorities, hospitals, schools and the police. This was an obvious outcome of how the news work was organised: institutions like these were covered on the local reporter's daily assignments. Very frequently these kinds of articles were oriented towards some problem. This could be problems that these institutions were working to solve—say, crime, diseases, environmental pollution, etc. But, just as often, the stories were about problems concerning the bureaucracies themselves, such as inefficiency, corruption or some controversy. To illustrate this latter type of 'minor irregularities' that were narrated on the local pages—major scandals would, of course, be published on the front page—I have picked out some examples from articles appearing in *Dainik Jagran* in early 1998.

One headline published on 4th February read 'Supply Department is unsuccessful in discovering false ration cards'. In the story, which had the byline 'Jagran correspondent', it was claimed that forged ration cards, especially for buying kerosene at subsidised prices, were available on the black market in Lucknow. Because of these fake cards goods had become scarce in some ration shops and people could not get what they needed and were entitled to. The reporter referred to anonymous residents in one area of the town, Rajajipuram, who had complained to the Supply Department without finding that any measures had been taken. The responsible civil servants were mentioned and accused of neglecting and even denying the existence of false cards.

A second example appeared on 5th February. One of the police reporters on the staff had a big story about the misappropriation of money at the Police Radio Headquarters. The headline was 'A deed of a well known DIG of Police Radio Headquarters: Efforts to destroy evidence of a scandal'. In the article a named high-ranking police officer, the Deputy Inspector General, was accused of having embezzled a huge amount of money intended for the purchase of some specific technical equipment. When the higher authorities started to investigate the case, the police officer had ordered his staff to break up and rebuild some of the equipment in order to hide the evidence, the reporter wrote. He also referred to employees at the Police Radio Headquarters who were for various reasons dissatisfied with their superior, thereby giving a hint of the sources of this story.

The third example is a small article that was published on 6th February with the name of a staff reporter in the byline.

The subject was the new appointment of a doctor at Lucknow University's hospital, KGMC (King George Medical College), despite the fact that all fresh appointments at the university had been frozen for some time back. Particularly interesting in this case was the fact that the doctor who had been appointed in contravention of the regulations was the son of the Principal of the Medical Collage. The two persons who had formally recommended and sanctioned the new appointment, a Head of Department and the Vice Chancellor, denied all knowledge of it when confronted by the reporter. The headline was: 'Controversy about appointment of KGMCs Principal's son'.

The society narrated on the local pages consisted to a considerable extent of departments, bureaus, authorities and public undertakings of various kinds, peopled and run by civil servants in different posts. These officials were often referred to by name and rank, the latter frequently with an unexplained acronym. Akhil Gupta, in an article in which he discusses the 'culture of politics' in an Indian context, recognises this feature of regional newspapers—and he makes a point of it in contrast to the national elite press. He claims that the latter, focusing almost exclusively on large-scale political events, tends to "reify the state as a monolithic organisation with a single chain of command" (Gupta, 1995: 387). The regional papers, on the other hand, are clearer in "delineating the multilayered and pluricentric nature of the state" because they write about different places, naming specific government departments and specific people (ibid.).

I think, Gupta is making an important observation. The readers of regional Hindi newspapers were presented with images of the state that were largely lacking in the English-language elite press. The state was made visible in its particular functions which, in turn, were run by public servants in various positions. On the local pages, the image of the state was clearly not an anonymous monolith. There was, however, another related feature of how the state was imagined in these newspapers. Routine local reporting was generally confined to one particular level in society. If, for example, a reporter with the city hospitals on his beat came across a story about extremely long queues for certain medical operations, he would collect all the information available from hospital officials and doctors. But he probably would not include the responsible politicians in his sources, or talk to any patient waiting to be treated. A result of this practice was that the image of society on the pages of the newspaper was somewhat segmented. Politics and the bureaucracy occupied distinctive spheres and were rarely described in interaction. State politics was covered by reporters in the political bureau, and the local administration by staff reporters in the local bureau.

The 'common people' also had their journalists. Besides the articles written by staff reporters with specific departments and bureaucracies on their beat, another kind of story appeared frequently on the local pages. These stories also had to do with the work of government undertakings, but from another angle. Quite a few shorter articles and news briefs consisted of reporting from localities where people, often named, complained about defects in public services, such as bad water or power supply, non-working telephones, leaking drainage, environmental pollution or roads which were in a bad condition. This type of story usually had the byline *samvad sutr* (news source), which indicated that they were written by a 'stringer' and not by a staff reporter (*Dainik Jagran* had an impressive network of freelancers who contributed small stories from residential areas and workplaces). If the first category of local news (articles produced by staff reporters) was characterised by the many names of departments and civil servants, the second type of stories referred to locations in the city and to 'ordinary citizens'. These stories were generally more uniform than the first category and can readily be illustrated.

The headline of a 20-line story, published on 4th February 1998, read 'Dirt everywhere in Tilhar Nagar ward'.[19] The story ran as follows:

> Lucknow, Tuesday. Tilhar Nagar ward has been trapped by dirt. There is dirt in several parts of the ward. In the drain muddy and dirty water flows. [...] Mr Deepak Sristava of Narayan Press Street in the ward says that for several years the drains have been in a bad condition and have not been repaired. Because of broken drains and blocked pipelines, dirt flows in the street. [...] Ramnagar Colony in the same ward is also in bad shape. The ground level of this

> colony is at least six feet lower than other colonies so it is always full of water. Colony resident Paramjeet Singh Pammy says that people are fed up with complaining time after time to the L.D.A.[Lucknow Development Authority] and the Municipal Corporation about their problems.

A similar article, appearing in the local section the following day, highlighted a problem that occupied people of another area. Under the headline 'Electricity theft by putting hooks on wires has increased', the article described in some detail the situation of the electricity supply for an area of central Lucknow that fell under Fatehganj Power Station and the sub-station of Gahru.[20] Because the electrification was not completed here, people who lacked power in their houses solved the problem for themselves by stealing electricity, using hooks that were put on the electricity wires. This in turn affected legal electricity consumers because the power station was not equipped for all the extra connections. Transformers often burned out or the voltage was low. Furthermore, streetlights were out of order on the main road. People from the area had, according to the article, complained to the Electricity Department and demanded a proper power supply. But "the Electricity Department employees, who are aware, just keep quiet".

Just as the staff reporters on the local bureau stick to their level of society, the local stringers are confined in their reports to the localities and their residents. They do not confront the bureaucracy or the politicians with the reality of the 'common man'.

Editorial

After the local pages comes the editorial page. This page was identical in all editions of *Dainik Jagran*. The head office in Kanpur produced and distributed it daily to the various printing centres. The page consisted of an unsigned editorial column commenting on topical political issues. It also included a section with 'letters to the editor', that was distinct from the letters that were published on the local pages.[21] The main part of the page was, however, allotted to the columnists, and at least two or three articles appeared every day. Among these columnists one could find several of India's best-known journalists and intellectuals, reputed for quite diverse political positions.[22] These were articles that often could be read in other papers as well, as they were syndicated to a number of Indian newspapers. But exclusive material also appeared and once a week the chief editor, Narendra Mohan, wrote a column under the vignette 'flows of thought' (*vichaar pravaah*). Furthermore, the editorial page of *Dainik Jagran* also contained articles appearing under weekly vignettes like 'health', 'law' and 'astrology'. *Dainik Jagran* did not, like several of the other papers, carry an additional 'opposite editorial' page.

District

The next section of the paper was the page with 'district' news.[23] Each of the local editions of *Dainik Jagran* had a mandate to cover districts adjoining the city where the editorial office was located. The office in Lucknow administered news coverage in ten such districts, composed of towns and rural areas close to Lucknow: Bahraich, Barabanki, Faizabad, Gonda, Hardoi, Lakhimpur Kheri, Raebareilly, Shajanpur, Sitapur, Sultanpur and Unnao. One should bear in mind that these localities were not sparsely populated hinterlands. Most of them had about the same sized population as Lucknow and together they were inhabited by nearly 30 million people. In a few of these places the newspaper had a small office and one or two staff journalists, but in most places the business was completely in the hands of stringers. News from the districts was reported every day to the office in Lucknow where the 'district desk' edited the material.[24] The district news was printed in special local supplements that were distributed only in those places to which they were related. Three such local supplements, with a number of districts covered in each, were produced at the Lucknow editorial office. A selection of district news was, however, placed in the main edition of the paper, on the 'district' page. The stories on this page never had bylines (nor in the local supplements); thus the district journalists would seldom or never have the pleasure of seeing their names printed in the paper. It is sometimes claimed by critics of the Hindi press that stringers in the districts work for a very small payment (or for no money at all) just in order to get their name in the newspaper. But it is not that simple. On the dateline one could only see which local office had contributed the story and if it was a staff reporter or a stringer who had written the piece.

National/International

Dainik Jagran had also one page in common for 'national' and 'foreign' news. The international material consisted of news briefs selected from news agencies (AP, AFP, DPA, PT and *Varta*)[25] placed in a broad column under the vignette 'view of the world' (*vishva darshan*). The foreign news briefs were quite short (about five to fifteen lines in a double column) and the number of items in a day could vary between three and ten. Nearby countries—dateline Colombo or Islamabad—appeared more frequently than other places among the foreign news. Apart from this, *Dainik Jagran* treated different places of the world fairly equally. The stories got the same exposure whether they had Washington or Nairobi on the dateline and the tendency to favour news from political and economic world centres seemed pretty weak.

The rest of the stories on this page were 'national' news, which meant stories from anywhere in India except Uttar Pradesh. Like the foreign news, all these stories were selected from news agencies (Press Trust or *Varta*) even though a majority of the articles had New Delhi in the dateline; material produced by *Dainik Jagran*'s editorial office in the national capital was never placed on this page. Generally, not more than half the page was used for editorial material as the national/foreign section was popular with advertisers; big advertisements for electronic equipment and other expensive consumer products often occupied much of the space.

Economy

Dainik Jagran had two daily pages dealing with the economy and business news (*aarthik jaagran*). One of these was dominated by stock market prices; listing companies on the Mumbai, Kanpur and National Stock Exchanges—except on Sundays and Mondays when the stock markets had been closed on the previous days.[26] Just as in newspapers all over the world, 'the economy' is depicted as something primarily having to do with industry, trade and commerce. But this page also included something that the English-language press lacked in their business sections: rates from the wholesale 'bazaar', listing daily prices of vegetables, grains, cooking oil and the like. The second economy page consisted of business news, mostly stories selected from *Dainik Jagran*'s own news network. As could be expected, some of these were reports from India's primary business centres—Mumbai, Kolkata, Bangalore and Chennai. But even though these cities were more frequent in datelines on this page than anywhere else in the newspaper, 'economic' news from New Delhi dominated. Occasionally, the staff in Lucknow did contribute stories of local business concerns, but not every day.

It could be justified to ask why a paper like *Dainik Jagran* set aside two full pages for specialised information like business news. In particular, the stock market prices seemed to be superfluous. Those Lucknowites who conducted business on the Mumbai Stock Exchange were probably quite few and almost certainly read the English-language papers anyway (even in *Dainik Jagran* the list of stock prices was printed in English). But, the economy pages were important for the newspaper in a particular way; they were essential in order to balance the newspaper's image of being very local and popular. Let me spell this out in more detail.

On one of my first encounters with Vinod Shukla, the resident editor of *Dainik Jagran*'s Lucknow edition, he explained the strength of the newspaper to me. He pointed out two examples of how the paper had improved during the last few years. One was the introduction of supplements with local district news, which was in line with the ambition to reach more readers among 'ordinary' people who had previously not been newspaper readers. The other example was the business news with the stock market rates, which, according to Vinod Shukla, was a novelty in Hindi dailies when *Dainik Jagran* first started to publish them in 1993.

Insensitively, I asked if *Dainik Jagran*'s readers really had any interest in the stock market. Did not investors stick to English-language papers for that kind of information? I hit a sore point. Vinod Shukla immediately called in the young woman who was responsible for marketing the paper. At his request she handed me some leaflets intended for advertisers and pointed out diagrams illustrating *Dainik Jagran*'s readership compared with other newspapers. The illustrations were aimed at persuading advertisers that *Dainik Jagran* was the best choice if they wanted to reach potential customers. In those leaflets one could clearly see traces of a dilemma that the Hindi press was facing. The image that was often an asset for *Dainik Jagran* and other vernacular dailies—that they reached the masses and were 'close' to ordinary people—could in other contexts be a problem. For example, advertisers could readily believe that the wealthier strata of society did not read these newspapers. Some businessmen preferred their products and company names to be exposed in a medium that was associated with power, influence, modernity and sophisticated lifestyles. The English-language press had a clear advantage in this regard; advertisement space was also considerably more expensive in these newspapers. The symbolical status of language was also shown in the strange fact that quite a lot of advertisements in the Hindi papers were printed in English.

The leaflets I was handed tried to suggest—in English, of course—that *Dainik Jagran* reached 'core segments' of readers in the main cities of Uttar Pradesh. With staple diagrams referring to readership surveys,[27] it was stated that this newspaper beat its main competitors (the comparison was between *Dainik Jagran*, *Aaj*, the *Pioneer* and the *Times of India*) in being read by the highest categories in the socio-economic hierarchy. This meant people in the age group 25–44 who were graduates or above, working as 'officers, businessmen, executives or professionals' with monthly incomes above Rs 5,001. The message was also clearly stated in the slogan printed on the leaflet: '*Dainik Jagran*. Puts your ads where the money is'.

It was essential for the publishing company to show that its newspaper was read by a socio-economic elite. Otherwise, it would have difficulties in attracting advertisers. And, to claim convincingly that *Dainik Jagran* was read 'where the money is' there had to be some material in its pages that was clearly intended for the wealthier sections of society. With an ambitious economy section, *Dainik Jagran* tried to broaden its image of being a paper mostly for the 'common man'.

Sports

There was, of course, a sports section on one or two of the last pages of the newspaper. It was usually dominated by the two favourite games in India, viz., cricket and hockey. Some stories were produced locally under the byline 'sports reporter', but most of the articles were agency news about sports events that had taken place somewhere else in India. In actual fact, the sports section seemed to be the least 'provincial' of all the news sections in the paper. The geographical location of an event mattered less than on other pages in the paper (aside from feature material). Every day, one could read stories from distant places, longer and more detailed than anything that would usually be printed in the 'foreign news' section: a hockey tournament in Melbourne, a tennis match in Stockholm or a world championship chess game in Holland could be highlighted in an extensive article. Certainly, the participation of an Indian team or sportsman in the event would increase the likelihood of its coverage. Another feature that made the sports section more 'universal' in appearance than other sections (I believe these pages would look quite recognisable to a non-Indian reader) was the pictures. On other pages the photographs were, as in all Indian newspapers, usually non-dramatic; Indian photo journalism seemed to have a particular preference for important people who were sitting or standing. Pictures on the sports page, however, showing athletes in various activities, made a striking contrast. Here people were running, jumping or hitting a ball. This 'action', combined with the well-known paraphernalia that was seen in these photos—the sports ground and the clothes as well as bats, sticks, rackets, balls and other equipment used—made the sports page appear less tied to a particular place or country.

Capital and miscellaneous

Two of the sections in *Dainik Jagran* did not have a fixed place in the newspaper, but could be placed anywhere between the local pages and the final page. One was a page called 'the capital' (*rajdhaani*), referring to the Uttar Pradesh capital and not to New Delhi. One might perhaps find this section a bit excessive considering that the newspaper already allotted five or six pages to Lucknow news. But, the section was distinct from the local news in that it was purely devoted to state politics. This was certainly not a page where one could read stringer reports about broken drains. Staff journalists who had state politics on their assignments contributed almost all the articles. Thus, the headlines on this page were to an even greater extent than the front page, filled with the names of political parties and state politicians.

Next to the local news, the biggest section in the newspaper was vaguely classified as 'miscellaneous' (*vividha*). Generally, three pages were marked with this banner. Two of these appeared in between the district page and the national/international page, with a third page further back in the paper. Articles that continued from page one took up half a page. The remaining space was filled with material that was really not very unpredictable, as the banner would suggest. If one was interested in news from other places in Uttar Pradesh, outside Lucknow and its vicinity, this was the section to look in. Previously, *Dainik Jagran* had a particular section for news from the state, but in 1998 this had been removed. Now, all articles from the newspaper's offices in towns like Meerut, Gorakhpur, Varanasi, etc. came in the 'miscellaneous' section, if they were not important enough to fit into the front page. But on these pages news also appeared that could have been placed in the 'local', the 'national' or the 'capital' sections as well.

Features

The last page in *Dainik Jagran*, always in colour, was the 'features' section. This was something all newspapers in Lucknow had in common; the last page was always used for some kind of 'light' reading, edited with colourful photographs and illustrations. In *Dainik Jagran*, each day had its own particular theme on the features page: on Sundays it was 'the economy', on Mondays 'miscellaneous', on Tuesdays 'sports', on Wednesdays 'women', on Thursdays 'films', on Fridays 'television' and on Saturdays the page was named 'children's club'. Like the editorial page, this section was produced by the head office in Kanpur and was common to all editions of the paper. This might have been a reason behind the very non-localised character of the material published in this section; most stories could have appeared in any Indian newspaper. In this sense, 'features' could be seen as something diametrically opposed to the local news that filled up so much space elsewhere in the paper. And, much like the sports page, material in the features section did not necessarily have to do with Indian issues. A story about Bill Clinton's dog and Tony Blair's cat was, for example, not particularly odd to read under the 'miscellaneous' banner on the features page.[28] And, in a story on Indian heroines, on a Wednesday's 'women's page', it could be claimed that the world is indeed today a 'global village' and one should also look for role models in places like South Africa (Winnie Mandela), Indonesia (Megawati) or the United States (Hillary Clinton).[29]

Looking at the features pages it becomes obvious that the Lucknow newspapers have to be understood in a wider mass media context. Several subjects that were common on the features pages referred directly to other media technologies. One could read about the latest Hindi films, the soap operas on television or about the Internet and new computer technology. Other subjects, such as beauty contests, design, house furnishings or 'lifestyle', were clearly inspired by the content in television or popular magazines. In particular, the parallel between popular magazines and the reading that was offered on the features pages was something that staffs were well aware of in the newspaper's editorial offices. Among those newspapers that put most effort into features it was explicit policy to hang on to the attraction of the colourful magazines—remember the scene at the news vendor's outside the Coffee House. These magazines, with their aura of a modern urban lifestyle, were inaccessible for many people because they were expensive, and furthermore, the most sophisticated were in English. The newspapers could offer the same kind of desirable reading at a reasonable price. As one resident editor, of a newspaper that was competing with *Dainik Jagran,* said, "We should be both a newspaper and a features magazine".

One argument, which was often heard when resident editors wanted to explain the importance of features material, was that the newspapers had to be a matter for the whole family. A daily morning paper should ideally be a 'family newspaper' and of interest to women, young people and children as well as to men (who are supposed to be mainly interested in political news). This way of thinking was guided by the idea that the modern family had changed. It was not only the husband's voice that counted nowadays, but other members of the family also had opinions—for example, on the choice of newspaper.

Even though the newspaper (unlike television) is a mass medium designed to be read by individuals, the family as a unit of consumption has a significant position. 'The viewing family' that Mankekar (1999) argues that Indian state television has participated in constituting since the 1980s, is also a 'reading family'. And it is precisely with regard to the section in the newspaper that most obviously deals with middle-class modernity that 'the family' matters.

Mapping society

What kind of society is emerging from the impressions one gets by browsing through a Lucknow newspaper? In order to provide an answer, I would like to return to a point made in Chapter One, regarding the differences between the imaginary of a novel and a newspaper. A novel usually consists of one story that the reader follows from beginning to end. All sub-plots and details are subordinate to the main narrative, the totality is more important than the parts. A newspaper is different: it is far from obvious which is the main unit of meaning in journalism. It might be the story, the page, the news section, the issue of a paper or perhaps the news reporting over an extended time (cf. Manoff and Schudson, 1986: 6). The newspaper could rather be compared with another printed product that in a straight-forward way attempts to map society: the demographic atlas.

The Oxford Atlas of India has two main sections comprising a large number of maps and diagrams. The first section presents "India at a glance, providing an objective view of the country's topography, federal structure, human habitation and infrastructural development, climate, religion, literacy, workforce and communication routes" (*An Atlas of India*, 1990: 1). The second, and much larger, section consists of detailed thematic maps of 25 states and seven union territories in India, providing information on nine subjects for each state: physical features, administration, population, transport and tourism, agriculture, industries and markets, minerals, economic development and mass communications.

Both the newspaper and the atlas attempt to provide a view of the conditions of human existence within physical entities at different levels, and the information is collected and compiled according to models with a limited number of categories and subjects. The newspaper, like the map, offers a 'spatial matrix' into which subjects and local communities can be inscribed and through which society can be imagined (cf. Radcliff, 2001). Comparing the Indian atlas with a Lucknow newspaper, some entities (nation, state, district) and subjects (administration, population, economy) also overlap; one can easily think that the newspaper is, in a way, trying to capture the processual aspects of the static reality that the maps are depicting. Furthermore, both the atlas and the newspaper have in common that they are aimed at a broad readership and that they are informative on very disparate topics. Someone who wants to know more about minerals in Maharashtra may consult the same atlas as someone else who needs a figure for the literate population of Punjab. Likewise, the same issue of a newspaper may satisfy the curiosity of both a hockey supporter and a stock broker. But few people would enjoy the atlas or the newspaper for its grand narrative, reading it with attention from first page to last. If one tries to understand how the newspaper constructs 'social imaginaries', the atlas is perhaps a more helpful analogy than the novel.

The totality, however, that is constructed out of all those maps and diagrams in a national atlas is undoubtedly the nation-state. Regarding a newspaper, I think, it might be deceptive to look for the single most important entity that all those disparate stories of the various news sections are 'really' building. Imaginaries of the nation are significant but not necessarily the primary construction in a local or regional newspaper. Nor would I emphasise the reinforcement of local identities as the single most important objective of the Lucknow newspapers. In this sense local news media in India seem to be different from, for example, in the United States where the major focus, according to Phyllis Kaniss, "has come to be placed on issues with the symbolic capital to unite the fragmented suburban audience" (1991: 4).

The Hindi newspapers of Lucknow are, as we have seen, much focused on local issues, but they do not neglect news of national concern. On the front pages stories from Lucknow are usually overshadowed by those with the dateline New Delhi (a similar concern with 'national news' would hardly be the case in local or regional newspapers in, for example, Sweden). In a significant way, the local is constructed in the context of the national, and the national in the context of the local. The great lacunae in the Lucknow newspapers are instead found at levels between the national and the local, particularly with regard to regions in other parts of the country. Importantly, these newspapers have a tendency towards bifurcation in their representation of society: state, politics and the bureaucracy are described in its centralised monolithic aspects and in localised specific practice. However, these levels are to a great extent kept apart: they are contextualising one another, but are not blurred into each other. John Durham Peters has argued that in modern society "our vision of the social world is bifocal" (1997: 79). What he has in mind is that we experience fragments of society with our own eyes and totalities through representations in diverse media. With regard to the Lucknow newspapers this bifocality is present also within the mediaised representations.

Notes

1. All the newspapers used cheaper newsprint for the inside pages.
2. The English-language press can charge more for advertising space and is therefore not so dependent on income from the sale of copies.
3. For a discussion of the universal practice of journalism to separate news into departments, see Schudson, 1995:13f.

4. Variations on banners that the different newspapers used for geographical categories were: (1) Lucknow, City, *rajdhani*, *sthaniya* or *apna shahar*; (2) Uttar Pradesh, U.P, State, Region or *pradesh*; (3) India, Nation, *desh*; (4) The World, Foreign, *deshantar*, *videsh*, *pardesh*, *duniya*.
5. Only one of the newspapers used the name of any district in the banner. *Hindustan* had one page named Raibarelli/Barabanki.
6. Newspapers surveyed were *Dainik Jagran*, *Hindustan*, *Swatantra Bharat*, *Rashtriya Sahara*, *Kuber Times*, *Pioneer*, *Times of India* and *Hindustan Times*. I examined articles on the first page of these papers between the 24th and the 30th of December 1997.
7. On the relationship between journalism and the political culture of a given society, see Schudson, 1995: 31.
8. In the Indian context 'communalism' refers to the use of religious identities in the political sphere; 'reservations' refers to government policies of affirmative action.
9. Nevertheless, one should not underrate the importance of face-to-face communication in this context. Politicians' travelling schedules and public appearances during election campaigns are often astonishingly ambitious.
10. The reputation of a newspaper being favourable to a particular party was sometimes readily admitted and confirmed by its journalists, and even by the resident editor himself. In other cases, political sympathies were more hesitantly acknowledged. I did, however, encounter only one resident editor who claimed that his newspaper was completely neutral and denied any leaning towards a particular party.
11. Its leaders often made a point of the fact that the owners of newspapers as well as journalist, were predominantly of the Brahmin caste. A name that they often used to denigrate the newspapers was *Manuvadi Press*, implying that the press was sympathetic to the ancient laws of Manu that prescribe how society should ideally be built on caste principles.
12. Cf. Chapter 2, page 56.
13. 'vidhayak nivas ki sirhiyo par sir kati lash mili'. *Dainik Jagran*, Lucknow edition, 4 February 1996.
14. 'Headless Corpse Sensationally Found at OCR' ('ocr me sir kati lash milne se sansani'). *Rashtriya Sahara*, Lucknow edition, 4 February 1996.
15. One should keep in mind the political dimension that was added to the story on this day. A politician of a major party was mentioned in

association with the murder. This might have been a consideration in some editorial offices. The two newspapers with a political reputation of being closest to BJP, the party in question, treated the issue completely differently, however. *Dainik Jagran* made the murder a top story and included the name of the political party in the front-page headline, while the *Pioneer* did not mention it at all.

16. 'ocr mein mili sirkati lash ke piche pulis ko "narbali" andesha: bajpa ke ek vidhayak sandeh ke ghere mein'. *Rashtriya Sahara*, Lucknow edition, 7 February 1996.
17. 'purv vidhyayak ke flet me hatya ka mamle aur rahstyamay hua'. *Dainik Jagran*, Lucknow edition, 7 February 1996.
18. As news-briefs I count only articles that are completed on the front page. Some of the stories that I have called secondary stories are also quite short one-column items on the front page, but are continued inside the paper.
19. 'Tilhar nagar vaard mein chaaro taraf gandagii'. *Dainik Jagran*, Lucknow edition, 4 February 1998.
20. 'Katiyaa daalkar vidhyut chorii zoron par'. *Dainik Jagran*, Lucknow edition, 4 February 1998.
21. The letters on the editorial page are called 'words from the people' (*janvani*) and those in the local section 'suggestions and complaints' (*sujhav-shikayat*).
22. Regularly one could read contributions by Arun Shourie, Kuldip Nayar, Nikhil Chakravarti and Khushwant Singh.
23. This page was called *janpad* in 1996 but in 1997 had changed its name to *zila*, both names having roughly the same meaning of 'district'.
24. The reports were mostly sent by modem, fax or courier, but sometimes reporters from the districts came to the Lucknow office and handed over their stories personally.
25. News from Reuters were supplied through the Indian agencies.
26. There are in total 22 stock exchanges in India, 20 of them being regional and 2 with nation-wide trading. Kanpur being the one closest to Lucknow (*India 1999: A Reference Annual*).
27. Such as *National Readership Survey 1995* (NRS, 95).
28. *Dainik Jagran*, Lucknow edition, 29 December 1997.
29. *Dainik Jagran*, Lucknow edition, 24 December 1997.

Four

On the Beat

Dainik Jagran's editorial office in Lucknow was located until 1997 in Hazrat Ganj, known as the posh area in the town for shopping. The building was within walking distance of the State Assembly and with several state and municipal functions close by. Along the main street—officially named Mahatma Gandhi Road, but still colloquially called by its colonial name, Park Road—there were plenty of expensive shops for clothes, home electronics and food delicacies, most of them housed in faded old buildings from colonial times. This was the most 'Westernized' area of Lucknow, a feature which was marked by some still living remnants of British times, such as the Mayfair cinema hall, the Café Royal and the British Library. All establishments did not have a colonial history, of course, and some were more recently opened shops that offered various 'modern' consumer goods. Hazrat Ganj was the obvious place to go if one was looking for a pizza, some rock'n roll on music cassettes or a paperback in English. In the evening, a couple of ice cream bars were popular hangouts for middle-class families who came in from the other side of the Gomati river in Maruti cars and on Honda scooters.

The office of *Dainik Jagran* was not posh, however, nor did it have many associations with 'Western modernity'. It was housed in a red brick building off the main street, reached through a muddy lane close to Moti Mahal, a popular sweet shop and eating place. The modest and shabby signboard announcing the entrance to the office was easy to miss. The premises were cramped and ill-suited to a big newspaper. When I made my first visit here in 1995, one of the first things the resident editor assured me, while showing me round, was that the whole business would very soon be shifted to a brand new building under construction. This building, located a kilometre to the east of Hazrat Ganj in an area where several other newspapers already had their premises, would be brought into line with the needs of a modern, expanding daily newspaper, equipped to print twice as many papers. The shift of premises, though, did not take place during my first period of fieldwork. Not until I revisited Lucknow in 1998 had the office moved into the spacious new building.

In the old building in Hazrat Ganj, the activities were scattered over three floors. The printing presses and the advertisement department were on the ground floor. Passing the doorkeeper, half way up the stairs was the room where the editorial meetings were held every morning and where the reporters on the 'political bureau' had their workplaces. The main editorial room was another half floor up. This was where the majority of the journalists sat when they filed their stories and edited their copies. The rectangular room was about 80 square metres, with spartan fittings—virtually nothing but four long tables with chairs. These tables were the equivalent of editorial 'desks'. The main desk, for the front page and other important stories, stood on a podium at one end of the room—much like a teacher's desk in a classroom. In front of it stood, first, the desk for local news, then, a common table for the sports desk and the economic desk; the table at the rear end of the room was the district desk. Shelves running from floor to ceiling, filled with bundles of newspapers, covered the wall behind the latter; this was the news archive. The other three light green painted walls were empty: no shelves, noticeboards, posters or decorations, except for a small space above the entrance door where a picture of *Dainik Jagran*'s founder, Shri Puran Chandra Gupta, hung. The four tables were almost as clean. If one visited the room in the morning, before any reporters had arrived, there were only a couple of telephones and maybe a few newspaper bundles or some notes left behind from the previous night's work. Later in the day, as the work proceeded, more notes and newspapers would fill the tables. But nowhere in this room were there any computers, typewriters, radios, television monitors, files, books or other things that one might have expected to find in an editorial room. The lack of technical equipment was explained by the fact that all the reporters wrote their stories with pen on paper. Manuscripts were then processed on computers by typists sitting in an adjoining room—air-conditioned and always kept closed in order to save the technical equipment from the dusty north Indian air. Behind another closed door—where a sticker with the message 'Avoid Getting Yourself and Your Boss in Trouble' was posted—the resident editor Vinod Shukla had his office. A third door on the opposite side of the editorial room led to an open-air terrace, from which the rooms where the pages of the paper were composed (print outs were pasted on screens) could be reached. The circulation department also had an entrance from the terrace.

The organisation of work

The main person in *Dainik Jagran's* Lucknow office was Vinod Shukla. He was resident editor and managing editor at the same time. According to him, he was the man required for everything in the office. He ran the place with a great deal of authority. Personally, he had control over the various divisions in the office: editorial, finance, circulation, advertisements, stores and machines, and the after-press departments. However, he seldom moved around in the building, except for the editorial meetings in the morning that he attended most days. He executed his will from his quite small room to which he called his staff to give them instructions or to get information. And, all mail for every department in the building first passed over his desk. That was how he knew all the details of the business, Vinod Shukla explained to me. He demanded absolute loyalty and obedience. Anybody called to his room for an order would listen quietly, and was not expected to have a divergent opinion. Nevertheless, the chief preferred to be addressed by the affectionate name *Bhaiya*, meaning brother. Shukla explained:

> Actually, they are my family, I live with them more than I live with my real family, my wife and kids. They are closer to me. Sometimes I take all of them off to one place, we go and live together for two, three days. They should feel they have free access

> to me. And they do come to me with different sort of problems: family problems, domestic problems, professional problems. We interact freely, I'm like a big brother in a joint family.

Vinod Shukla's 'family' was, however, only a small part of a large clan. The Lucknow edition of *Dainik Jagran* was one of twelve editions (in 1995) that were brought out in Uttar Pradesh and New Delhi by the newspaper conglomerate. The main edition was produced in the industrial town of Kanpur, some 80 kilometres south of Lucknow. And newspaper publishing was only one branch within the Jagran Group of Companies. Other commercial interests were in electronics, real estate, sugar and textiles. Certainly, the fundamental aim for the resident/managing editor in Lucknow was to make money for the company. Every edition had to be profitable and this was something that Vinod Shukla was keenly aware of: he might be ever such a good editor, but if he was not selling, if the edition was not economically sound, the management in Kanpur would immediately replace him. But, as long as he fulfilled this objective, he felt free to run the edition according to his own mind. The chief editor and owner, Narendra Mohan, sometimes had opinions and suggestions to make, also on journalistic issues, but not very frequently. Vinod Shukla met him every third month when he was called to a meeting in Kanpur with the other resident editors.

If Vinod Shukla's position in the office hierarchy was clear—he had the power, above him there was only the chief editor in Kanpur—the editorial positions under him were more confusing. In the first phase of my fieldwork one of my aims was to get a picture of the division of work in the editorial department. I wanted to know how the news production was organised, what was the formal hierarchy and who held the different positions. With my own brief personal experience of working with a newspaper in Sweden and my familiarity with the kind of functions that are normally involved in news production, I thought the best way to begin my study of *Dainik Jagran* was to draw a chart of the organisation hierarchy.[1] To my mind it was a simple task. Anybody on the staff should be able to tell me the proper names and responsibilities of the different positions in the editorial department. Even in my initial fieldnotes on my encounters with Vinod Shukla and some of the senior journalists, I thought I had a pretty good picture. I had noted down positions like 'senior editor', 'news editor', 'chief sub-editor', 'sub-editor', 'bureau chief' and reporters on various 'beats'; and I had started to fill the positions with names and routines. But I soon discovered many inconsistencies, and often when I asked journalists about their designations they were unspecific. On a few occasions I was also told in confidence by some journalists, commenting on what they had overheard a colleague say to me, "he pretends he is a ... but actually he is not". After some time I took up the subject with Vinod Shukla and told him that I had a problem grasping the organisation in the editorial department, and that I was not sure who was actually on which designation.

"I understand your confusion", he said and explained to me that he was not in favour of having a strict system.

> Once you give a man a formal designation, I feel that he becomes half as useful to us. He will only look to his own rights, not to his duties. And it becomes a little difficult for us to sack him. The rest of the team suffers.

To clarify his point he mentioned a senior journalist in the political bureau who had recently telephoned reporting sick and had not come to the office for some time. Vinod Shukla was very dissatisfied with him: "He could at least come and sit here in the office. I could even send a jeep to pick him up. But only because of this—that he is a senior member of the staff and has got a designation—he does not bother about his service and his work." It was better to keep the posts floating, was Shukla's opinion: "We don't have news editors, senior sub-editors ... nothing. If you are efficient, if you can influence people, if you are wise—then you become the chief. And as soon as you are losing, then you are off."

An illustrative example of the vague designations on *Dainik Jagran* was a journalist by the name of Girish Mishra. He stood out among others on the staff in several ways. He was rather snobbishly dressed, most days in a 'Western-style' shirt, jacket and with a silk scarf round his neck—but occasionally he would come to the office in *kurta-pajama*, the homespun variety popular with Gandhian-minded intellectuals. He was also particular about his intellectual image, and was fond of referring to classical literature. (For example, once when we talked about the state of journalism in India he told me: "It's like Shakespeare said, there are three kinds of men. Those who are born to a vocation, those who learn one and those who think they are born to one.") Among the staff he held a unique kind of position, somewhere on the higher rungs of the hierarchy. He always kept a high profile at editorial meetings, sitting next to Vinod Shukla and giving his opinions on different matters. But he did not file a story every day, was not involved in the routines of desk editing and was not responsible for any particular task. He explained to me that he was recruited to the paper in order to write 'special stories', particularly on 'social issues'—most of his writing appeared in a regular column called 'perspectives'(*Pahal)*—and also to guide the other journalists on how to improve their stories, what approach to take, how to present a story, what kind of words should be used. In one person he seemed to combine the roles of 'associate editor', 'special reporter', 'columnist' and 'adviser'. The latter was the nearest label he could find to describe his job. But Vinod Shukla had not given him any formal position. He was employed on a contract basis, and in addition to the work at *Dainik Jagran* he also taught journalism at Lucknow University.

It was in the positions immediately below Vinod Shukla himself that the designations were particularly unclear—a fact which, no doubt, emphasised *his* control over the paper. It was significant that *Dainik Jagran,* unlike most other newspapers, had no associate editor or assistant editor. Two years after I started my fieldwork, the organisation in the editorial department had undergone a number of changes, but the main features remained same. When I met the staff again—in the new premises—I noticed that Girish Mishra had left the paper (he had gone to the newly launched Hindi daily *Kuber Times* to become a resident editor of its Mumbai edition). Instead, there was a new man with an important but unspecified position. This man, Gyanendra Sharma—who was previously the resident editor of the rival Lucknow paper *Swatantra Bharat*—had not, however, replaced Girish. He had a different role: quite clearly he was doing a job that in most editorial offices was that of 'assistant editor'. Being in charge of the morning meeting and coordinating the daily newswork, he had apparently taken over many of Vinod Shukla's responsibilities. But he was without designation, formally *Bhaiya* was still all-powerful. Just like Girish, Gyanendra was employed on contract and called himself an 'adviser' or 'consultant'.

So it was not easy to draw a chart of the hierarchy in the editorial department of *Dainik Jagran*—at least not a chart with unquestionable designations. This did not imply that there were no routines or a practical division of labour in the everyday work of the department. As scholars of media production have often emphasised, newswork is definitely not a haphazard affair (see, for example, Schlesinger, 1978; Tuchman, 1978). Vinod Shukla's idea of a 'floating system' was more a potential system than a system in full effect. People *could* be shifted around on different functions but this was not done every day. The division of functions and work routines on *Dainik Jagran* would be familiar to a journalist involved in news production anywhere in the world. The main division of labour in an editorial office is between journalists who gather the news and journalists who process the news. The former are called reporters and the latter sub-editors (or desk editors or copy editors).[2] In a rough sketch of these two functions, the reporter is the one who starts off with a small piece of information (or an idea) on a potential news story, collects whatever extra information he needs and writes up a story ('files a copy'). The sub-editor takes over the copy, makes the changes he finds necessary, gives it a headline and decides where on a page it should go (and if it should be illustrated with a photograph or some graphics). One could say that the main objective for a reporter is to produce a story, while for the sub-editor it is to produce a page.

Now, there are also divisions of labour among reporters and sub-editors. A functional division among reporters is in the form of 'beats', which are particular areas that the various reporters are assigned to cover. And, the processing of news is divided into 'desks' where different sub-editors have responsibility for certain pages or sections of the newspaper. There is a hierarchical dimension to this functional division of labour. Not all beat reporters or sub-editors have the same status, some beats and desks are more important than others. Journalists reporting politics are generally higher in status than those on the crime beat; desk editors doing the front page are above those doing the district page. Another hierarchical dimension is in the form of 'seniority', which is a matter of experience and promotion rather than of age. A 'senior' reporter or sub-editor is better paid than one who is not 'senior'. The hierarchy of seniority may compete with the hierarchy of beats: a senior crime reporter may actually be more experienced, have a higher status and get a better salary than a non-senior reporter on a more prestigious beat.

Two of the reporters on *Dainik Jagran* were designated (in practice at least) as 'chief of bureau'. One was in charge of the political reporting and the other of the local reporting. In the political bureau five or six reporters were working on different beats. There was one journalist assigned to each of the three main political parties of the state: Bharatiya Janata Party, Samajwadi Party and Bahujan Samaj Party. Parties of minor importance in the state, such as Congress (with two factions), Janata Dal, the Communist parties and some small Dalit parties, were also covered regularly. Furthermore, the political bureau was in charge of covering the state government and administration. On its list of responsibilities were the State Secretariat, the Chief Minister, the Governor (who represents the central government) and various state departments. The individual beats could be quite wide in scope. When Hemant, one of the reporters, introduced himself, he told me that on his beat he had "state crime, the home department, Congress (I), industrial development, the jail and the home guard".

In the local bureau 10–12 reporters were working on beats that included crime, education, the trade unions, health, public works, science and the municipal administration. Besides the reporters working under the bureau chiefs, there were two reporters on the sports beat, one who wrote for the economy page and one (part-time) who covered law. A team of eight sub-editors processed the stories filed by the beat reporters. Two senior journalists led the work in the function of 'news editors' (one working daytime, the other nights). This team also edited material from the news agencies. In addition, three sub-editors worked on district news, only a small part of which went into the main edition (the bulk was edited into special district supplements).

As mentioned in Chapter Three, *Dainik Jagran* also had a huge network of affiliated freelancers who contributed small stories from residential areas and workplaces in Lucknow.[3] One of the main changes that took place between my visits to Lucknow was in the way this type of reporting was organised. In Spring 1997 *Dainik Jagran* had introduced an innovation among the Lucknow dailies, by starting a kind of 'trainee class', enrolling 15–20 inexperienced freelancers. These were not considered as proper journalists but were called 'news sources' (*samvad sutr*). They gathered round a big table in the editorial office every morning for three or even four hours. A senior journalist acted as their teacher, criticising and suggesting improvements to the news stories they brought with them. Several of the competing Hindi-language papers adopted the system very quickly and started their own 'trainee classes'. None of the English-language newspapers did it. In the editorial offices of the latter I often heard severe criticism of the *samvad sutr* system, which was believed to damage journalistic competence, and was only a means to exploit young people's career dreams for very little payment. The latter criticism certainly had some basis. At least on *Dainik Jagran* there was an explicit promise that those who performed best in the 'trainee class' would have a chance to advance to proper journalistic assignments.

Reporting and sub-editing were in principle discrete functions. A journalist was either employed as a reporter or as a sub-editor. The functions, however, overlapped to some extent. For example, every day, the reporters got a lot of press releases, not all of which resulted in a new story; some were just lightly edited by the reporters and went into the paper as news briefs. And occasionally it happened that a sub-editor wrote a story. In these cases it was mostly young and newly recruited sub-editors who were called to fill a temporary vacancy on a beat, or filed stories on their own initiative. Being new to a paper—and working on a trainee basis—it was important to show your talents and usefulness in order to secure a permanent job. Furthermore, reporting and sub-editing were not separate as careers. Someone might very well work in sub-editing for some time and then shift over to reporting or vice versa.

Within the division of reporting and sub-editing the functions were quite flexible. Every journalist had his or her primary task defined but always had to be prepared to do someone else's job. And every day somebody was shifted to another task, partly because of the work schedules (the paper was being published seven days a week but all employees had one day off) and other reasons for people being on leave, but also because of unexpected developments in the newswork. Local reporters in particular had to be prepared to cover stories far from their regular beat; a crime reporter could be assigned to a story concerning the economy or someone with the Municipal Corporation on his beat could occasionally cover a sporting event. A particular occasion when the flexibility of the staff was used to a great extent was at the time of an election. I was present in Lucknow at the time of the elections to the Central Parliament (*Lok Sabha*) in both 1996 and 1998. When the parties started their election campaigns—officially one month before the election—the newspapers adjusted their organisation in order to cover the political game even more closely than normally. At *Dainik Jagran* an election desk was set up with three or four journalists—relieved from their usual duties—who were in charge of two extra pages in the newspaper completely devoted to the approaching election. In addition, special election supplements were produced every week. And even among the reporters who were not particularly assigned to follow the election, political meetings and rallies took up much of their work. Everybody was more or less a political reporter during the month preceding the election.

The news net

Each day a newspaper has to be filled with stories, and no news organisation can take it for granted that news fodder will appear in an even stream on its doorstep, nor can it trust each reporter's initiative to find stories wherever he likes. A news net is an instrument that news organisations construct to ensure a steady input of information (Tuchman, 1978). The metaphor of a net highlights the premise that no news organisation can, or even wants to, capture everything. A net has holes, and the way it is tied, the strength of its fibres and the spots where it is laid out will determine the catch. The news net metaphor also emphasises that newswork is a deliberate and selective act; it stands in sharp contrast to the view of news as a 'mirror' of society. Studying news organisations in the US (a television station and some metropolitan newspapers), Gaye Tuchman (1978: 23–31) has pointed to three characteristics of the news net as a method for news organisations to disperse reporters. According to her, "the news net is flung through *spaces*, focuses on specific *organizations*, and highlights *topics*" (ibid.: 25, italics mine). Of these methods she considers geographical territoriality (space) to be the most important. Looking at the product published by *Dainik Jagran*, or by any of the editorial offices in Lucknow, that is certainly true here also. As I have stated in the previous chapter, most of the material in the newspapers is classified according to geographic territoriality, such as national, local, state, district and foreign. But if one looks at the reporters who are operating from a particular editorial office, the effort to disperse the net geographically becomes less marked.

The reporters in Lucknow all dealt mainly with local or state (Uttar Pradesh) news (with an approach from the capital); they were physical beings and their area of operations was not unlimited. News from other geographical levels came from news agencies, stringers or other *Jagran* offices. When looking at those 20 or so reporters who each morning were receiving their assignments at *Dainik Jagran*'s office in Lucknow, one can see that the news net was rather flung over organisations and topics. These two methods, furthermore, blended into each other and were not sensed as different types of beats by the reporters. The police reporter covered a topic, 'crime', but in practice it meant that he got more or less all his information from the same organisation, the police—although from various headquarters, stations and departments. Reporters with 'education' or 'health' on their beat found their stories at a limited number of educational institutions (schools, colleges and the university) and hospitals which they visited regularly. It was not much different from having an organisation, such as the Municipal Corporation, defining the beat. Moreover, apart from the police reporters, most journalists did not have one single organisation or topic as a beat but covered several issues.

The reporter who covered the hospitals also had, for example, 'the environment', 'science' and the Public Works Department on his beat. One of the reporters even had a mixed beat from both the political and the local bureau; he covered a couple of minor political parties as well as schools and 'Muslim issues'.

If we use the metaphor of a net for the organisation of news gathering we have to imagine a very odd net, not at all like the homogeneous, symmetrical one that fishermen use, which catches all fish above a certain size that come its way. The fibres of the news net are very unevenly tied and some of the holes are gigantic. It would also be a net that strangely enough could let the big fish pass through while trapping the small ones. May be it is better to imagine the beat reporter as on a fishing mission equipped with a spinning rod, hoping for a catch at some favourite spots. And, to complete the fishing metaphor, one would have to think of a sea inhabited by fish with quite some initiative themselves to be, or not to be, caught. That news sources are not passive suppliers of information would be obvious to anyone who spends some time with journalists (Ericson et al., 1989: 377, have defined news as a product of transactions between journalists and their sources).

Work routines

The working day at *Dainik Jagran* started, for most of the reporters, with the morning meeting at 11 a.m. It took place around a big rectangular table that dominated the rather dark and gloomy room of the political bureau. At most 15 journalists (all of them men)—including the two photographers—attended the meeting. Usually, there were fewer people. A few reporters were always out on early assignments, some might have reported in sick and others would be on leave. A couple of ambitious reporters usually appeared well before the meeting started and spent some time reading from the bundles of newspapers that were supplied to the room every day—not only the local papers but also a few selected national newspapers. Most of the other reporters dropped in just before eleven, took a seat at the table and joined their colleagues in usually relaxed small talk. The reporters did not have fixed places, but there was a system to how they were grouped during the meeting. Reporters in the local bureau always sat at the rear half of the table, political reporters at the portion closer to the door. When Vinod Shukla made his entrance, they would all get to their feet until *Bhaiya* had settled in his armchair at the end of the table among the political reporters; on days when he was absent, that chair was left vacant. Journalists who entered the room after this point excused themselves for their late arrival and often also made an attempt to touch Shukla's feet in the traditional Indian way of showing respect towards a superior.

There was no formalised procedure for the morning meeting. Nothing announced that it had actually started. When Shukla had settled down he just joined in the conversation with the reporters sitting next to him, or more often started to go through that day's newspapers—*Dainik Jagran* and its local competitors. He was constantly chewing on betelnuts, tobacco and fennel seeds with which he generously filled his mouth from tins and small bags that he placed on the table. Anyone within reach could help themselves. Another pleasurable routine was the tea, brought by a boy to everyone in the room soon after they had all arrived. Shukla was the natural centre of the gathering, but not in the sense that he was necessarily *holding* a conference. It was more a matter of his presence being felt very strongly in the room, regardless whether he was talking or not. Occasionally, he had some critical opinions on the most recent issue of the paper. It was mostly a critique on a general level, that some news in the other papers was missing from *Jagran* or that the editing was not good enough. Or it could be more specific questions: why had nobody followed up the *Havala* case (a major scandal of corruption) during the last ten days? Who made the decision to give the Indian cricket victory against Pakistan—"the event of the year, the whole Hindustan was brought to a standstill" —only four columns on the front page? Why wasn't there any photograph of Netaji (Subhas Chandra Bose, the Bengali freedom fighter) today, the anniversary of his birth? Nobody who was criticised would try to argue with Shukla or come up with an explanation as an excuse. Even the most senior of the journalists would remain quiet and shamefaced.

On other days Shukla would make long speeches, explaining his views of what journalism was really about, why *Dainik Jagran* was so successful (and the competitors so miserable) and how they should improve to be even better. There were occasions when this kind of lecturing became extra long and passionate. The outrage when a prominent Delhi journalist had questioned *Dainik Jagran*'s credibility (see Chapter Six) was such an event, which gave an input to Shukla's sessions during several morning meetings. So was the day when the resident editor brought with him the news that a survey[4] had found *Dainik Jagran* to be India's most widely read newspaper; the success was celebrated with *samosas* and sweets that Rajesh, the *chaprasi* (peon), was ordered to fetch from Moti Mahal. Another topic that could turn the meeting into a Shukla monologue was reminiscences of journalism in the olden days, i.e., some twenty years ago when Shukla himself was doing the reporting. A favourite subject was the coverage of *dacoit* (bandit) activities during the late 1970s. This was a topic that he could now and then slip into because the former 'Bandit Queen', Phulan Devi, was still in the news, these days as a *Lok Sabha* candidate for the Samajwadi Party.

However, most days, after Vinod Shukla had glanced through the newspapers, he did not address the whole group of reporters but talked about current political events with the political reporters next to him. Not as a particular journalistic subject, but more or less in the same way (although of course better informed) as 'politics' is talked about among any kind of politically interested citizens: Who would be getting a 'ticket' (be an official candidate) from this or that party? How many seats could party X possibly win in the coming election? Would party Y go into an alliance with party Z? Is not politician X a spent force?

Very rarely did Vinod Shukla interfere in the practicalities of everyday work. He was not involved in planning the day's schedule and did not hand out assignments or instructions about the coverage of stories. Nor did he keep himself particularly informed about the details of newswork. As he saw it, his role during the meeting was to inspire. The reporters handled the practical routines better themselves, he told me on one occasion; he did not know much about it. The newswork, however, had to be planned and organised each day, and the morning meeting was the only opportunity to do so. Simultaneous with the conversation or monologue that had the resident editor as its centre, there was parallel activity going on in the room. In lower voices the reporters were planning the day's work. This activity had two centres, equivalent to the two bureau chiefs sitting at different parts of the table, with the reporters working for them clustered around. The daily planning was mainly a matter of coordinating assignments that the bureau chiefs had in their daybooks with activities that the reporters had on their own schedules. The bureau chiefs distributed jobs that they wanted done, and noted down what the reporters intended to contribute from their own knowledge of their beats. The bureau chiefs' influence in suggesting and selecting stories was, however, often rather limited. Their role did not conform very well to the task of an 'assignment editor' who deliberates on story ideas collected from various sources (including reporters) and then assigns each selected idea to the most appropriate reporter (see Ericson et al., 1989: 181–220).

The usual procedure was that the bureau chief asked a reporter about what he intended to come up with that day, rather than giving him assignments. This was especially true of the political bureau. The chief of the local bureau had somewhat more influence on the reporters' activities. But there were always some stories, originating from the bureau chiefs' daybooks, that had to be distributed to unwilling reporters. The restrained mumbling heard during the morning meetings from the part of the table where the local reporters sat, was often a dispute concerning some assignment that nobody wanted to take on. It was always unpopular to get assignments that meant long trips (that is, outside the city centre), took up too much time or were topically remote from one's usual beat. Arguments commonly heard when a reporter tried to convince the bureau chief that he was the wrong man for a particular story, were that he had no means of transporting himself that distance, because his scooter had broken down; that he had other more important stories that would take a lot of time; or that this assignment was really on someone else's beat.

The morning meeting usually broke up after one hour, by noon. Some reporters immediately left the room and hurried down to their scooters to be on time for a press conference or some other scheduled event. Others, in less of a hurry, stayed for a second cup of tea and some small talk in the yard outside the office where the *chai-wala* (tea vendor) put up his equipment. A couple of reporters might go for a stroll to visit a *paan-wala* (vendor of betelnuts for chewing) across the road. And almost every day there seemed to be a few reporters who had unsettled problems to discuss in a somewhat agitated manner after the meeting had been closed. Or some kind of important matters to mull over in confidence—in a low voice at some distance from the others. If the former kind of discussion was mostly related to work, such as annoyance about the distribution of assignments, the latter often seemed to be about more personal matters.

In the editorial office it was usually a peaceful quiet time from noon up to late afternoon. Except for one of the "news editors", the sub-editors did not attend the morning meeting. A few started work before noon, but most of them dropped in after twelve o'clock and others who worked on the night shift came around five in the afternoon. During the early afternoon only the tables at each end of the main editorial room were occupied: the main desk on the small podium and the district desk at the rear end of the room. At the main desk the day's work started with material that came from other *Jagran* editions. The sub-editors got photocopies of stories that had been published in the latest editions of these papers, which they edited and put in heaps intended for different pages in the paper. They went on with copy from news agencies, mostly using the Hindi-language services *Bhasha* and *Varta* that were supplied by the Press Trust of India (PTI) and United News of India (UNI) respectively. Some material, however, was used from the main English-language services of these agencies. It was then the sub-editor's task to translate the stories. In contrast to reporting which was an all-male affair, there were a few women among the sub-editors. One of them worked in a senior position at the main desk, while two other were editing district news supervised by Rajiv, the energetic chief of the district desk. There was a fourth woman in the room who contributed much to the relaxed and happy atmosphere. She was quite young and did not do any sub-editing but had various clerical assignments and also wrote small pieces for a regular 'gossip' column (when I met her on the second part of my fieldwork, she had become a regular reporter on a rival newspaper).

There were, of course, other people in the house during the afternoon, such as the staff working in the non-editorial departments, but apart from a couple of clerks they did not move around the premises very much. Then, little by little from five o'clock or so, the desks filled up with reporters returning from their beats with stories to write up, more sub-editors started their working shift and journalists of other kinds (writing sports, economy, columns) appeared. The atmosphere became hectic but concentrated as the reporters filed their stories on page after page of unlined sheets of paper that were pinned together and sent on to the sub-editors. News stories began to pile up, telephones were ringing, people hurried back and forth; by six o'clock the tempo was high as the time for the first edition to go to press was approaching. This bustling activity remained throughout the evening up to two o'clock in the morning when the last edition was completed. By that time the reporters had all left the office (a few might have stayed until ten o'clock) and the production of the newspaper was a matter for the sub-editors and the technical staff.

On the beat

The editorial office in Hazrat Ganj was the natural hub of the news-producing activities for the journalists working on *Dainik Jagran*. Sub-editors spent their whole working day here except for an occasional stroll out to the Hazrat Ganj market. For reporters it was the place where they started their working day, coordinated their activities and where they returned at the end of the day to file their stories. But, in the same way, as the hub only makes up a small portion of the wheel, an editorial office is only one of the locations essential for the production of a newspaper. There would not be much to print in the paper if the journalists stayed in the office all day. This is a truism for journalism everywhere, but is especially valid in countries like India for the simple reason that telephones are not very useful working tools, unreliable as they are. All reporters moved around between places in Lucknow on their daily beats and actually spent most of their working day outside the office. Occasionally, the news archives were consulted to get background information to stories, and sometimes a few facts could be checked over the telephone, but otherwise not much stuff for stories could be obtained from within the house.[5] There was not much reason to visit the office between noon and the time for writing up. If reporters did come in, it was mainly because they wanted to socialise with colleagues. Even writing up stories could be done outside the office. Reporters who were living close by sometimes did the writing at home.

When the morning meeting came to an end by noon, the reporters soon dispersed over the city. Lucknow is a sizeable town and even though the editorial office of *Dainik Jagran* was centrally located, places of interest to journalists were spread out over a vast area. Many beats were also defined in such a way that they meant some distance to be covered between places that had to be visited; Lucknow has many schools, hospitals and police stations and they are naturally scattered all over the urban area. A beat reporter certainly needed some means of transportation. The most practical vehicle to use is a two-wheeler that can move fast in the dense and chaotic Lucknow traffic, as well as through narrow lanes and crowded markets. The scooter (or more rarely a motorcycle) is a fundamental working tool for the journalist, as essential as the pen. The journalists' scooters were their private vehicles. As far as I know, no newspapers in Lucknow provided their reporters with two-wheelers. (*Dainik Jagran* had a couple of cars but reporters rarely used them, except for missions outside Lucknow.) The journalists, however, received a monthly allowance of Rs 600 to cover the cost of petrol and repairs. Even though the scooters were practical and necessary, there seemed to be constant troubles with these vehicles; there was always somebody on the staff who had problems getting around because his scooter was being repaired. Part of the reason probably was that no one was eager to invest private money in a brand new, reliable vehicle;

they were all using old machines that had been roughly handled on bad roads for years.

It was not always that a reporter headed for the first stop on his beat when he left the morning meeting, started the engine of his scooter and became absorbed in the traffic jam on Park Road. In principle the reporters were free to spend their days as they wished—as long as they delivered their stories on time. So, the first thing to do might very well be to return home for lunch, to take care of some private business or to visit a friend. Generally, however, most reporters were busy on their beat. There was not much time to waste for a reporter who wanted to perform well on his job. The hunt for stories could be very time-consuming.

How many stops a reporter made on a daily beat varied from just a couple of places up to ten different locations. There was no simple correlation between how many places a reporter visited and how many stories he filed. One story could involve sources in several locations, but then a single stop could generate more than one story. Big organisations on a beat generally involved visits to several departments and people who could supply different information. A reporter with the university or a main hospital on his beat often walked through lengthy corridors and knocked on many doors after he had parked his scooter at the gates. Locations on a beat could be related, such as different departments or branches of the same organisation. While working on a particular story, a reporter might go from place to place in search of information. People in these different places worked with related issues and often knew (or knew of) each other. In other cases the places visited were totally unrelated—except for being on the beat of the same newspaper reporter. Between visiting two branches of the police, a crime reporter could make a call on the fire brigade or a halt at a hotel where a political party was holding a press conference. All locations were not visited with the same frequency; to some places a reporter would come almost daily, to others maybe once a week or more rarely. Sometimes he would go to totally unfamiliar places, although that was the least common category.

When a reporter went to a particular place he could have a few different purposes for the visit. One was to find a source for a story that he already had an idea about. It was a search for specific information: the reporter knew what to ask for and often from whom to get it. A second purpose was to get new ideas for stories. Places were visited without preconceived ideas about what to look for. I would say that the second purpose was generally the most common and it was also an aim present in all situations; even when a reporter had a specific story in mind he was always open to new ideas. A third kind of objective for a visit was to maintain contacts. Sometimes a reporter did not actually expect to get anything concrete out of a place, but it was anyhow important to drop in with some regularity. It could always be useful to keep up a familiarity with a potentially newsworthy organisation, to meet new people on the staff and learn about future events or projects; not least it was important to be a familiar face oneself.

It was unusual for a reporter to have to introduce himself in locations on his beat. At several, if not most, of the places he was a regular visitor, on friendly terms with many of the people who worked there and recognised by all. As Sigal (1986: 16) has remarked about news gathering generally: "Reporters are not free-floating atoms in a mass of humanity. They occupy fixed places, geographically and socially, that bound their search for news." Sometimes one might get the impression that the reporter was an integral part of the activities going on, and not an external guest and observer. Of all the people who usually moved around in many offices (especially those of public undertakings), the reporters of local dailies were certainly among the more regular figures. One might even say that a reporter 'belonged' to some of the locations on his beat just as much as he 'belonged' to an editorial office, because in particular situations the reporter certainly had a key role as one of the most important actors in the non-editorial environment. This was most obviously in the headquarters of political parties where reporters were entertained as main clients—or rather co-actors in the play. But, of course, in some places the reporter was not always appreciated as a welcome guest, and could at least occasionally be regarded as an intruder poking about. However, constantly hostile places were rare—and would simply be useless as halts on a reporter's beat. In cases where a journalist became involved in a major conflict with an important source he simply had to be shifted to another beat.

One aspect of those places that were major stops—such as political party offices, hospitals, police stations, the State Secretariat or certain government departments—was that they became places of interaction between journalists from different media organisations. During his working day, the beat reporter constantly encountered other journalists on a similar beat. These encounters were most often friendly, the reporters often knew each other well, exchanged jokes and gossiped. And, they quite freely exchanged information they had come across. The tough competition between the Lucknow newspapers seemed to be remarkably absent in this context. On the whole, reporters were always keen to look up places where it was likely that they would encounter fellow journalists, even if they were places outside their own beat. If a beat reporter was on his way from one state department to another, driving on Vidhan Sabha Marg, he would probably do an extra turn through the lanes in front of the State Assembly building where it was likely that other journalists' scooters would be parked. And if there was a political rally taking place in Begum Hazrat Mahal Park, there were always a lot more reporters stopping by (at the enclosure reserved specially for journalists) than just those assigned to cover the event.

There were also some places frequented by journalists that were on nobody's beat, places for which there was no other excuse to go than to socialise. One of these places was a small bookshop in Hazrat Ganj, just across the road from the *Dainik Jagran* office. It was called the *Chetna Kitabghar* and was run by the CPI (Communist Party of India). Dropping in here any time in the afternoon, one could be almost sure to meet a few journalists, usually reporters from the Hindi-language dailies. Apart from journalists, some artists, writers, students, junior bureaucrats and communist friends of the shopkeeper Durga Mishra—a soft spoken, slender man in his sixties—also frequented the place. Rarely did it happen that any of these regular visitors looked at the books on the shelves—much less bought anything. The bookshop was a place to go in order to pass some time in the company of friends; for the reporters that meant in-between assignments. In the semi-darkness of the small shop the visitors sipped tea, smoked and engaged in small talk, balancing on the few stools available, standing or half-lying on pieces of cardboard on the floor. News and rumours concerning newspapers, journalists and editors about town were always popular subjects in the company of these men (there were never any women among the regulars). When some journalist was promoted, fired or moved to another paper, it was from here that the news would rapidly diffuse out to the community of journalists. There was always some journalistic matter to discuss: a newspaper was employing new staff, some 'function' would be taking place at the Press Club, or a political party was making travel arrangements for reporters to attend a rally in another town.

In this milieu it became evident that the journalists of Lucknow could be understood as a community. Not that all the journalists in the city came here or regularly visited other common meeting places (such as the Press Club), but everybody seemed to have an interest in and a vast knowledge of virtually anybody that mattered in the press. Resident editors and others in senior positions on the various newspapers rarely moved around among ordinary journalists, but their names and backgrounds were all part of a common knowledge, as were details about a large number of beat reporters. During the part of my fieldwork when I mainly conducted interviews with journalists and editors on the various papers, I often started off from the bookshop. I was always given a lot of information, rumours and opinions about whoever I was about to meet later in the day from someone in the company. Often this was done in a joking fashion, trying to make me feel insecure when I was about to meet someone, such as when I had an appointment with a senior editor about whom everybody seemed agreed that this was really an 'one-eyed man'. When I met him I realised that this was not metaphorically speaking; the man had got only one eye. My visits to the bookshop also offered several opportunities to experience how the solidarity between journalist friends often exceeded the loyalty to the interests of the newspaper. If somebody had missed a story, there would always be a colleague from a competing paper who could brief him. Sometimes a reporter did not bother to attend a routine press conference, confident that he could get the details from his fellows and write the story anyway.

Among the bureaucrats

Let us return to the more proper activities of the Lucknow beat reporters. How does a reporter go about his beat? What is the interaction like between the reporter and his sources? How does he get access to information? Naturally, a newspaper reporter covers many sectors of society, beats may be very different and places that could possibly be visited by a reporter highly diverse. Nevertheless, it is not impossible to generalise. As I described in the previous chapter, a large part of the material in the newspaper—particularly on the local pages—consists of reporting from various public institutions. Likewise, most of the locations on a beat are government undertakings, and the sources public officials. Neither the physical milieu nor the interactions between reporters and sources are without similarities, whether the office is in a police station, a hospital, a government department or at the university.

One of the 'mental hang-ups' that I struggled with during my fieldwork was my perpetual inclination to compare the Lucknow journalists with my knowledge of the profession back home (both from my own experience of practising the profession and from a kind of general knowledge—journalism is a phenomenon that virtually everybody in a country like Sweden come in contact with and have some ideas about). It was also an inclination that was often fuelled by the Lucknow journalists themselves, through questions about how things were in 'the West', how the job was different here. Often I found myself hesitating on this issue. I thought it was possible to find arguments for diametrically opposite opinions. On the one hand, I could argue that journalism is a universal occupation, a form of cultural production that is strikingly similar in otherwise diverse settings. On the other hand, it would be equally true to claim that Indian journalism must be understood first and foremost in its own context, that it was not 'the same' as anywhere else in the world. The question was somewhat easier to handle if one looked at specific parts of the phenomenon, such as the form and content of the newspaper and the organisation and practice of the work. It would then be obvious that form and organisation were more universal than content and practice. A Swedish journalist would no doubt recognise one of the Lucknow dailies as a newspaper and would be familiar with much in the organisation of the newswork, even though she would be struck by some peculiarities. If the journalist got some articles from a Hindi daily translated she would find more notable differences but still be able to see parallels with her own writing. But if she followed one of the Lucknow reporters on his beat, saw him in the offices of government departments, police stations or hospitals, interacting with those public officials, the Swedish journalist would be quite lost. This is really the point where Indian journalism appears most culturally specific. The Lucknow reporter on his beat does not behave like his professional cousin in Stockholm.

I have already touched upon some features of the everyday practice of the Lucknow reporters. One small but crucial detail was their infrequent use of the telephone, which meant that practically every piece of information had to be collected 'out there'. Another point was their close familiarity with some locations on the beat, which to some extent followed from the former fact: they spent a lot of time on the beat. But these intimate relations between reporters and sources were also grounded in another sheer necessity. Indian journalists have very little access to open information, and they can rarely demand to see any document. They are always dependent on the goodwill of their sources to hand out information.[6]

The Lucknow reporter on his beat moves around in settings that mostly fall within the sphere of Indian bureaucratic culture, because to a great extent the news net is flung over bureaucratic organisations. Reporters doing their job on the beat have to conform to the practices of this culture—or rather, they are part of this social world (which strengthens the fibres in the news net). There seems to be quite a strong resemblance in how this culture looks, both in different organisations and at different levels of the bureaucracies. The scene Akhil Gupta (1995: 379) has described from the very lowest rung of the state bureaucracy—the office of a *patwari*, a keeper of land records, in a village of western Uttar Pradesh—would look almost the same in offices on the highest rungs of the state bureaucracy in Lucknow. Typically, a fairly large number of people cluster in the grounds of places like police stations, hospitals, local courts and offices of the state administration. At district headquarters the district magistrate's office draws a crowd every day, and Lucknow as a state capital has many of these places where people come to get in contact with the bureaucracy. When entering these kinds of premises one normally finds an officer in charge (or, in big departments, several) sitting at a table in a sparsely furnished room in the midst of a considerable number of people. Gupta aptly used the expression 'holding court', to recapitulate how the officer handled people who had come to see him on some business or other, because the mode of operation is reminiscent of an Indian *darbaar* at a royal court. The room of an 'important' public official should ideally be crowded all the time, and the officer would talk to all the visitors at the same time, switching from one to the other without attempting to complete any case in a hurry. Intermittently a clerk will come in with documents to be read and signed. Apart from people seeking his services, there will also be a group of friends, colleagues or rather prominent individuals that he simultaneously entertains around his table. Any privacy in this kind of contact with the bureaucracy is simply out of question. All those present can not only overhear each other's business but may also join in the discussion of any case. The more prominent of the visitors will be offered tea and occasionally some *namkin* (snacks), sweets or fruits.

This was a characteristic scene for the reporters in several locations on their beat. The reporter rarely had to stand outside a closed door, waiting for an officer to complete his business and have time free for an interview. The reporter would just drop in and join the crowd. If he was a journalist from one of the main dailies, he would be among those semi-prominent and familiar guests who were offered tea and invited to take a seat on one of the chairs in front of the desk. As may be obvious, the situation was not exactly set for efficiency if the reporter had a specific subject in mind and needed the public servant's undivided attention for a while. It could take some time before the officer turned to the reporter and gave him the opportunity to put forward his query. If the subject involved some information that had to be dug out from office files, a clerk had to be put on the case to deliver the documents, a somewhat long-drawn-out procedure. And, if the officer was unwilling to answer a particular question or hand out the desired information, he could just offer another cup of tea and ignore the subject, occupying himself with so many other things. I never witnessed a reporter applying pressure and demanding to get an answer. On the other hand, the environment was ideal for picking up pieces of information on all kinds of issues and ideas for unexpected stories. A reporter had excellent opportunities to hear for himself what was topical in this office on that particular day. If something big or notable was going on it would be before wide-open curtains. Not only cases that were dealt with by the officer could be of journalistic interest; those other guests and friends in the room might also very well have something that they wanted to share with a newspaper reporter. No doubt, in many situations, it was a sign of 'importance' to have information that could attract a reporter and possibly end up in the newspaper. All in all, for anyone new to the scene it would not be obvious who was the reporter among those people discussing various subjects. Frequently the reporters did not take notes, sometimes they had not even bothered to bring a notebook and a pencil with them, if they needed to put something down on paper it was perfectly alright to borrow the equipment from someone else in the room.

Of course, there were other types of locations and situations on a reporter's beat. The scene just outlined, a crowded room with an officer in charge 'holding court', was often the first stop in the premises of a particular organisation. Following up on the information gathered here, the reporter might need more that could be obtained from other sources—located in the same building or in a branch elsewhere. This could include moving up in the hierarchy (to see the Chief Medical Officer, CMO, if the reporter was on the hospital beat, or the Director General of Police, DGP, on the crime beat). One might then walk into rooms considerably bigger than those just described, but devoid of the crowd, and be greeted by men behind spotlessly clean and polished desks, men with the power to provide all the information that could possibly be available—by pushing a button and calling a clerk to find the right document or fetch the required person. In these kinds of encounters the reporter's (and the newspaper's) reputation and previous cooperation with that person or issues falling under his jurisdiction would be crucial. A reporter who had performed to the satisfaction of the officer could be met with open arms, treated with respect—the usual tea and snacks could even turn into the offer of lunch—and be given really exclusive information. A similar situation could appear lower down in the hierarchy if the reporter had good relations with people in specialised positions that were not so exposed to the media and the public. Between four eyes, and frequently 'off the record', a reporter who had nursed his contacts well could be highly rewarded.[7]

A third type of location of sources in a bureaucracy was on the lowest rungs, among those officers or workers who in practice implemented or executed the tasks. These kinds of people and sites would not usually be among the routine stops of many reporters; even though there were exceptions such as the mortuary in a hospital which was always checked both by crime reporters and medical reporters. Often these locations were difficult to handle. Junior officers or workers were often afraid to speak to the media—even though they were flattered by the interest—and asked the reporters to apply to a superior for information. These locations were also quite crowded with staff and workers, and it was seldom possible to get somebody to 'leak' in privacy. But, on the other hand, among people in these positions discontent about conditions could often be strongly expressed. Not least, in these locations, the reporter could see for himself how a particular task was performed in reality.

To give an example of how a reporter may penetrate a bureaucratic organisation and search for information in several types of location, I shall illustrate with some ethnography collected from the beat of *Dainik Jagran*'s medical reporter.

The malaria prevention story

"Today, I'm going to try to do a story on malaria", Sadguru said one day after the morning meeting was over and I was hesitating about which reporter to accompany. It surprised me because this was in early February and not really the season for malaria in the city. Furthermore, just a week ago I had been with Sadguru to the office of the government Malaria Control Programme in *Jawahar Bhavan*, the huge building on Ashok Marg which housed several state bureaucracies. We had just dropped by, because Sadguru happened to be in the building for other reasons, and the officers assured him that they had nothing for the press. This brief visit had, however, had the effect that one person on the staff decided later in the week that there certainly was something that could be of interest to a reporter. Now Sadguru had in his hand a document showing statistics on how cases of malaria had increased during the last few years, at the same time as state expenses for malaria prevention had decreased. The state government was not fulfilling its object of allocating the same amount of money for this purpose as was allotted to the state by the central government.

I decided to go with Sadguru on this assignment and seated myself behind him on his scooter. First, we drove down to *Jawahar Bhavan*, but no officer in charge of the state malaria programme was to be found anywhere. Back on the scooter again, we continued to the Medical Directorate in another part of the city, but Sadguru could not find the director he was looking for here either. Resolutely he tried another way to go about it and took me down to the basement of the Medical Directorate. Here was a big room filled with barrels containing the insecticide that was used to spray in drains to prevent mosquitoes from breeding. At a desk amidst these barrels sat an officer responsible for the practical execution of malaria prevention in the districts. Sadguru approached the man, who welcomed him with a smile. Turning towards a colleague sitting at his side, he said, "This is a good friend from *Dainik Jagran*, he has a very constructive approach towards our division." The officer openly started to give Sadguru information concerning areas of the town that were particularly malaria-infested, efforts that were being made to deal with the situation, the staff available and so forth. After a while, however, he suddenly said, "Please, don't quote me". When Sadguru, dissatisfied, asked why not, the officer explained that they had a policy in this division that all communication with the press should go through only one particular officer. Despite this, the man continued to talk, obviously happy to be useful to a journalist. He sent a clerk for tea and tried his very best to be helpful. When we left the place, Sadguru had a pretty clear picture of the state of things. There was no lack of materials, machines and chemicals for malaria prevention—which were supplied from the central government. The problem was resources and personnel to get the job done in Lucknow. It was the coordination between the different authorities that did not work.

There was still a lot missing from the story. Out in the traffic again we headed for the authority that had the ultimate responsibility on the matter—the Chief Medical Officer (CMO). Again, this was in another part of town, in Kaiser Bagh a short ride away. Without even entering the building Sadguru could see that the CMO was not in the office, because his car was not parked in the yard. We went up anyway and were told that he was coming in later during the day. The next stop was the *Nagar Nigam* (the Municipal Corporation), conveniently housed on our way back to Hazrat Ganj, which had a medical division with malaria prevention among its responsibilities. This was a place that did not usually occur on Sadguru's beat, and he was unfamiliar with the premises. Not recognised by the civil servants, he had to introduce himself and explain what he was looking for. After some confusion, he found the correct officer, in charge of spraying insecticide in residential areas. In despair, the man told us about the bad state of the machines they had at their disposal, and the lack of resources to carry out the work. "But don't take this as official", he concluded.

Being close to the *Dainik Jagran* office, we stopped by and met a couple of colleagues in the political bureau. Brijesh, the BJP reporter, was just about to have his lunch and invited all those present to help themselves to dishes that the wife had sent with him in a food-flask. Back at work again, Sadguru had to do a job that the bureau chief had assigned to him. This was to attend a press conference given by a Dalit organisation at

Darasafula (a building complex which housed both the living quarters of bureaucrats and the offices of several political, social and trade union organisations). This was an assignment clearly outside Sadguru's beat, and he tried to get it done as quickly as possible. As soon as he had a brief idea of what it was all about, we were out on the street again. After exchanging a few words with a reporter from *Amar Ujala,* we got back on the two-wheeler and went for another attempt at the office of the CMO.

This time the white Ambassador car (the typical vehicle allotted to government administrators of the highest rank) was parked outside the entrance to the building; the CMO was present in the office. A public servant showed us into a room where we had to wait for ten minutes. When the CMO appeared, he greeted Sadguru with a welcoming gesture and invited both of us to take a seat in his office. I had been here with Sadguru once before, when he was working on a story about the pollution of the Gomati river, so I knew that the chief of the medical administration had a friendly attitude towards the *Dainik Jagran* reporter. The CMO had explained to me, while showing me an album of newspaper cuttings, that all the media, and *Dainik Jagran* in particular, had given very good coverage to a recently accomplished polio vaccination campaign. For the pollution story the CMO made a considerable effort to supply Sadguru with information and even called a chemical expert in to the office to explain the technical details of the case. This time it was not primarily information that Sadguru needed, but rather some comments and clarification on the facts that he already had. My impression was also that he wanted to inform the CMO, as a senior and powerful person in the bureaucracy, about a story that would expose deficiency in government undertakings. The CMO had no objections to the story that Sadguru presented to him. He acknowledged that there was a problem with the implementation of the malaria prevention programme. The culprit for the inaction was, according to him, *Nagar Nigam* (the Municipal Corporation).

"Now, the story is ripe", Sadguru said as we walked down the stairs of the building and out to the scooter. "I am very satisfied, but it did take a lot of effort." He explained that he intended to break the story in two parts: first an article about the situation in Lucknow, and then a follow-up with an article about the districts out of town. We went back to the *Dainik Jagran* office and I left Sadguru there to file his story. The first part was published some days later and dealt with the inability of different government authorities to coordinate their resources in order to run the malaria prevention programme in Lucknow. The second article, dealing with the state malaria control programme in general, appeared the next day. Both of them were published on the front page and Sadguru's name was in the byline.

About a month later I was reminded of this story when one morning I got a lift into town with Sadguru (we both lived in Indira Nagar, across the Gomati river). He told me that his articles about the malaria programme had now resulted in some action from the authorities. The mayor of Lucknow had taken the initiative to hold a meeting with all the departments and authorities involved in malaria prevention. The aim was to coordinate the different resources and activities in order to implement the programme. Now, it was hoped that the drains would be cleaned up and sprayed with insecticide, with the use of the workforce, machines and chemicals already available in town. Sadguru, who was usually modest and never boasted about himself, claimed that these efforts were the direct outcome of his articles.

Benefits of being a reporter

"Everybody wants to be a beat reporter", a senior journalist once told me when we were talking about different designations in the editorial office. Even though going on a beat often involved quite hard work compared with sub-editing, it had some significant advantages. A beat reporter had good connections with important people, in politics and in the bureaucracy. He mingled daily with very powerful individuals and often came to know them in a friendly way. I have dwelt at some length on the often intimate relationship between reporters and sources in the bureaucracy, but the informality and relaxed atmosphere struck me even more on occasions when I accompanied reporters to encounters with the most powerful politicians of the state. The journalists never conformed to the usual procedures of showing respect to people with power—no bowing or feet touching. Press conferences at political headquarters were often held in a quite joyful and egalitarian mood. The politicians and the reporters engaged themselves in conversation on various issues, exchanged jokes and laughed together. On the other hand, challenging or intricate questions to the politicians were rather uncommon.

This familiarity with politicians and bureaucrats could also be useful for the reporter privately—for himself, his relatives or friends. The advantages could be an innocent matter of knowing how things worked in bureaucracies which were not very transparent to ordinary people: where to go and what to do if you wanted to get something done. In a kind of grey zone, good connections could also be used to speed things up when you knew whom to approach. I witnessed this several times, and the reporters did not seem to have any second thoughts about using their connections in this way. One example was a reporter whose mother-in-law needed an eye operation. Knowing the director of the hospital very well, the journalist could get a date booked for her within a few days' time; she did not have to wait all the months it would have taken via the official queue. On another occasion a relative of one of the reporters was waiting outside the *Dainik Jagran* office one day after the morning meeting. He had some problem with the registration of a property at the Lucknow Development Authority (LDA); the fee had been paid, but nothing had happened and he was even asked for more money. The reporter related to the man did not have the LDA on his own beat, but he approached the colleague who covered the *Nagar Nigam*. Together the three men talked over the problem, and the municipal reporter agreed to see what he could do about it.

These kinds of benefits were more or less taken for granted by the reporters. Of course, they made private use of their good connections, they said. Anybody would. In fact, this was how things worked with the bureaucracy. To get something done, preferably you go through somebody with good connections; it might be a distant relative, a friend or somebody from the same village. The reporters just happened to be in those positions themselves.

Other minor favours that came with the job were the treats on the political beat. Politicians of all colours were often 'generous' to journalists. A press conference held by a political party always involved some sweets, light dishes with delicacies, or sometimes a buffet lunch—treatment probably familiar to journalists in many parts of the world. When a major political rally was taking place somewhere outside Lucknow, the parties would generally arrange transport facilities, hotels and food, and take care of telephone and fax bills for the journalists. On some occasions it could be quite spectacular. One day when I was sitting with a few reporters at the People's Bookshop, they described with enthusiasm the previous day's flight in a small private aeroplane together with one of the party leaders down to a political rally in Kanpur. For a less extraordinary event, I travelled together with a reporter to the nearby town of Faizabad, for the purpose of doing a story about a particular constituency in connection with the approaching election. We arrived unannounced in the town by bus late in the evening and checked into a hotel. In no time at all a local politician had got to know that a reporter from one of the main newspapers of the state was on a visit to his town and came over to welcome us. Entering our room he asked what we would like to drink. When my journalist friend mentioned that whiskey would not be a bad idea, the politician took out a bottle of 'Indian Made Foreign Liqour' from somewhere under his *kurta-pajama*. While we consumed the bottle together with a hearty dinner, the politician remained seated by our table in the room, not eating or drinking but eager to be of any help. However, the reporter mostly ignored him and did not even ask which party he represented. The next day, when we checked out of the hotel, the bill for our dinner had already been taken care of.

A main topic, when journalists talked about the advantages of beat reporting, was the possibility of obtaining government accommodation: a centrally located flat of good standard for a reasonable rent. Government housing in India is primarily something that concerns public servants and politicians of different ranks. The system is elaborate and implies that houses and flats are allocated according to the rank of the public servant. The higher up you are in the hierarchy, the better and bigger flat you are entitled to. A very senior civil servant or a minister in the State Cabinet might even get a colonial bungalow with a huge garden in a green area; in Lucknow that could mean Mall Avenue. The fact that journalists, who are mainly employed in the private and commercial sector, are also included among those who may apply for government accommodation suggests a unique privilege. It might be interpreted as an illustration of the historical intimacy between journalism and the nation-building project in India.[8] All journalists working on a daily newspaper could in principle apply for a flat. But just putting in an application would not quickly give you accommodation. You must have the right connections. Some journalists had much greater opportunities than others to pull the proper strings, especially reporters on a political beat. Several journalists told me that it was the Chief Minister (who had a discretionary quota of flats for allotment) who had to be approached if one needed housing quickly.

The allotment of government flats was not a particularly controversial subject among the journalists. To my knowledge, it was not a source of jealousy and I never heard anyone talking about the distribution procedure in terms of unfairness. It was more a matter of good luck if one was in a position to enhance one's chances of getting a flat. Nor was this favour sensed in everyday discourse as something questionable, with regard to professional morality. There was normally nothing shameful about the fact that some journalists were living in government flats. However, the allocation of flats was among a number of other favours handed out by various state governments to journalists, which since 1995 had been under severe criticism from the Press Council of India, which had undertaken an investigation into the matter.[9] At the time of my fieldwork this investigation was a burning issue in the media world of Lucknow. What had originally aroused the Press Council's concern was the scale of financial benefits that the former Chief Minister of Uttar Pradesh, Mulayam Singh Yadav, had extended to certain journalists during his tenure of office. The Press Council had demanded that all state governments and union territories supply information about the various kinds of favours bestowed on journalists. The information received from the Uttar Pradesh government listed favours such as free bus travel and rail concessions, free medical facilities, financial assistance to journalists and their dependants in distress, free life and accident insurance, plots of land and flats supplied at concessional rates, allotments of government houses and the establishment of Press Clubs. Furthermore, cash had been disbursed from the Chief Minister's discretionary fund amounting to Rs 10,788,000 between December 1993 and June 1995 alone (Press Council of India, 1998).

When the issue was discussed among the Lucknow journalists, it was primarily the financial favours that aroused interest. Nobody seemed to bother much about the rest. A list had been circulating in Lucknow (compiled by a political opponent of the former Chief Minister and presented in the State Assembly as well as published in the newspapers) which named the journalists and the amount of money or other kinds of favours they were suspected of having received. It was common knowledge that one of the reporters on *Dainik Jagaran* had been on that list. His fellow journalists in no way froze him out, although in an insinuating manner they sometimes mentioned his 'exceptionally good connections' with the former Chief Minister. The reporter never denied that he had received money, but neither did he brag about it. A few other journalists I met, who had been on the list, strongly denied that they had taken any money and claimed that the list was a fake.

The opportunity for getting close to powerful people and moving in prominent milieus is also a feature of beat reporting that is desirable in a less material sense. It definitely gives status to the reporter. This kind of status was clearly a part of his professional reputation. A successful journalist was not only someone who broke good stories, but also a person who was intimate with influential people. Once when I was invited to dinner at the house of a *Dainik Jagran* reporter, we talked for several hours about his successful career. He had started as a sports reporter in a small town edition of a Hindi paper and was now, at the age of only 29, a senior journalist in the political bureau. To underscore how remarkable his career had been, he showed me his photograph album in which important family events had been documented. The most precious pictures were those of ministers in the State Cabinet who had obviously attended a big feast held for the reporter's first-born son. Even the famous Chief Minister Mulayam Singh Yadav had paid his tribute on this important occasion in the life of a 'simple' newspaper reporter.

In this chapter I have tried to sketch a picture of the practice of news reporting and some of the predicaments of working as a journalist. But who are the people who work for the newspaper offices in Lucknow and how have they achieved these positions? This will be the subject of the next chapter.

Notes

1. In Chapter Six I shall dwell somewhat on the implications in the field of my own experience of journalism.
2. Sub-editor is the term usually used in British journalism and has therefore also become common in India.
3. Most reporting from the districts was also organised on a freelance basis. Their news was, however, somewhat wider in scope.
4. Indian Readership Survey 1995.
5. An exception was during election time when all tasks were re-organised. Several reporters were assigned to the special election page and spent a lot of time in the office, editing material from news agencies and rewriting from other papers.
6. On this point my own experience of journalism might stand out as too sharp a contrast, because few countries in the world come close to Sweden with regard to legal accessibility for journalists to documents in government undertakings.
7. A way to keep the sources happy was to give them some positive publicity occasionally—to write stories that were really not motivated journalistically (and were disliked by the news editors). This was a common way to make up for an article that had exposed mismanagement.
8. See Chapter Two.
9. The Press Council is a quasi-judicial body with a "two-fold function of preserving the freedom of the press and maintaining and improving standards of the press". The Council, headed by a sitting or retired judge of the Supreme Court of India, consists of representatives of the press, members of the Houses of Parliament and representatives of the cultural, literary and legal fields. It is financed by fees levied on registered newspapers and by grants from the Central Government (Press Council of India, 1997).

Five

The Journalists

One of the recently recruited young journalists working with *Dainik Jagran* was D.P. Shukla. Since he was working nights on sub-editing I had not noticed him in the editorial office during the first weeks of my fieldwork but he recognised me at Lucknow University one morning when I was visiting the journalism division in the Hindi Department. I was there to see Girish Mishra, the 'adviser' employed on contract on *Dainik Jagran,* who was also teaching at the university. After attending one of Girish's lectures where he had been speaking about newspaper layout and news values before a group of students taking a course in 'Public Relations and Advertisement', D.P. approached me in the whitewashed arcade in front of the classroom. He introduced himself, saying that he had seen me at the premises of *Dainik Jagran* a couple of times and suggested that I should come with him to the university canteen for a soft drink. We talked and spent several hours together that day. For a large part of my fieldwork D.P. became one of my main informants and a good friend.

D.P. was doing his second year of the master's course in journalism while he was working full-time at *Dainik Jagran*. It seemed like a tough schedule, but it was workable because all the lectures were in the morning, and his working hours at the newspaper were between six in the evening and two o'clock in the morning. Furthermore, as he said, the course did not take up much time, it was mostly a matter of attending lectures and doing a little reading in order to pass the examinations at the end of the semester. The course was purely theoretical and involved no practical exercises in journalism. Besides this, he was also taking a course in law—"one has to know some of that as a journalist", he said. He had already obtained a BA, which included philosophy, international relations and economics and, on top of that, an MA in social work.

D.P., at this time 25 years old, was from a Brahmin family which originally came from a village in the Pratapgarh district of eastern Uttar Pradesh. The family still had relatives living in the village and D.P. went there a couple of times during my fieldwork, staying a week or so to deal with family matters. Even though he had never lived in the village himself, it certainly played some emotional role for him, and he sometimes referred to other people originating in Pratapgarh as fellow villagers. In Lucknow the family had a house in a residential area called Old Hyderabad across the Gomati river. This was where D.P. stayed most of the time but sometimes he used the room of a friend in the university's student hostel. His father, recently retired, had been a civil servant working in the Department of Telecommunications. D.P. had a brother who was a businessman and a sister who was a welfare officer at a government undertaking. Except for D.P., the sister was the only family member who had a university degree. Like him, she was also interested in poetry—writing some herself—and she had been a main intellectual inspiration to him, he claimed. Another relative he admired was his *Tau* (father's elder brother) who had been a freedom-fighter associated with the famous Chandrashekhar Azad during the Independence Movement; "from him I have learnt idealism", D.P. stated. While most members of the family were devoutly religious, follower of a south Indian guru, D.P. called himself non-religious.

Leaving the canteen and walking together through the lush greenery that surrounds the university buildings of beautiful Nawabi architecture, we encountered some of D.P.'s friends with whom we exchanged a few words. As we continued he explained that they all formed part of an informal group of students who had been very close to each other for some years, meeting regularly to discuss political, cultural and philosophical topics. The group was 'leftist', he said, and they had met each other originally as members of a student organisation associated with the CPI (Communist Party of India). D.P. was rather sad that the group was splitting up because several of them were completing their studies and were about to leave the university. They were now busy looking for future careers. Some were preparing for the examination enter to the IAS (Indian Administrative Service) and a couple of others were aiming at a military career in the army or the BSF (Border Security Force). His closest friend had just got a job at the Lucknow branch of the Press Information Bureau (a government organisation under the Ministry of Information and Broadcasting).

D.P. had started his journalistic career by contributing articles to a publication called *Lucknow Magazine* (which, despite its English name, was published in Hindi). The first article he wrote for this publication was on Urdu poetry. That was a couple of years ago. The collaboration came to an end when the editor of the magazine put his own name under a story that D.P. had written—a story, by the way, about the former Chief Minister's 'generosity' towards journalists (mentioned in the previous chapter). However, one of his contributions to *Lucknow Magazine* was an interview with his teacher in journalism, Girish Mishra. Apparently, Girish had been very pleased with this article, because he had suggested that D.P. should go and talk to Vinod Shukla, the resident editor of *Dainik Jagran*, and ask for a job. Vinod Shukla accepted Girish's recommendation and gave D.P. an opportunity to show his abilities for one month. He did this to the satisfaction of the resident editor and was invited to continue to work as a sub-editor. Of course, it was not a proper job, he was recruited as a 'trainee' and instead of a wage he was given a 'grant' of Rs 2,200 a month—for full-time work. Still, in the process of learning the profession he pointed out that it was completely on his own initiative that he was improving his skills: "They don't *teach* you anything. I have to study carefully how they do it, watch how they select the articles to be published."

Besides sub-editing, D.P. occasionally wrote articles on his own initiative for *Dainik Jagran*. This was always in the form of contributions to the regular column '*Pahal*' (the perspective) and he had done stories, for example, about 'the cultural invasion from the West', 'women's liberation' and 'the lack of honesty in politics'. It gave him intellectual satisfaction to write these kinds of stories, he said. Convinced that he would have a future in journalism, he hoped to secure a permanent job with *Dainik Jagran* in the nearest future. But he realised that this was solely in the hands of Vinod Shukla and it did worry him a bit that he had not yet been able to establish any personal relationship with him.

In the event, D.P.'s career with *Dainik Jagran* did not last very long. Shukla never gave him a proper job. Two years later, he had left *Dainik Jagran* and joined the newly started *Kuber Times*. In joining this paper he had taken a major step in his career; he had become a senior sub-editor in charge of the front page. But he did not stay long here either. And, contrary to his expectations when I first met him at Lucknow University, he did not even remain a newspaper journalist. At New Year 2000 I received a greeting from him by e-mail announcing that he had moved to New Delhi and started work as a publications editor with the Food Corporation of India.

The story of D.P. may serve as a point of departure for an account of the Lucknow journalists. In this chapter I want to give a picture of the people who make up the editorial staff of the newspapers in the town, with particular reference to *Dainik Jagran*. Who are these individuals who decide what's news for the readers in Lucknow (and much of Uttar Pradesh)? How did they get into the profession and what routes had their careers taken before they ended up in an editorial office in Lucknow? Without proclaiming D.P. as 'the typical Hindi journalist', I shall suggest that several features of his biography are not uncommon among his colleagues, for example, with regard to age, gender, caste and education. Other parts of his story hint at characteristics that appear quite typical but need to be somewhat more qualified—such as family background, method of recruitment into the profession, career, ambitions and political engagement. Focusing on elements like these, I shall try to sketch some answers to the above questions. My description of the Lucknow journalists is not, however, composed from quantitative survey data; I have no material with which I could statistically map the journalists with respect to a number of criteria. So, I do not pretend to present the Hindi journalists in the same prototypical way as Weaver and Wilhoit (1991) have described their professional cousin in the United States—the white male Protestant with a bachelor's degree, married with two children, middle of the road politically, and earning 19,000 dollar a year. As an anthropologist more at home with soft data, I have chosen to rely on impressions from my encounters in the field.

This chapter will not, however, focus exclusively on the Hindi-language journalists. I shall also refer to journalists working with the English-language dailies of Lucknow. The point about this is obviously comparative. The Hindi- and English-language journalists are in the same occupation and most of their work routines are the same. They explicitly relate to each other and are part of a common professional sphere. But, in some respects, the journalists of the two languages work in different media worlds: to some extent they belong in different journalistic traditions and write for different readers. However, what matters in this context is that they come from different backgrounds, and that their career routes in the profession rarely cross each other.

Gender

First, Hindi-language journalists are, as I have mentioned before, predominantly male.[1] This is particularly true with regard to reporters. During the first part of my fieldwork all the reporters on *Dainik Jagran* were men. The few women in the editorial department worked as sub-editor. When I revisited Lucknow in 1998 two young women had, however, been employed as reporters in the local bureau. The situation at the other Hindi dailies of the town was much the same: female journalists were very rare, especially as reporters, even though not totally unknown. In this respect, the contrast between the Hindi and the English press was striking. Not that women were in a majority on any paper, but they were certainly a much higher proportion in the editorial departments of the *Pioneer*, the *Hindustan Times* and the *Times of India* than they were on any of the Hindi dailies. On the *Times of India* women were not far from making up half the staff. To explain this difference I believe one first has to consider what kind of workplace a newspaper is, and what is the popular image of journalistic work.

An Indian woman from an educated background would look for a 'respectable' job and place of work—or rather, the parents of a young woman would be particular about the kind of work their daughter took up. As one female journalist told me:

> Many parents regard teaching as the ideal job for a daughter who has just completed her education. Preferably working in a girls' school. She can take a rikshaw to work in the morning, teach in a protected and all-female environment, and then return home safe and happy. And after some time in that occupation she will be suitable for marriage. The conditions of work as a newspaper reporter would not readily match these requirements.

Moving around on a scooter, meeting all sorts of people in various, and predominantly male, settings is to many minds not a suitable occupation for a woman. The image of the English-language newspapers could, however, to some extent make up for these circumstances. Whatever the reporters are doing in practice, these papers are known to be a matter for the elite in society, dealing with 'important' issues of national concern. One does not primarily think of a journalist on an English paper as one who spends much of her time in police stations or among junior bureaucrats and petty politicians. Working as a reporter in the Hindi press, with its local focus and its reputation of being closer to the common man, is more difficult to picture without these practical predicaments of the job.

But also on the English-language papers female journalists would more often be found working on the editorial desk or with features writing rather than as hard news reporters. Female journalists told me that their male colleagues often behaved protectively towards them and refrained from sending them out on certain assignments. Few, however, complained about this. As one woman said: "It works both ways; if there is a crime in the middle of the night a girl won't be assigned to that, but she would also not be keen on it." Features writing on a freelance basis seemed to be a principal entrance for women into the English-language press. The editors in charge of the features pages of both the *Pioneer* and the *Times of India* claimed that most of the freelancers they relied on were in fact women. The reason for this, they said, was that it was easier to find women with a good English education, who could write well and were willing to contribute stories occasionally for a rather small payment. Young men are not good freelancers, said one editor: "Only those who can't get any other job, who are good for nothing, are interested. The girls, on the other hand, are from good families and are doing it while waiting to get married." Some of these young women eventually get hooked and continue with journalism, whether they marry or not.

Religion

All the journalists but one in the editorial office of *Dainik Jagran* were Hindus by origin (the exception was a Sunni Muslim reporter in the political bureau). Most of them would also describe themselves as Hindus by faith, even though the majority had a quite profane approach to life. It was unusual for anyone on the staff to come to the morning meeting with a coloured *tika* on his forehead, showing that he had visited a temple before coming to work. Other paraphernalia of religious-minded men were also rather low-key. On the beat the reporters often encountered lower middle-class bureaucrats with sacred bracelets on their wrists and amulet rings on almost every finger—in offices where incense was burnt in front of deities on the wall. The editorial office had none of that atmosphere. But not many of the journalists would, like D.P., straightforwardly call themselves non-religious, much less atheists. 'Secular' was the word some preferred to use. But this is a term that in the Indian context has a specific political connotation and history.[2] Those who sympathised with Hindu nationalist ideas and organisations (BJP, RSS, VHP and so on) would not use it, even though they never showed any religious inclination. When it came to journalists who were emphatic about their non-religious image one could sometimes be surprised. One of the staunchest 'secularists' came back to the office after a week's holiday and revealed that he had been with his family on a pilgrimage to Gangotri—a famous religious site in the Himalayas.

The staff of the English-language press were somewhat less homogeneous when it came to religious identity. All the English papers had several Muslim journalists on their staff. I met a few Shia Muslims from well-off families associated with the former 'splendour' of *Nawabi* culture in Lucknow, though Sunni Muslims with more modest backgrounds were really more numerous—but not to the extent that the English-language press would risk getting a reputation as a Muslim stronghold. The British presence in Lucknow—another important theme in the history of the town—had not left any significant traces with regard to the background of English-language journalists. The Anglo-Indian community was once quite influential in Lucknow, and journalism, like education, was one of the occupations where they had a chance to make use of their mastery of the English language. But this community had largely vanished from Lucknow and I never met any Anglo-Indian journalists, and few other Christians for that matter.

Caste

If women and non-Hindus were rare as journalists working with the Hindi press, the staff of these newspapers mirrored Indian society even less in another important respect. Like D.P., most of the journalists had a family name (and thus a byline) indicating that they were of Brahmin origin. On *Dainik Jagran* not more than a handful of the editorial staff were from castes other than Brahmin, most of them from *jati*s usually understood as falling within the *varna* of Kshatriyas.[3] The situation looked much the same in other Hindi-language papers in the city. Brahmins, whose proportion of the population is somewhere around 5 per cent, dominate Hindi journalism. Thus, in this important part of the public sphere, the traditionally most powerful caste in society today has a stronger presence than in politics and in the government administration—where the practice of positive discrimination puts a limit on the domination of the higher castes. Probably, the Brahmin presence in journalism is stronger than in most other educated professions. One study of three educated professional groups in Indian society—civil servants, industrial managers and university teachers—found for example that Brahmins constituted nearly half of the Hindu respondents. The greatest dominance, 52.7 per cent, was among industrial managers (Navlakha, 1989: 65). Despite not having access to precise statistics, I would find it safe to say that the proportion of Brahmins among all (Hindu or non-Hindu) journalists who worked with the Hindi-language press in Lucknow was considerably higher.

If the Dalits (the 17% of Indians traditionally belonging to the lowest rung of the caste hierarchy and officially classified as 'Scheduled Castes' or SCs) were poorly represented among Lucknow journalists, this was not particular to the profession in this city. Robin Jeffrey states that in ten years of studying the Indian-language press (which included visits to twenty towns and interviews with more than 250 journalists), he never, as far he knew, met a Dalit journalist working for a mainstream publication (2000: 160, note 80). *Dainik Jagran* in Lucknow had one SC journalist on its staff—the only one I met, as far as I know, among the journalists in this town. The man was working as a reporter in the local bureau. He was not, however, in charge of covering issues associated with the SCs. During the time when I met him daily together with his colleagues in the office, I never heard anybody talk about him as a Dalit, and people never turned to him when Dalit questions came up for discussion during morning meetings. This was in sharp contrast to the other 'odd' journalist on the staff: the Muslim reporter who was always assigned to stories concerning his community and who was a kind of authority on Muslim affairs. Nor did the SC reporter himself invoke his caste identity in any situation when I was present. That he was from a SC was obvious from his surname but otherwise he seemed to keep as quiet as possible about his caste status. (One Dalit journalist, who had only worked on minor political publications, pointed out to Robin Jeffrey that this was the only practical option, ibid.: 162). I am not sure if this was a conscious strategy or not. Whatever the case, the journalist was successful in the profession. His colleagues regarded him as one of the best in the local bureau and he was popular with the management. When the editorial office was reorganised at the time of the central parliamentary election, he was put in charge of the special election pages.

Later, he was among those who left *Dainik Jagran* for new publications that were launched in town. He was recruited by *Hindustan*, perhaps the best reputed (and best paying) of all the Hindi dailies in Lucknow.

How should one explain this unrepresentative composition of the newspaper staffs when it came to caste? I do not believe that there was a deliberate recruitment policy behind it. Probably—and as far as I understand it—neither the resident editors nor the chief editors or the owners had taken a decision that Brahmins were the most suitable for journalism. Nor would it be true to say that Brahmins are culturally preferred as journalists in the same way as a priest ought to be a Brahmin. The discriminatory process is subtler. According to the traditional ideology, the Brahmin's superior status is closely related to his learning. "The respectable Brahman is a scholar and a teacher rather than a priest" (Parry, 1989: 53). Insofar as journalism is considered an intellectual, literate and learned occupation, it would not be far-fetched to regard it as quite suitable for a Brahmin. Furthermore, the idea that "the Brahman's knowledge is theoretically something to be disseminated" (ibid.) rather than kept secret, fits quite well with the work of a reporter. An ideology revolving around a sense of idealism—most journalists would say that they have a kind of 'mission' in their work—adds to the potential of regarding the profession as a respectable one. One could also imagine how the process of discrimination works once the Hindi press has built a reputation as a Brahmin stronghold. To the extent that the ideological pre-eminence of the Brahmins still has some cultural significance, it must take some amount of self-confidence for a non-Brahmin to enter their domains. But this is purely my speculation. No journalist ever said that he had chosen the profession because he was a Brahmin. Nor did those who were not Brahmins claim that they had trespassed on a restricted arena.

Ethnographically, is it not simple to put a finger on how the phenomenon of caste does become visible in the editorial offices?[4] Certainly, it is not possible to describe it as a rigid set of rules regulating the interaction between people, as it once permeated social life in India—and still does in many contexts.

No one on the staff refrained from drinking water from the common jug on the table. I never witnessed anything that could unambiguously be described as caste discrimination. In fact, it would have been easy to say that caste is something irrelevant among these modern urban professionals, at least in their role in the editorial office (cf. Appadurai, 1988; Béteille, 1994: 448).[5] That is, if it was not for the uncomfortable fact that Brahmins were in such a strikingly dominant number on the staff. Caste cannot simply be written off.

One opinion I sometimes heard when middle-class people (journalists as well as others) dwelt on how caste is still a prevalent phenomenon in contemporary modern India had to do with self-confidence. Some claimed that in a group of educated professionals one could always make out who was a Brahmin and who was of lower caste by the way they behaved. A Brahmin takes comfort from his caste identity and acts with a high degree of self-confidence. Those from lower castes, according to this opinion, are always more modest, silent and less self-assured. Thus, in modern contexts, caste is more of a mental phenomenon than a system of regulations and rules. Translated into the language of social science, it would mean that Brahmins have a 'habitus'—a set of dispositions associated with a particular social class, which structure practice and perception (Bourdieu, 1990: 52ff)—which puts them at ease in a professional field. I am not sure that this popular perception would hold if it was empirically scrutinised, at least not in the most general version implying that all kinds of Brahmins all over India have a common habitus. (Certainly, I have met modest Brahmins as well as presumptuous Dalits.) But, according to my experience among journalists as well as among other educated professionals in India, the idea does not appear completely without foundation. With regard to caste identity, being a Brahmin seems to be unproblematic at least in one sense: that one *is* a Brahmin and not 'actually' something else. When I asked my informants about what caste they belonged to, those who were in the highest *varna* category without hesitation or roundabout explanation answered straightforwardly that they were Brahmins. A few times I tried to be cunning and told someone that I did not recognise his surname;

was he perhaps Bengali? No, Brahmin, would come the reply. For people of other castes the answer was less obvious and they often felt some specifications were needed. A non-Brahmin might invoke one or several of a whole range of classifications: a *varna*, a *jati*, a religion or an official category (Forward Caste, Other Backward Caste, Scheduled Caste or Scheduled Tribe). He would often clarify the traditional occupation of the caste and mention the father's occupation or the region from which the family originated. Furthermore, even though it would not be possible to make any generalisations from my limited material, those journalists who kept a low profile in the editorial offices were in fact often non-Brahmins.

As an instance of when the subject of caste cropped up unprovoked, I recall a conversation with one of the journalists on *Dainik Jagran* in which I mentioned a senior colleague using the suffix *ji* added to his name, which is a common way of addressing people with respect. I was reproved and told that I should call the man *Babu Sahib* like everyone else, because he was a *Thakur* and very pleased to be called by that name. I was aware that the senior journalist was often addressed in this way, but I had never followed this practice. *Babu Sahib* is another term of respect and the journalist might very well have liked to be so called, but the name also has a kind of feudal connotation and I did not feel that I had the cultural competence to use it. To me a *Babu Sahib* was a wealthy landowner sitting on a *chaarpai* (string bed) in a village and commanding other people to work—which is also the common image of a *Thakur*. I explained my doubts and said that I felt it strange to address a professional journalist in that way. "Yes, you are right", said the colleague, "but he *is* a *Thakur*". Later, the older journalist told me that he was from a family of farmers, but by caste they were Kshatriya (warriors, the second highest *varna* category). When I asked more specifically if they were *Thakur* (which is a *jati* conceptualised as within the *varna* of Kshatriyas), he showed deep disapproval. "No, no ... well some say *Thakur*, other say *Rajput*, but actually we are Kshatriya." Obviously he was not happy about the rural and unsophisticated (however wealthy) association that came with being a *Thakur* and preferred the more general *varna* category. Kshatriya is a lot more compatible with an intellectual vocation than is *Thakur*. But every time someone addressed him as *Babu Sahib,* the latter identity was invoked.

Again, with respect to caste, the English-language press was another story. On these newspapers the caste background of the staff was much more diverse, and though Brahmins were present in large numbers they were less dominant than on the Hindi papers. As I have mentioned previously, there were several Muslims on the staffs of these newspapers. Among the Hindus most were from the higher or intermediate strata in the traditional caste hierarchy, but not necessarily Brahmins. One caste which was common among English-language journalists in Lucknow, as well as all over northern India, was the *Kayasth* a, which in fact conforms to the traditional Hindu social order in which members of this *jati* (within the *varna* of Kshatriya) had the profession of writers.

Education

Something that initially surprised me when I started my fieldwork and regularly appeared in editorial offices in Lucknow, was that most journalists seemed to take my presence and my interest in their work completely for granted. I was an academic studying the media, nothing very strange about that (apart from the academic being Swedish). A few journalists remarked that anthropologists usually stayed among tribal people in remote settings and not among writers in big cities. But I rarely had to explain what social science was about, or justify what good it would do to study them and their work. I soon understood that academia was not a world apart for the journalists: practically all of them had a university degree and were familiar with academic research.[6] With a few exceptions, all of them were at least graduates, many had obtained master's degrees and a few had even started on a PhD programme (I met none with a doctorate, however). And due to the fact that most of the journalists were quite young, university life was not a very remote experience. A couple of them, like D.P., were still students, and most of the others had good friends (or relatives) at the university. Furthermore, adding to the familiarity of academic life, the university was among the regular beats, covered in particular by one reporter but frequently visited by several of the others: on the local pages there were news items every day from the campus.

The journalists working with *Dainik Jagran* had most commonly read some social science or arts subject, like political science, sociology, history, Hindi, English or literature. But there was great variety and the most diverse educational backgrounds could be found among the staff. One had a degree in business, another was a graduate of law school, and a third had read biology and chemistry. All of them matched the resident editor's minimum requirement when recruiting journalists to the newspaper: they should at least be university graduates. To have an education in journalism was not a qualification he particularly favoured. Like many senior journalists (in India as elsewhere, I believe) he was sceptical about the idea that this occupation could be taught in courses; a proper journalist was born with the talent and learnt the skill by practical work. Nevertheless, there were several people on his staff who had a university degree, or had taken some course, in journalism. A quite common qualification was to have a Bachelor of Journalism from Benares Hindu University (in Varanasi). At least half a dozen of the journalists working with *Dainik Jagran* in Lucknow had this background and several of them were senior. This was one of the few places in north India in which Hindi journalism was established early on.

Apart from the MA course in journalism at the Hindi Department of Lucknow University—which did not seem to supply the editorial offices in the city with any great number of journalists—there were other options in Lucknow for young people wishing for a career in the mass media. Several private, or semi-private, institutes ran courses in newspaper journalism and other mass media occupations. Most of them were recently started institutes offering part-time courses of one or two semesters. These institutes were quite clearly trying to make a profit out of young people's dreams of making a career in the glamorous new mass media, preferably television. Thus, the courses offered were mostly concerned with English-language journalism. It was also among the youngest staff working on the English-language papers that I found many who had topped up a university degree with a course in journalism from a private institute. One of the better known of these places was the Lal Bahadur Shastri Institute of Communication and Management, which ran a government-approved diploma course in journalism. The institute was affiliated to a government education centre in Mumbai, part of the well-reputed *Bharatiya Vidhya Bhavan;* it was by the latter name that the Lucknow institute was known among the journalists. The director of the institute as well as the course was a 26-year-old journalist who was also working on the *Times of India*, writing feature stories. He had only two years ago graduated from the same course at another branch of the same institute. (His rapid career might be explained by the fact that his uncle was the institute's 'Head of College'.) The one-year course charged a fee of Rs 4,500 and offered lectures between 9 and 11 a.m., six days a week. Every year 50 students attended the course, which, according to the director, was very popular; they short-listed their students from a couple of hundred applicants.

There is one significant difference in the educational background of journalists working with English and Hindi papers. Journalists in the English press have usually had most of their primary education in English-medium schools of good reputation. The most prestigious institutes of Lucknow (and among the best known in north India) are La Martinière and St Francis' College, both housed in marvellous historical buildings in green surroundings south of the city centre—the former famous for being described by Kipling in his novel about 'Kim'. More commonly the journalists had been students at places such as Christ Church College, the Cathedral School or Lucknow Christian College. Invariably, all English-language journalists have had access to schooling reserved for a privileged stratum in society. Few others would have sufficient command of the English language.

Social background

On one level the staff on the Hindi newspapers seemed far more homogeneous than those on the English-language papers. As I have shown above, it is in no way an overgeneralisation to describe the Hindi journalist as a quite young, male, Hindu,

Brahmin with a university education. The English-language journalists were more mixed with regard to gender, religion and caste. But if one looks more closely at the social background of these journalists, the reverse picture appears; it is among the latter that one can perceive a pattern.

When I started conducting interviews with journalists working with the English-language press, one thing soon struck me as recurring in many life stories. So many of them complained about being rootless, and narrated how they had been moving around with their families to different places in India during childhood. Very few regarded Lucknow as their native place. Subodh Gildiyal, one of the latest recruits to the *Pioneer,* could serve as an example. He had joined the paper six months before I met him in January 1998. Although Subodh was only in his mid-twenties, he was designated as a senior correspondent, in charge of covering the biggest political party of the state—the BJP. His surname, ending with an *-iyal,* indicated that the family came from the northern hill region of Uttar Pradesh. Born in Dehradun, just in the foothills of the Himalayas, he had, however, spent most of his life in other places in northern India. His father worked with the Indian Air Force and was frequently transferred, so the family had moved about and lived first in New Delhi, then in Jamnagar (Gujarat), Mumbai, Ludhiana (Punjab), New Delhi again, and Bhubaneshwar (Orissa). On top of that Subodh had lived without his family in Bangalore (Karnataka) where, after attaining a bachelor's degree from the prestigious Jawaharlal Nehru University in New Delhi, he did a diploma course in journalism. His first job was with the *Indian Express* in New Delhi, where initially he was a sports reporter, and then shifted to cover crime and the courts.

Why, then, was this background of mobility common among the English-language journalists (and less so among those working with Hindi papers)? It was probably not the rootless experience of living in many places that was the determining factor in becoming a journalist. The reason for this mobility during childhood was that their fathers had been working in the military or in high positions in the civil service, which meant that they were regularly transferred to new postings. Another characteristic of these careers is that to a great extent they have been English-speaking since the colonial days. People in the higher echelons of the military and the civil service are part of a pan-Indian English-educated elite that has been dominant in certain sectors in Indian society since independence (Sheth, 1995: 191; Shils, 1961; Weiner, 1965). This class also has strongholds in national politics, corporate business and higher education—and, of course, among the prestigious 'national' mass media that communicates in English. The social background is closely tied to a common educational background because the English-educated elite naturally put their sons and daughters in the best English-medium schools.[7]

Among the Hindi-language journalists it was difficult to find a similar denominator of the same strength when one looked at the social background with regard to the father's occupation. Certainly, many came from families where the father had a government job. But these were in diverse departments or undertakings, and at different levels; they did not give the same uniform picture of the family background as for the English-language journalists. Few had the same experience of moving with their families to different places, and hardly anyone could be said to belong to the English-educated elite (even though many of them spoke some English). It was more common for the Hindi-language journalists than for their colleagues on the English-language newspapers to regard Lucknow as their native place. Nevertheless, many were originally from other places in north India and, in contrast to the English-language journalists, several had a rural background. Moreover, to the extent that any journalists were from simple social backgrounds—coming from relatively meagre circumstances and from families without a tradition of higher education—they would be people working with the Hindi-language papers.

One female Hindi journalist stressed the difference in social background as the main explanation of the fact that the English newspapers had many more women working on them. She claimed that young journalists in the English press all came from 'good middle-class families with liberal ideas'. Their parents worked for the education of their children and put them in English-medium schools. They gave their daughters the same education as their sons. And, the daughters had their parents' full support in taking up a career. But to the Hindi press people come from Hindi-medium schools, she said. They have all kinds of background. Some parents do not want to educate their daughters, or, when the girl is educated, her education is pushed into the background and she is supposed to get married. The few girls who enter journalism are often not up to the mark, the journalist claimed.

It was not unusual to meet journalists for whom the profession was in the family. *Dainik Jagran*, for example, had two brothers on its staff—one a political reporter, the other a columnist—whose father as well as two more brothers and one sister were likewise journalists. Furthermore, one of the local reporters had two brothers in the profession, one being bureau chief in *Dainik Jagran*'s district office in nearby Faizabad, and also father who had been a freelance journalist. The resident editor himself was from a family of journalists; both father and grandfather had been newspapermen. It was a similar situation on the other newspapers, both the Hindi and the English-language: I always met a few journalists who had the occupation in their family—often it was among the senior staff. But this was far from characterising the whole profession. More often journalists made a point of being the first in their family to choose this occupation. They explained that the choice of career had been solely their own, and was discouraged rather than encouraged by their parents.

Recruitment

The question of getting into the journalism profession and to a particular newspaper in Lucknow can be dealt with from two angles: from the point of view of those who have entered the profession, the journalists, and from the perspective of those who decide to employ particular people as journalists, mainly resident editors. The journalists have their explanation of how they came into the profession and why they applied for a job on a particular newspaper; the resident editors have their reasons to employ certain people as journalists. However, even though in a few instances I have been around when people have been recruited to a paper or have decided to shift to another job, these are occurrences that are not easily studied in practice. When listening to people elaborating from both these angles, one often has to consider their stories as 'narratives' rather than objective accounts. For journalists, the question deals with a crucial decision in their lives: why they entered this career and did not take up something else. The narrative consists of events, episodes and motives with which the teller builds up an understanding of why his life took this particular route, thus trying to impose some kind of order on sequences of happenings that are seldom connected in a transparent way. What they produce are versions of reality that are born out of experience and which give shape to experience (Ochs and Capps, 1996). For resident editors, the question does not have the same existential weight; employing staff is a routine matter. But, on the other hand, they are more inclined to interpret their practice according to an ideal policy. While a journalist might very well say that it was just lucky circumstances that made him end up in this particular job, a resident editor cannot say that he 'accidentally' and without any consideration hired a particular person. He feels a compulsion to justify his action.

When the journalists told me how their careers started, the narratives were mainly of two kinds. First, there were those who claimed that they had chosen a career that they had wanted for specific reasons. They described the decision as a prime choice, even though some might mention that other careers were also considered. The 'positive choice' could be expressed as a strong desire to become a journalist. In those cases the choice of career was often coupled with resistant parents who wanted another future for them. For others the 'positive choice' was less emphasised and the narrative was more 'as a matter of fact' without much emotional involvement. As one reporter told me: "After graduation I was considering this career for a couple of months. My father [who was a journalist] encouraged me and my older brother had already started to work with *Aaj* in Kanpur. So I came over here, met the resident editor and put forward my wish to become a journalist." As the reason behind the 'positive choice' some journalists mentioned personal skills and interests—that they were good at expressing themselves in writing or that they liked to read news. Others put forward idealistic objectives and said that they entered the profession because they wanted to do something good for society. (Some combined the personal and the idealistic motives: they had a mission *and* they could write.)

D.P., introduced at the opening of this chapter, is an example of a journalist who saw his choice of career as a deliberate decision motivated by what he described as social and political commitment. A good journalist was 'a lighthouse in society' (not unlike the 'freedom fighters' of the Independence Movement) and he worked single-mindedly to become one, by taking useful courses at the university and by contributing articles on 'socially relevant' issues on his own initiative. Parts of his motive in the narrative were also personal skills and interest. He considered himself an intellectual, particularly interested in poetry, and had no doubt about his ability to write well.

Some journalists, however, produced a totally different narrative to account for how they came into the profession. Instead of stressing a positive choice, they claimed that originally they had had no idea of becoming a journalist, but circumstances turned them into one. Sometimes they straightforwardly admitted that they had wanted another career but failed in some way, for example, they had not obtained enough high marks in examinations to be admitted to a particular course. Or, more specifically, they had not succeeded in the entrance examination to the Indian Administrative Service (IAS). For these people, journalism was obviously a second choice or a substitute for something else. There is a huge oversupply of well-educated people in India and the competition for attractive jobs at one's education level is very tough. One particular feature of journalism as a career route is that formal competence is not necessary to obtain a job or to be successful. Furthermore, in contrast to very desirable government careers, for people from the Forward Castes, journalism had the advantage of falling outside reservation policies; it was never a disadvantage to be of high caste. Several young journalists were of the opinion that this career was a relatively easy route to take. Some saw a job on a newspaper as a springboard to something else. The young women in the English-language press were often hoping for a career with the more glamorous 'electronic media'.

Others, among those who pointed to 'circumstances' rather than a 'positive choice', did not stress journalism as a substitute for some primary desired career. Instead, the plot of their narrative illustrated how luckily things might unexpectedly turn out. P.J., now a resident editor of one of the Hindi dailies, said, while narrating his story, that he had never thought about becoming a journalist when he was a young student at Lucknow University. In fact, he had wanted a career in the IAS but had had no money to put down for the examination fees; his family was in deep financial trouble after his father had died in the late 1960s. Instead, he was doing his MA in political science and was planning to continue with research. At the same time, he was interested in painting and drawing and had developed some skill from a correspondence course. The circumstance that changed P.J.'s career was an incident in 1973 when there was a lot of political unrest among students in Lucknow. During some serious agitation a kind of student 'mutiny' broke out and parts of the university were burnt down. A classmate of P.J. had a brother who was the editor of *Dinman*, a weekly magazine of the *Times of India* group, and wrote a report on the incident for that publication. P.J., who was also a witness to the agitation, did some drawings as a supplement that were published together with the report. This was his first contact with the news media and during his student years he continued to make drawings and cartoons for newspapers as a means of earning some money. He already then established contact with the paper that he was now heading; and he was put in charge of the cartoon page. On completing his studies and looking for a job, the experience of working with newspapers came in handy. He easily got a job as a sub-editor and soon found himself in a fast career in news editing, shifting between positions and the editorial offices of Hindi dailies in Lucknow, Jaipur and Kanpur. Finally, after 25 years in the profession, he had reached the top position of resident editor. Clearly, he was satisfied with the way things had turned out.

Broadly, the editorial staff had been recruited in two ways. The initiative might have come from the person who applied for a job on a particular newspaper and was accepted by the management to start work. The other way was when the management approached a particular journalist (either from a competing newspaper or from another edition in the organisation) and offered him a position. The former procedure was, according to my impression, the most common. When I asked journalists how they got their job, the usual answer was that they simply went to see the resident editor and put forward a wish to work on the paper. From what I know it was rare for the newspapers to advertise their vacancies, but it did happen in some special circumstances. *Dainik Jagran,* for example, advertised when they started recruiting their *samvad sutr* (see Chapter Four).

On a few occasions I had been present when someone in search of a job had visited a resident editor or some editor in charge of a particular section of a newspaper (The office of an Indian daily is just like an office in the bureaucracy in the sense that people are constantly coming and going and that not much really takes place between four eyes). Once I was sitting in an editorial office, talking to the features editor, when two girls came to see him. One of them was apparently acquainted with the journalist. They had recently met on the occasion of a local 'beauty contest' that had taken place in one of the more prestigious social clubs of the town; the girl was actually the previous year's 'beauty queen'. But it was in fact on her friend's behalf that the two had come to see the features editor. She had recently quit a job with an advertising bureau and she now had a desire to get into journalism—an occupation she had always dreamt of. Would there be any chance for her in this paper? She was aware of the fact that there were no vacancies that she could apply for, but someone had told her that there was a shortage of freelance writers. The features editor confirmed that this was true, and that he was always interested in finding material for the page he was responsible for. He took time to explain what kind of writing he needed—on virtually any topic except politics. Without asking about her qualifications, experience, interests or ideas for stories, he said that she was welcome to write whatever she liked, whenever she wanted. If it was good enough, he would certainly publish it and pay something between Rs 300 and Rs 500 for a story. When the two women had left, the journalist turned to me and said that she would probably never come back, and if she wrote anything it would most likely not be good enough. Every day, he said, people who wanted to write, or had already written something they wanted published, came to him. But rarely was anyone up to standard.

An inexperienced journalist, or a complete novice, who wanted to work for a newspaper certainly needed some luck with the timing of his request. Someone looking for a job when a paper had recently recruited new people would not stand much of a chance. But if the newspaper was looking for new staff, who would be considered? Vinod Shukla, the resident editor of *Dainik Jagran*, explained that among the first qualities he looked for was loyalty; "the basic thing is that I feel a person can live with me". He preferred to hire people without any previous experience of journalism because they were better able to adjust to his system of running a newspaper (which was, as he said, 'like a family' with him as an elder brother). Other important criteria were enthusiasm and conviction. A person he would consider hiring must have a desire "to do something for society, for the people", he claimed. It was also useful if the person had "a nose for news", but if it was lacking the situation could always be improved on. First and foremost, they should be 'fighters'. If the applicant seemed suitable, he (rarely she) was given a chance to show his abilities for a few weeks. Provided that he passed the test, he would be accepted as a 'trainee'. This had been the procedure when D.P. started on *Dainik Jagran,* with the important addition that he also had a recommendation from his teacher in journalism, a senior staff member on the newspaper. The latter circumstance, that an applicant had a connection with someone known at the newspaper, was common but did not seem to be an absolute condition; several journalists claimed that they had had no connections at all when they asked for a job.

Other newspapers were less particular about 'breeding' their own staff and more open to employing already experienced journalists. For those papers that were recently established in the town it was, of course, necessary to hire skilled journalists rather than potentially good people. And journalists were moving between newspapers for various reasons (see below). To the extent that Vinod Shukla wanted to raise journalists who would stay with him until retirement, perfectly attuned, as he said, "to the movement of his conductor's baton", he was certainly fighting against the odds. Shifting between newspapers rather than sticking to the same one was definitely a feature of the profession. *Dainik Jagran* in particular had lost many staff with the launching of the two latest Hindi newspapers in town, *Hindustan* and *Kuber*. The half dozen journalists who went to *Kuber* were recruited in a special way. I was told, when I met some of the people who had moved jobs, that the management of the new paper had not invited job applicants via advertisements nor offered posts to particular journalists whom they selected. Instead, they had approached one of the journalists at *Dainik Jagran*, and persuaded him to join them and to bring with him a number of colleagues whom he would like to work with. Clearly, it was an ingenious way of overcoming the problem of setting up a completely new organisation and putting it to work smoothly within a short time; the staff were not completely unfamiliar with each other, but a core of journalists who had worked well together before.

For the newspapers' management, the frequent changing of people between posts was a serious problem. Although a new staff member, with some experience in the profession, could easily fill a vacancy without much instruction—reporting and editing is basically the same job on any paper—it was difficult to get him to work in a manner that suited the particular organisation. The journalist needed to be socialised into the organisation to get a 'feel' for what was expected of him. Resident editors needed at least a minimum of continuity in the staff around them: a few journalists whom they had worked with for a long time and could rely on—not least some people whom they could trust to be loyal. During interviews several editors mentioned particular journalists whom they relied on, often people they had worked with for decades. Sometimes it was a person they prided themselves on having raised from a manual labourer to a significant position. (*Dainik Jagran*, for example, had such a person as circulation manager. "He started on the newspaper as a bundle boy", Vinod Shukla told me. "We educated him. Now, he is the best circulation manager in U.P.")

Resident editors who were fresh to the city, either on newly established newspapers or as successors of someone else in the post, often brought with them a few journalists from their previous workplace. Sunil Dube, the resident editor who launched *Hindustan*'s Lucknow edition in 1997, had five or six journalists on his staff who had accompanied him from Patna where he previously held the same position. At least one of them moved with Dube to a new town for the second time. Another example was the chief reporter on the *Pioneer*, who was from West Bengal where he had spent most of his career. Explaining why he had come all the way to Lucknow, he said it was because he knew the resident editor of the *Pioneer* since they had both worked on The *North East Times* in West Bengal: "You could say he brought me along when he moved".

Career

Thus few journalistic careers are committed to one particular newspaper. Among older journalists whom I met I cannot recall anybody who had been faithful to the same newspaper throughout his working life. To have shifted workplace, either newspaper or edition of a newspaper, a dozen times or more during a career, was not rare. The English-language journalists were particularly on the move (being able, unlike their colleagues in the vernacular press, to take up a job anywhere in India, but also, as it seemed, because they were largely from a mobile social class). But also among Hindi journalists, a regular change of workplace was a common feature of their career. As a fieldworker eager to get the details right, I often had difficulties following my informants when they recapitulated their careers in brief, not always narrating them in chronological order. Years, places, newspapers and positions often seemed to get mixed up, giving me a headache when I tried to bring some order into my fieldnotes. Take, for example, what I had in my notebook after an interview with Jai Prakash, principal correspondent of *Hindustan*:

> He came to *Hindustan* when it was launched in Lucknow. His beat was the BSP. Before that he was for five and a half years chief of bureau at *Swatantra Bharat* in Lucknow, having the SP on his beat.

> Before that he worked with the weekly *Dinaman Times* in New Delhi. Earlier on he had been correspondent of *Jansatta* in Lucknow but in between chief reporter of the same newspaper in Bombay. In Bombay, however, he had found it difficult to find a place to live and this had meant problems for his family, so he returned to Lucknow, now as a special correspondent of *Dainik Jagran*. His career, by the way, started with *Dainik Jagran* in Gorakhpur in 1975. Four years later he was admitted to a master's course in journalism at the Indian Institute of Mass Communication in New Delhi. When the course was completed he got a job with *Amrit Prabhat*, in an editorial building located in the very same premises where the *Hindustan Times* building stands today. Then he worked for a while with *Ravivar*, a weekly magazine part of the Amrita Bazar Patrika Group; that was also when he started as a reporter, previously he had been at the desk.

If I interpret my scribbling correctly, for 22 years Jai Prakash had been working in nine different offices, for seven newspapers, in four cities. This did not appear exceptional. His younger colleague, Ragvindra, with ten years in the profession, had already a list of experiences to reel off. Starting on *Hindustan* in Patna he had passed through *Navbharat Times* (Patna), *Rajasthan Patrika* (Udaipur and Jaipur) and *Amara Ujala* (Agra) before he came to *Hindustan* in Lucknow.

Journalists, who had shifted between newspapers and places numerous times, usually described their careers briefly but with great precision. Even though I was often confused, they never hesitated in their story and could often remember the very date when they started their career in journalism. Sometimes I felt as if I was being presented an oral *curriculum vitae* when I asked somebody where he had worked previously. It came out fluently, even if not chronologically. The impression I got was that the route of their career was important in their presentation of themselves, like some kind of pedigree. The renderings were often interspersed with details of remarkably fast promotions or significant contributions. Sunil Dube, the previously mentioned resident editor of *Hindustan*, had during his career been responsible for the launching of three new newspaper editions. He recapitulated his career as follows:

> I started my career in 1975 from *Dainik Jagran* of Kanpur. I was there for 13 years and I rose from trainee sub-editor to joint editor

> of that newspaper. I also worked as chief reporter and news editor, then as joint editor. After that, in 1988, I switched over to *Hindustan* in Patna, which had started in 1986. From 1988 to March 1991 I was there. Then again I switched over to *Jagran* in Delhi. As executive editor, I was there for just three months. Then I switched over to *Rashtriya Sahara,* which was being started at that time in Delhi. So I started there on 15 August 1991, as editorial adviser. Then I was transferred to Lucknow, for the launching of the Lucknow edition of *Rashtriya Sahara*. That was in February1992. I was there till January 1994. Then I switched over again to *Hindustan* and went to their Delhi edition. Then again I switched to *Hindustan,* Patna after two or three months. And I was there for about 26–27 months. Then, when this Lucknow edition was being launched, I was transferred here.

Some journalists depicted their careers as being very calculated. They had shifted newspapers, positions and places, with the deliberate intention of climbing professionally. But a change of job did not always imply an obvious step in one's career, like going from a badly-paid job on a small newspaper to a well-paid position on a better publication. There was a combination of factors to consider, and the factors could be valued differently in relation to each other. Reasons for changing jobs as mentioned by journalists included improvements in pay, terms of employment, beat or position, size of newspaper, status of newspaper and place of publication. It was not unusual for people to accept a new job that implied a lower wage because they could claim a gain in some other factor. Once I was present when a senior crime reporter of an English-language daily was negotiating for a new job with one of the other English dailies in town. "Please, pay me a little less, but give me this opportunity", he begged the resident editor. The reason, he claimed, for desiring this job was that he would get a political beat. And several times I met journalists who had traded a contractual job for less well-paid but safer employment (others, however, had taken the opposite path). Thus, a gain in some points made up for losses in some others.

Sometimes the gain from a move could be rather diffuse. The new job had been taken, not because it was particularly attractive in itself, but because it would be a better position from which one can go further. This was something that people claimed particularly with regard to Lucknow as a place to be in journalism. For example, Subodh, mentioned earlier in this chapter, had quit a job on the *Indian Express* in New Delhi for the *Pioneer* in Lucknow. This appeared somewhat odd—going from one of the most prestigious national newspapers in the central capital to a far smaller paper in a regional centre. Most of his colleagues were aiming in the other direction. Subodh explained that he had left Delhi because the competition in the field of journalism was so tough. There were so many good and ambitious people around, and all the best journalists from the regions were coming in to Delhi. In Lucknow he would simply have a much better chance of making a career. For others, Lucknow was a springboard for New Delhi. I heard this, for example, from some of the journalists who had left good positions on newspapers in Kolkata. The newspapers in West Bengal are generally regarded as some of the best in India, and journalism in that part of the country has a very good reputation. But obviously even some Bengali journalists felt their place of origin to be regionally limited and were looking towards the 'national' scene. The step from Kolkata to New Delhi being great (geographically as well as politically and culturally), they thought their chances would improve if they first took a job in Lucknow—particularly with a paper that had an edition in the capital.

Nevertheless, even though career considerations were undoubtedly a subject often spoken about, the journalists were not all completely calculating people. Not every change of job was made rationally in order to advance one's career. In many cases the shift of job was forced or at least not desired. A journalist could lose his job for various reasons. The newspaper business is not a stable one. Editions of a paper may cut down in staff or reorganise so that some people become redundant. Or they may close down completely. A couple of years before I conducted my fieldwork, the Lucknow edition of *Navbharat Times* (the Hindi paper of the *Times of India* group) suddenly and unexpectedly closed down, throwing almost the entire editorial staff out of work (except for a small number of people who were transferred to other editions within the organisation). I found many of these journalists working with other Hindi newspapers in Lucknow, often bitter at having lost a job with a well-reputed national daily. In senior positions on both Hindi- and English-language papers I also sometimes came across older journalists who had worked with the newspaper house that in the early 1970s was the leading one in town, the *National Herald* (which published both an English-language and a Hindi edition, *Navjivan*). Since this publishing house had been going downhill after the emergency, most of the best people on its staff had gradually dispersed to other papers. Nevertheless, these journalists often talked with great pride of their earlier association with this once respected newspaper and its famous editor Chalapathi Rau,[8] often in a way that overshadowed their later career.

Another reason for changing jobs, outside the calculated career route, was that one had come into conflict with the management or other seniors on the staff. In these cases the journalists most often seemed to have quit voluntarily. Even if resident editors sometimes mentioned that they did not hesitate to 'sack' journalists who had misbehaved or whom they were dissatisfied with, I never heard a journalist explain his resignation using that word. Virendra described a resident editor he had previously worked under as a '*goonda* and hoodlum type of personality'. It had been a terrible experience to work with him and Virendra had confronted his boss on several occasions. But as a reason for shifting to another newspaper he stressed the fact that the wage was so low and that he had had no opportunities to advance with that paper. The distinction between voluntarily quitting a job because one is not happy with it and discharge is not always clear.

It was very common that during the course of his career a journalist was transferred between several editions of the same newspaper. Not always did the journalist initiate the transfer. The management of a newspaper could move somebody because he was needed more urgently on another edition. And even if this could sometimes be interpreted as a promotion (for example, if a beat reporter in Lucknow was made a bureau chief on a smaller edition somewhere else), it was not always desired by the journalist. But, in many cases, the transfer seemed to have been an offer that could not be refused. Some people told me that they had spent years on an edition with a standing request to be transferred back to where they had come from. Other journalists had moved to the new posting with good hopes but had found that they could not adjust and had soon started to long to go back. Often they described how a transfer (or a voluntary move) had created difficulties for the family—the wife might not have been happy—and problems in finding a place to live. Younger journalists, who were not yet married, complained about how they felt lonely on postings far from their relatives.

Even though the career of a journalist usually involved frequent changes—of job, position, newspaper, edition of a newspaper, city and so on—one kind of shift was very rare: the borders of language were seldom crossed in the course of a career. Less than a handful of journalists that I met in Lucknow had gone from a job on an English-language newspaper to a Hindi one, or vice versa. Basically, journalists of the two languages made their careers in different labour markets. One explanation for this, usually invoked by the journalists themselves, was technical. Most Hindi-language journalists were not fluent enough in English to apply for a job with an English-language newspaper. Likewise, English-language journalists, who had had most of their education in English-medium schools, often claimed that they could not master the written language (although they, of course, spoke fluent Hindi). But a technical explanation is hardly sufficient. I met several journalists of both languages who could very well have been able to change their language of work, but who never considered crossing the border. The barrier is cultural as much as linguistic. Journalistic experience with a Hindi-language newspaper does not carry much weight in an application for a job with the *Times of India,* and an English-language journalist would consider it a backward step in his career to take up a job even on a well-reputed Hindi-language paper. This is a theme that will be elaborated on somewhat further in the following chapter, which deals with the professional ideas of the Lucknow journalists.

Notes

1. Sonia Bathla (1998) has discussed the gender perspectives of Indian journalism, though she has focused on the English-language press.
2. For a discussion about 'secularism' in the Indian context see Madan, 1987; Nandy, 1988; Upadhyaya, 1992 and Hansen, 2000.
3. Varna is the fourfold hierarchical division of Hindu society according to the religious scripts: Brahmins (priests) have the highest rank, followed by Ksatriyas (warriors and kings), Vaisyas (merchants) and Sudras (artisans and workers)—the Dalits (untouchables) are below all, outside the *varna* system. *Jati* is the more sociological aspect of caste, consisting of thousands of endogamous groups, traditionally practising a particular occupation and ranked hierarchically in each social setting.
4. My discussion on the issue of caste is concerned with the relevance of this concept among the journalists. Another question is the significance of caste for the journalists' practice on their beat. The reporters interact with a large number of individuals every day, people who become sources for their news. It is, of course, very likely that caste identities play a role in these encounters. This is, however, a subject that I have not addressed in this study. The prime reason is methodological. During my fieldwork I followed the reporters and have only their points of view on what happened in specific situations. Most often I was not even aware of which caste a source belonged to. Caste is an intricate subject and to study it in this context would have required a differently designed fieldwork. I recognise that this is a limitation of my study.
5. André Béteille claims, for example, that in the modern occupation system "caste has ceased to be a significant agent of social control" (ibid.).
6. Occupied with people who had a similar level of education and social status as myself, I was clearly 'studying sideways' (Hannerz, 1998a) rather than the more common situation when anthropologists are studying people with considerably less influence, 'studying down', or, very rarely, 'studying up' (Nader, 1972).
7. Quite a few of the English-language journalists had surnames that showed that their family originated in regions of India outside the Hindi belt. Andhra Pradesh and West Bengal in particular seem to have exported journalists in significant numbers. These happen to be regions that since colonial times have had a strong English-medium intellectual tradition.
8. See Chapter Two.

Six

Professionals for the People

One morning in mid-March, the chief of *Dainik Jagran*'s local bureau called for me when the editorial meeting was over and all the reporters were about to leave on their assignments. "Suppose you were going to cover a *mela* (festival)", he said, "How would you do it?" Beside him stood Prem Prakash, one of the local reporters who primarily had trade union issues on his beat but often had to take on other kind of jobs. Today, he was obviously assigned to cover the Sitala Ashtami *mela*, a festival held for the goddess Sitala, popularly celebrated in North India for her ability to cure smallpox (Kinsley, 1987: 204). It was a local holiday in Lucknow and the celebrations were going to take place some four kilometres north of the city centre, close to the temple dedicated to the goddess. For any of the journalists, this was quite an unattractive assignment. There was no prestige or excitement in covering a popular festival of this kind: there was nothing controversial about it, it was not big enough to create problems, and there were no prominent people around. It would just be a crowd of ordinary people celebrating and enjoying themselves in a temporary marketplace. There was simply no 'news' in it. The story would probably be placed far down on one of the last local pages, and published without a byline.

Why did the chief of the local bureau bother to ask for advice on this assignment? I was a bit puzzled but answered him that if I had been given that job I would just go there, look around and talk to people—ask them who they were, why they had come to the *mela*, what it meant to them, and so on. "Okay, why don't you go with him today?," the bureau chief said and nodded in the direction of Prem Prakash. As both of us had respect for the bureau chief's authority, we raised no objections and left the office together. Prem Prakash looked rather unhappy but tried to raise some enthusiasm for the job. The only problem with this assignment, he said, was that the site for the *mela* was so far away and that his scooter was (as usual) out of order. Otherwise, he actually liked this kind of job, it was important that the newspaper paid attention to events that ordinary people were engaged in. And, as he said without sounding completely convincing, the bureau chief often assigned the festivals to him because he trusted him to treat them seriously.

After a quick lunch at Prem Prakash's home—he lived in a government flat just a few blocks from the newspaper office—we managed to get his scooter going and were on our way. Before arriving at the site for the *mela* Prem Prakash started telling me about the assignment. It was the first time he had covered the event but he seemed to know all about it. The Sitala Ashtami, he explained, was also called *Atho mela* because it always falls on the eighth (*atha*) day after *Holi* (another, and more important, festival). It was an important but simple local festival, very popular among Lucknow people. Hindus, particularly women, from all over the town and nearby places brought their children to the temple of the goddess. They had fasted since the day before and would come full of joy and expectancy, dressed in their best clothes. In front of the temple they would sit down and consume food that they had brought with them. A lot of vendors would be there and would do good business selling sweets, bangles and toys to the people. All in all, some eight lakhs (800,000) of people would be taking part in the celebration. Prem Prakash came up with this figure by estimating that "not all, but most, of the Hindus in Lucknow will come".

We parked the scooter at Prem Prakash's brother's house, which was fortunately in this part of the town, and approached the site on foot. So far there were not many signs of a big festival. As Prem Prakash did not know the exact location of the temple, we had to ask people the way several times. It was only when we were quite close to the temple that it started to look like a *mela*: here and there garlands were hanging across the street and vendors of sweets, ornaments, kitchenware and toys had put up their stalls. On an open field a simple amusement park for children had been set up. At a crossroads a rather small stage had been built and some people were checking out the sound system. Certainly, there were people around, but the place was far from crowded. To me it appeared more tranquil than an ordinary market day in Aminabad, the central shopping district.

Prem Prakash, however, saw it differently. The majority of people will come tonight, he said. But look at those women and kids—he pointed to a couple of overloaded cycle-rikshaws: "See how full of joy they are and how nicely they have dressed themselves". With great haste we walked through the place, passing the temple where Prem Prakash made a quick halt to pay his respect to the goddess. Otherwise we did not stop and talk to anyone. Prem Prakash continued to point out scenes that confirmed what he had already told me: families eating from their provisions, children playing, women shopping and so on. He already had his story, no need to waste any more time here. We hurried back to the scooter, which, of course, was impossible to start; we had to leave it at the brother's house and return to the office by cycle-rikshaw.

In the newspaper the following day, one could read about the *mela* in a three-column article on page four.[1] Prem Prakash's story (the byline, however, said only 'Jagran reporter') had been given the headline 'Bustling festival on Sitala Ashtami/abundance of joy for families'. Quite surprisingly, it was illustrated with a photograph of people greeting the goddess in front of the temple; one of the photographers must have been sent after we had left (or perhaps it was a photo from the archives). The text offered a somewhat lengthier version of the same story that I had been told by Prem Prakash. It went on about women, children, smallpox, sweets, joy, nice clothes and food, and it was written in a completely general style, merely summarising what most people living in Lucknow seemed to know about the festival. No individual people were cited or referred to.

Putting one and one together I began to understand why the chief of local news had given this assignment some extra thought before he sent his reporter on the job. On several occasions since I began to attend the editorial meetings I had heard Vinod Shukla, the resident editor, talk about how important it was for the newspaper to be 'close to the common man'. *Dainik Jagran*, he said, was a newspaper for everybody, it should write about things that concerned people of every *mohalla* (neighbourhood) of the town. Girish Mishra, the 'adviser', often supported him on this issue and called for more stories with 'human interest'. A new attitude seemed to being promoted: not only politics and the 'serious' news counted, small or trivial events were also important to cover. The readers had to 'recognise themselves' in the news.

Those discussions were, however, somewhat unspecific. No examples of 'good' stories were ever mentioned, nor any advice on how to approach particular subjects. For political news, crime stories, news from the bureaucracy and other 'important' issues, the journalists had models to follow. They seldom hesitated about how to approach a new assignment. But for popular, 'trivial' events, there was no obvious way to cover them 'seriously'. Most commonly, the newspaper coverage of religious festivals was reminiscent of stories in primary school textbooks: idealised and stereotyped.[2] The head of local news had probably become aware of the fact that the genre needed some improvement. After all, the festivals might not have much of news value in the journalistic sense, but they were certainly the kind of event that many readers took part in. They were 'close' to the common man's interests.

A global profession

The reason why the bureau chief thought that I could possibly provide a clue as to how his reporters should deal with an assignment like this was not that he considered me to be a media oracle. Not that I, as a foreigner and an academic, had a very different approach to journalism from the one he had. He asked for my opinion because he knew that, apart from being an anthropologist, I had also been working for newspapers. Aware of the fact that I had never been to a Sitala Ashtami *mela* before, had little knowledge of Lucknow culture and had never worked for any Indian newspaper, he nevertheless supposed that I would know a way to approach the assignment—because I was a journalist. This was not a rare attitude among the journalists that I came to know in Lucknow. When I began my fieldwork and introduced myself to the newspaper offices I mentioned that I had been working as a reporter myself, but it was not something that I made a big deal out of. For me that experience was years back and quite short. I had graduated from a journalism school in Sweden just before I started my doctoral programme in social anthropology. For a number of years I worked during summer breaks from the university as a reporter on a local daily in south Sweden, covering all kinds of small-town issues. It was a way of getting some extra income and at the same time keeping the door open for an alternative choice of career. I gave it up when I became more engaged in my doctoral studies, and I never really developed a strong journalistic identity. In Lucknow, however, the journalists soon found out that I was also a journalist of some kind, and they gave it some importance. Probably, it made more sense as to why I had come to study them if I was in the same profession. Although I did not write a single sentence in a newspaper during the whole of my fieldwork, I have never felt more like a journalist. The Lucknow journalists looked upon me as an occupational brother as much as an anthropologist. They took it for granted that we had a common frame of reference and that I was familiar with the conditions of the occupation. Quite often they had an attitude of "you know how it can be" towards me, particularly when facing obstacles. When following reporters on their beat and meeting their sources in various offices, I was even sometimes introduced as a fellow journalist from a foreign country.

Early on I was encouraged to write stories for *Dainik Jagran,* maybe, as much out of courtesy as for the value my contributions would have. After all, I was a journalist and the resident editor on one occasion asked the staff to consider me as a colleague. This caused me some trouble. Obviously, I was not in the position of being a beat reporter of a north Indian Hindi daily. My knowledge of the language as well as of the local state of things was too poor. Possibly I could contribute with stories of the kind "A Foreign Journalist Looks at ...". But that would hardly help in my purpose of understanding the world of Lucknow journalists, and it could easily get out of hand and be quite time-consuming if half a dozen of the other newspapers in town also insisted on the same contribution. I had to make it clear that I preferred not to take part in the work of the newspaper. Eventually, I was accepted as a regular but more or less passive visitor in the editorial office.

To some extent the Lucknow journalists were right when they supposed that I was familiar with their occupation. I could relate to their daily routines as well as to a lot of things that they said about themselves and their work. A reporter working on the local beat of a Hindi daily in Lucknow does have important features of his everyday activities in common not only with the journalists of more prestigious papers in India but also with people in the same occupation worldwide. He or she might be dealing with very local and particular events in a Lucknow *mohalla*, but still basically be doing the same daily job as numerous reporters all over the globe—whether the reporter works with a newspaper in London, Lucknow or Lusaka. The reporter turns up at the office in the morning for an editorial meeting, gets his assignment for the day and disappears out into the city on his hunt for a story. He visits his sources, usually in various government offices. In the late afternoon he returns to file his copy to be edited and printed in the next day's paper.

Furthermore, universal features of press journalism are not confined to the production process and the product itself. Professional ideas have also undergone a process of diffusion. This is not to say that the Lucknow journalists conformed to an occupational role and held professional values that in every detail would be recognisable to colleagues all over the world. But during the time I spent with newspaper people in Lucknow it became obvious that many of the ideas that flourished among the journalists were hardly particular to this locality. There was, for example, the preoccupation with 'the people', the ordinary man whose interests one had a duty to look after; the problematic relationship with powerful people whom one should scrutinise but simultaneously was so dependent on; and the concern with objectivity and neutrality in reporting. These and many more were subjects that I was familiar with both from the literature on professional journalism and, not least, from my own experience as a newspaper reporter in Sweden. When a senior journalist of a Hindi daily told me that "you cannot make anybody a journalist—either you are born for the profession or you are not", it was like listening to a former colleague on the local newspaper in Sweden.

Professionalism

In sociological studies of journalism and news production—usually about conditions in Europe and North America—a great deal of attention has been given to norms, values, attitudes or the consciousness of the journalistic occupation. Most scholars see the work of a journalist as guided by ideas that are shared among the practitioners as much as it is formed by the 'nature' of the occupation. To understand how events in society are selected and presented as news, one has to look into the journalists' own views of their occupation. This is usually discussed in terms of 'professionalism' and related to the vast literature on that subject.[3]

The 'sociology of professions' has as its ideal model some highly specialised occupations in which practitioners are trained to deal with abstract knowledge, such as medicine, the law or natural sciences. These practitioners have a professional norm system strongly focused on their special competence and crucial role for society as a whole, particularly as bearers of a rational value system characteristic of modern society. They serve society rather than the particular organisations that they might work for, and they are confident that modern society is dependent on their services. Ideally, they are free from economic considerations in their work. The journalistic occupation has not been regarded as a perfect fit for the professional model,[4] but in the conception of their role as a crucial one for society, journalists seem to be as confident as 'proper' professionals.

When scholars of the mass media discuss professionalism, it often covers a wide variety of issues linked to the occupational culture and practice of journalists. Some tend to see professionalism primarily in terms of the practical routines of the occupation. Professionalism in this sense guides the journalists by setting 'norms for behaviour'. A whole set of professional knowledge is tied to the practical execution of the job. To function as a journalist one has to have, at least, an idea about what makes news (news sense), where to find it and how to write it down in the form of an article. Kaniss, in her study of local news in the USA, writes about 'Standard Operational Procedures' as a form of professionalism:

> [Journalists] do not begin each day wondering where to look for news and how to define news [...] they learn to internalise certain professional values that guide them in the search for news and in the way they package what they find (1991: 73).

Other scholars focus on the journalists' perception of their occupational role, that is, professionalism as an ideology describing the journalists' place in society. In this sense, professionalism might offer a strong occupational identity without necessarily being of much help in the routines of daily work. It gives an answer to questions such as, why do we write news and for whom? The journalists' image of their profession, as it has been projected in Europe and North America, is, however, not unequivocal. Rather, it seems to be built around two (or several) models that sometimes stand in conflict with each other. Elliott (1979), in an overview of studies in media sociology, distinguishes between 'straight reporters' and 'committed journalists'. The former perceive their role as being neutral fact collectors and cherish professional values based on "factual accuracy, speed at meeting deadlines, style in presentation and a shared sense of news values" (ibid.: 149). 'Straight reporters' are of the opinion that their job is to inform people, but that interpretation and the valuation of facts should be left to the readers. 'Committed journalists', on the other hand, believe that it is their duty to provide backgrounds and analyses in their news reporting and do not regard it as unprofessional to make judgements on behalf of the readers.

Kepplinger and Köcher (1990) have looked into how different perceptions of the journalist's role are unevenly distributed in Western European countries. They claim that the institution of journalism has developed differently in countries like France, Germany and Great Britain and point out that legal foundations, editorial structures and work arrangements are not the same everywhere. Nor is the status of the journalistic occupation exactly the same all over Europe. In different countries it attracts people from different backgrounds and with different ambitions. Thus, professional ideas vary. As a case in point, Kepplinger and Köcher contrast the professional roles held by British and German journalists. The former perceive themselves as neutral reporters, they like working under pressure of deadlines and are attracted by the exciting and eventful nature of the work; they do not consider themselves to be intellectuals. German journalists, on the other hand, view the occupation as a form of political career; they see themselves as critics of negative conditions and as advocates of disadvantaged groups in society. They also like the analytical and creative aspect of the work and do see themselves as intellectuals. To a considerable extent the role perception of British journalists seems to coincide with that of the straight reporter, while the Germans appear more like committed journalists. In Renate Köcher's (1986) terms, British journalists tend to be 'bloodhounds' and their German colleagues 'missionaries'. Yet, as Köcher points out herself, a strict distinction between the journalists of these two countries is misleading. The idea that journalists of the two countries prefer contrasting occupational roles is to some extent a theoretical construction, showing up only in statistical material. In reality it is more significant that the two roles exist in mixed forms. "More than two-thirds of the journalists in both countries include the roles of a neutral reporter of events, a guardian of democracy, and a critic of abuses among their job" (ibid.: 57). The same conclusion has been reached by studies that have tried to put categorical labels on American journalists. "Despite the fact that neutral and participant values tend to be antithetical ... it can be concluded that most newsmen do in fact hold patterns of belief that combine elements from each perspective" (Johnstone, Slavski and Bowman, quoted in Köcher, 1986: 57).

Hindi journalism under criticism

No doubt, it would be possible to identify the 'bloodhounds' and the 'missionaries' among the Lucknow journalists. If one looks at them with these labels in mind, some were definitely found to be more 'hungry for news', very efficient on their beats, nursing their sources well and always looking for a 'good story' for the front page. Others were reflecting more on issues that they found important, priding themselves on writing stories that made an impact on society. On closer inspection it would also be revealed that many seemed to be both 'bloodhounds' and 'missionaries'. Like chameleons many journalists changed colour when the subject under discussion shifted from "how we do it" to "who we are" (cf. Schudson, 2002: 263). If I was talking to a journalist about his practical work, I often had a 'bloodhound' in front of me; the 'missionary' appeared when the discussion concerned the role of journalism in society. This confusing accommodation of conflicting roles seems to be an illustration of the basic difference between norms (how things should be done) and representation (how things are) (Holy and Stucklik, 1983: 50).

Nor is the image of the journalist uniform in India. The professional role is a debated subject, within the occupation as well as in public discourse more broadly. But even though there certainly are similarities, it would be not fair to interpret the Indian debate as a conflict between the values of the 'bloodhound' and the 'missionary'. The debate in this country is closely connected to changes in the whole newspaper business during the last few decades. The great newspapers that previously dominated the market were prestigious ones published from the metropolises, and the occupation of journalism was inhabited by an English-speaking (though sometimes Hindi-writing) and 'nationally minded' intellectual elite. But with the rise of the vernacular, regional press, the professional culture was challenged. New types of editors and journalists appeared in the Hindi-language press as well as in the press of other regional languages. People less committed to the intellectual ideals from the days of the independence movement have entered the profession with new ways of thinking. The attitude, particularly towards the tremendous success of the Hindi-language press, has been ambivalent, to say the least, in the old quarters. One place where this has been apparent is in the pages of the Indian Press Institute's magazine *Vidura*. An obvious example was an article published in 1992 in the form of a discussion between some leading Hindi-language journalists. The title of the article 'Who is afraid of Hindi journalism?' and the starting point of the discussion was a belief that the tremendous growth of the Hindi press had been at the expense of professional competence (*Vidura*, 1992: 4–19). Four years later—when the Indian Press Institute had adapted to the changing media scene and started a Hindi section of the previously all-English magazine—the editorial made a point of the two-edged character of the recent growth of Hindi-language newspapers:

> These developments could have constituted a big step forward in grassroot democratic awakening if the contents of these papers had kept pace with technological improvement. But most of the owner-editors have failed to devote as much care to locating and training good journalists to man their far-flung empires as they have to expanding the circulation of their papers and earning quick returns. Some have yielded to the temptation of exploiting their influence to secure favours or influence decisions at various levels, from the State Capitals to District Headquarters. (*Vidura*, 1996: 1)

In the Hindi section of the same issue of *Vidura* two New Delhi-based editors of prestigious 'national' Hindi-language papers contributed articles that were very critical of the current condition of Indian journalism. Prabash Joshi from *Jansatta* (belonging to the same publishing house as the English-language *Indian Express*) was deeply disappointed in the Hindi-language press because, in his opinion, it was no longer guided by ideals from the days of the Independence Movement, when journalism was a mission and economic considerations played no part. According to him, there was neither self-respect nor talent in Hindi journalism any longer, and the press was therefore unable to do its proper work, namely, to build public opinion in the Indian democracy. What Joshi had in mind was primarily the regional press, but he was also sceptical about the 'national' Hindi press to which he belonged. This press (in his opinion neglected by its publishing houses) had lost its popular base, and was suffering from a lack of inspiration (Joshi, 1996: 45–47).

Mrinal Pande of *Hindustan* (sister publication of the English-language *Hindustan Times*) showed even more clearly in her article how journalists on 'respectable' national papers regarded their colleagues writing for regional papers. She described 'the typical journalist' on an average Hindi-language newspaper in a caricature that nevertheless probably represented a widely held conception:

> The senior member of the editorial board of an average Hindi newspaper is not a thinker, an intellectual or a professional with a devotion; but he is a cunning small town businessman in a safari suit, or a person of medium stature belonging to the band of a manoeuvring politician. Do not be surprised if you most of the time will find him behaving like a politician or a businessman equipped with mystical manners, 'fixing' secret 'deals' in the office of collectors, tax inspectors or political parties; instead of collecting and selecting news or using his pen with sharpness and without fear. He will have 25 amulet rings on his ten fingers, in his pocket a gold pen (which he has received as a gift) and on his wrist a costly watch (again, from an unknown benefactor). Outfits in homespun cotton and heavy reading glasses have become a historical past and the concern for the future of Hindi is a completely different matter. (Pande, 1996: 48)

The model of journalism that these critical voices adhere to appears quite clearly. The profession is honoured for its role of building public opinion in the Indian democracy. A journalist should be a devoted intellectual serving his country altruistically and with great seriousness—more the 'missionary' than the 'bloodhound'. Both editors cited above explicitly relate this ideal to the role of Indian intellectuals during the Independence Movement (symbolised according to Pande by the figure in homespun cotton and heavy reading glasses, who had a concern for the Hindi language). At that time journalism was an important weapon in the fight for freedom, whether it was published in English or in Hindi (see Chapter Two). Today, many journalists and intellectuals of the 'old stock' feel that this kind of ideal is under threat. The culprit is the journalism associated with those regional vernacular newspapers that have enjoyed such a success during the last few decades. And certain parvenus in the Hindi-speaking belt of north India have the worst of reputations: corrupt, incompetent, politically biased and commercialised.

As Bourdieu has stated about 'fields of cultural production' in general, the boundary between insiders and outsiders—in our case, who is a proper journalist—is always a subject of heated debate:

> The field of cultural production is the site of struggles in which what is at stake is the power to impose the dominant definition of the writer and therefore to delimit the population of those entitled to take part in the struggle to define the writer. (Bourdieu, 1993: 42)

Dainik Jagran is among those newspapers that have often been explicitly mentioned by the critics. When I commenced my fieldwork I was aware of this. The path that brought me to the journalists working in the cramped editorial office of *Dainik Jagran* in Lucknow passed through preparations that included reading all I could find in 'national' Indian newspapers and magazines that mentioned the Hindi press. I spoke to media people and academics in New Delhi. The unambiguous picture I got, of a press that was a commercial goldmine but a professional problem, fuelled my interest but also worried me. Some critics even called this press 'criminal'. How would such unscrupulous people receive me? Would they take it for granted that I was interested in them because they were a 'problem', like other social evils that foreign scholars like to study?

But a shift from the media world in New Delhi to the media world in Lucknow also implied a changed perspective. The journalists working with the Hindi newspapers here were not particularly affected by the bad reputation they might have in certain circles. Not that they were unaware of the critique against them, they knew very well what prominent journalists of reputed dailies in Delhi thought of them. But these people were far away, in Lucknow the Hindi-language newspapers were viewed differently. Of course, they had their local critics but few people would dismiss these papers outright as incompetent, corrupt and untruthful (though I occasionally met members of an English-speaking elite who would never trust a word of these papers). Even though journalists working with the local English-language press often believed themselves to be superior and more 'professional' than colleagues reporting in Hindi, they generally regarded those Hindi-language newspapers with the biggest circulation as important and serious. In certain respects they could indeed admit that the Hindi press was often better.

And the dominant view, I would say, was that Hindi-language journalism had improved a great deal over the years.

Thus, the journalists on *Dainik Jagran* and other Hindi papers in the town did not experience that they were working under constant contempt. They did not feel that they had to defend themselves all the time and formulate their own professional identity in an ongoing argument with their critics. But there were occasions when the critique reached them and they were forced to respond. These were also events when occupational attitudes and values became more explicitly formulated than otherwise. I shall dwell at some length on one such event when questions about the occupational role of journalists were actualised. It was an incident that connected the local editorial office of *Dainik Jagran* with an intellectual debate about journalism and its role in the Indian democracy.

The illicit daughter

At the end of December 1995 *Dainik Jagran* published an article, which aroused astonishment and agitation among many of its readers. The article was printed on the lower half of the first page of the paper. Running over two short columns it was not edited in a particularly conspicuous way. "Bhaskar says that Mayawati has a twelve-year-old daughter" were the words of the rather modest-sized headline. The article consisted of an interview with a minister in the former state government of Uttar Pradesh. The politician accused his former Chief Minister of telling lies about her background. She prided herself on being an unmarried woman who had denied herself a family and children for a political mission; but the politician claimed that she had a twelve-year-old daughter from a former 'love marriage' and that the girl was now hidden in New Delhi.[5]

This was a sensation. To be an unmarried woman, moreover a powerful politician, and to have an illegitimate child was a very serious accusation. Among ordinary people, in workplaces and tea stalls, this became a topic to talk about: could there really be any truth in what the paper wrote? In the city of Lucknow, a couple of weeks later, the political party (BSP) of the former Chief Minister arranged a rally at which people were exhorted to march to the office of the newspaper, to demonstrate their resentment. Thousands of agitated party supporters blocked the office for a day, and the reports spoke of people throwing stones and also about other types of violence. The journalist who had written the signed article was threatened and for some time had to work protected by three security guards. Later on, journalists demonstrated against the former Chief Minister's party—in support of a 'free press'. A number of newspapers in Lucknow stated that they would boycott this party and not cover it during the approaching election campaign. However, only *Dainik Jagran* strictly upheld this boycott.

The article published in *Dainik Jagran,* and the events that evolved from it, were followed closely also outside Lucknow. It was widely debated among journalists and intellectuals throughout northern India. The focus of the debate was not the virtue of a female politician, but rather the ethics of journalism. In many editorials the publication of this kind of material was condemned as sensationalist journalism, and the aspiration of *Dainik Jagran* to be a serious newspaper was questioned; in other contexts the article was defended by people who claimed that the newspaper was only doing its proper duty.

The story was obviously at the limit of what could be publicly stated in the media, and in the reactions that followed norms and ideas, that are often implicitly understood, were explicitly spelled out.[6] Those who criticised *Dainik Jagran* were not a uniform group; they reacted on different grounds, with different arguments and in several ways. The defamed politician, Mayawati, was probably indignant on a personal level, but she and other leaders of her party, formulated their criticism in terms of caste politics. They were of the opinion that the publication of the story was only one instance of the mud slinging 'the Brahmin press' was constantly engaged in. From the horizon of this mainly low-caste party, the media in India are an inseparable part of the Brahmin-dominated establishment that from time immemorial has oppressed low-caste groups. It was just as expected; the establishment would try to defame a Dalit woman who had held the highest political office in the largest state in India. The BSP is the politically most important organisation within the contemporary Dalit movement, but if this movement has been recently successful in the political sphere, it is still largely denied a public voice on its own terms (remember how extremely rare it was with journalists of Dalit origin and with newspapers sympathetic to their cause). To the extent that the Dalit movement is involved in a 'cultural struggle of meaning' (Hardtmann, 2002), its relationship with the mass media is certainly crucial.

There were also attempts in the intellectual debate to interpret the issue in terms of caste politics. Some commentators pointed to the uniqueness of the media boycott of the BSP after its manifestation against *Dainik Jagran*. On several occasions supporters of Hindu nationalist parties and organisations have used violence against journalists, but this has never resulted in a boycott. Others expressed their criticism in professional terms: the journalist who wrote the article should have checked whether the facts were correct and he should at least have given Mayawati a chance to comment and defend herself. However, probably the most common point of view among those who criticised *Dainik Jagran* was to look at the issue as an ethical problem. Irrespective of whether Mayawati had a child or not, this was part of her personal sphere into which the media had no admittance. The fault with publishing the story was that it crossed the boundary from the public into the private, where 'the freedom of the press' is not valid.[7]

Those who supported *Dainik Jagran* in the debate interpreted the event in much the same terms as the critics, that is to say, politically, professionally or ethically. The political interpretation focused on BSP's manifestation against the newspaper office, rather than on the publishing itself, and claimed that this was only the latest of the party's repeated attacks against the media. The comments were often cynical and remarked that the 'defamation' was used by the BSP as an opportunity to unite its supporters against a visible enemy at a moment when the party was about to split. The professional defence of *Dainik Jagran* claimed that the newspaper was only doing its proper duty, reflecting the political debate by publishing accusations between two politicians. It was also remarked that Mayawati had been given a chance to comment on the facts before the article was printed, but had refused.[8]

Concerning *Dainik Jagran*'s defence in ethical terms, it is interesting to note how the chief editor (and owner) of the paper, Narendra Mohan, himself commented on the issue in an editorial. He asserted that *Dainik Jagran* was basically against the kind of journalism this issue was about. He regretted that the article had ever been printed. But then, when he tried to explain the mistake, he alleged two different things. First, that this kind of scandal writing in the press only showed that Indian journalists had unfortunately been affected by norms from the West, where 'sex scandals' are accepted subjects for the media. Second, this situation had come up because politics in India had become unethical. He argued that Mayawati herself represented a new political style, often using an 'ugly' language. She therefore had only herself to blame when journalism had also become unethical. As a solution to the problem, Narendra Mohan suggested that a 'code of conduct' should be formulated for journalists.[9]

Also engaged in this debate was the national chairman of the most important journalists union, the Indian Federation of Working Journalists, K. Vikram Rao, himself a resident of Lucknow. He maintained what was needed was a more rigorous system of self-control within the press. He was, however, sceptical about a 'code of conduct' and suggested instead three other measures: a national register of legitimated journalists should be maintained, the Press Council should have more powerful means of penalising journalists, and it should be compulsory for journalists to have some specialised training before being recruited to a newspaper (Rao, 1996).[10]

I arrived in Lucknow soon after the first article had been published. The 'defamation' of the former Chief Minister was one of the issues that marked the atmosphere in which the journalists were working when I started my fieldwork on *Dainik Jagran*. It continued to be a hot subject for several months. The journalists often talked among themselves, as well as with people they met on assignments, about this article and the debate it had triggered off. I was present at several editorial meetings when the event came up for discussion. On some occasions the subject was talked about in an agitated manner: staff members could indeed admit that a fault had been committed, but reacted strongly against the assertion that *Dainik Jagran* was not a serious newspaper and lacked professionalism and credibility.

As I understood the case, it was not the content of the criticism directed against the publication of the article that troubled the journalists in the *Dainik Jagran* office: even if they did not agree with it all, they comprehended it very well. What disturbed them was rather the way in which the case was used in a broader context. Permeating the debate was a general view of the status of the press in India—a view that emphasised a particular hierarchy. This was clearly formulated in a seminar that was held in Lucknow about a month after the incident. The title of the seminar, organised by the Indian Society of Professional Journalists, was 'Media Credibility under Threat'. Prominent among the participants were Judge P.B. Sawant, the chairman of the Indian Press Council, and Prabash Joshi, the earlier mentioned chief editor of the Delhi-based Hindi-language paper *Jansatta*. The message from this seminar reflected an image of the media that is quite well founded in the intellectual debate in India: in certain parts there are serious problems with corruption, incompetence, commercialisation and politically biased reporting, and because of these problems the media have lost credibility among the public. The examples and arguments that were used to describe this situation pointed unambiguously to one problematic sector of the mass media: the regional vernacular press. More precisely, it was newspapers of the Hindi-language press that were mentioned by name. Speakers referred to instances of biased reporting during violent confrontations between Hindu and Muslim groups. The regional Hindi press has been accused of aggravating, and even creating, violent conflicts by inaccurate reporting and the printing of false rumours. The Indian Press Council has in some cases severely criticised the newspapers, for example, for reports of the dispute about the Babri Masjid Mosque in Ayodhya (see Engineer, 1991; Jeffrey, 1997b; *Vidura*, 1992).

Critics have also pointed to circumstances that are prevalent in these newspapers, such as journalists not getting appointment letters but working under insecure contracts, or the system of using unpaid 'stringers' to report from village districts. It has also been considered suspect when the owner and chief editor are sometimes one and the same person, or when owners of these papers are involved in other commercial activities where the political strength of running a paper is an asset. The commercialisation of the newspaper business itself is often commented upon with an argument which could have been formulated by the mass media critics of the Frankfurt school: "media are treated as a commercial commodity and sold like soap or toothpaste".

Preceding the controversy about the Mayawati article, there had recently been two other occurrences in which this kind of criticism of the regional press was heard. First, there was the action that the Press Council had begun to take concerning the widespread system of journalists' receiving substantial favours from ruling state politicians, in the form of money or allocations of land and housing at subsidised prices (see Chapter Four). The second topic involved *Dainik Jagran* more directly. A year earlier, the newspaper, together with the competing paper *Amara Ujala*, had been involved in a conflict with the then Chief Minister, Mulayam Singh Yadav. The conflict started with a violent clash between police and a group of demonstrators, who were demanding a separate state for the northern hill region of Uttar Pradesh. In all the media the attack by the police on the demonstrators was described as brutal—the incident went down in history as Mulayam's *halabol* (tumult)—but *Dainik Jagran* and *Amara Ujala* had gone too far, in the eyes of the Chief Minister, in the reporting and in criticising the government as responsible for the incident. A committee from the Editors' Guild, which investigated the incident, also criticised the newspapers. The Chief Minister stopped all government advertising in the two papers for several months, which was a considerable economic setback, and he accused them of being socially and politically reactionary. Furthermore, journalists and newspaper vendors complained that activists from the Chief Minister's party were harassing them.[11] Looking back at all the difficulties he had faced during the previous ten years, resident editor Vinod Shukla described this as the worst event he had been forced to deal with.

Reactions in the Editorial Office

Among the loudest voices criticising the regional vernacular press were leading journalists from the more established and 'respectable' Hindi-language newspapers—that is to say, journalists from papers with a national profile that, in comparison with the regional vernacular papers, had not been particularly successful in commercial terms over the past decade. One of these well-known critics was the chief editor of *Jansatta*, Prabash Joshi. At the seminar mentioned above he had an opportunity to speak in a setting where the ears of those who were the subjects of his criticism were not far away—even though attendance from the regional Hindi press was low on this occasion and no direct dialogue was ever established. From *Dainik Jagran* only one reporter was present, the one who was covering the meeting for the paper.

At the editorial meeting of *Dainik Jagran* the next day, the rumour had already reached everybody that Joshi had explicitly named *Dainik Jagran* as the least credible of newspapers. "From top to bottom there is not one competent person in *Dainik Jagran*" was apparently what he had said. These words were, of course, not referred to in the article published in the paper. The reporter showed his discontent in more careful words. "On the one hand, the chairman of the Indian Press Council, Judge P.B. Sawant, gave several useful suggestions in relation to the problem with credibility of the press. On the other hand, the journalist Prabash Joshi made a personal criticism of certain named newspapers. Because of the latter, private interest was unfortunately given room at this seminar."[12]

The journalists were upset and the resident editor, Vinod Shukla, could barely control himself: "Prabash Joshi is an insignificant newspaperman. He is running a paper that is not selling more than 1.5 lakh (150,000) copies all over India; we have a circulation of over 5 lakh (500,000) only in Uttar Pradesh. Our readers have trust in us. And who is making money?" But this kind of criticism was nothing to bother about, editor Shukla explained after a long and agitated speech at the morning meeting. "Our task is to improve, we should concentrate on that." But, the subject kept on appearing among the journalists during the following days. Shukla said that the accusations against *Dainik Jagran* were disturbing their work, they were like an alien infection penetrating the body.

It was evident that it was the article about "Mayawati's daughter" which had made the critics focus on *Dainik Jagran* at this time. Vinod Shukla did not deny that a mistake had been made on their part. "I am not accusing my staff, they are doing their job. But this time things went wrong everywhere. We should have made more effort to get a comment from Mayawati, and in any case there should have been a line stating that we had tried to reach her."

In the editorial room it was considered unfair that *Dainik Jagran* and this isolated event had come to represent all the bad journalism in India. "Why are only we being attacked, why not other papers?" the journalists asked themselves. People at *Dainik Jagran* could also see connections with previous mistakes. "This was the second big mistake we have made, the last one was Ayodhya", Vinod Shukla said at an editorial meeting later in the week (for a moment forgetting more recent incidents, such as Mulayam's *halabol*). He explained to me what went wrong on that occasion:

> I had a young female reporter in Ayodhya. She phoned in the news. It was the first time she had ever seen blood and dead bodies. "There are hundreds of dead bodies", she said. We wrote, "More than a hundred people dead". Then there came news reports, with low figures of casualties. We tried to stop the edition; we even tried to withdraw papers that had already been distributed. We sat here at this table and discussed the figures.[13]

The incident had happened five years ago, and there were several papers that exaggerated the number of casualties at the time. To Shukla it was obvious why *Dainik Jagran* was still the focus of so much criticism. "They are jealous," he said. "We are the biggest. We are the most successful." To underline this, and suddenly in a better mood, he called for an internal report showing *Dainik Jagran*'s share of the market in relation to other newspapers.

During all the conversations when "Mayawati's daughter" was the topic, I never heard anyone from *Dainik Jagran* criticise the reporter who had written the article. This reporter, the only Muslim journalist on the paper, always kept a low profile when the subject he was responsible for was raised. But this young man was also normally a quiet person, a fact that did not, however, prevent him from being very efficient and ambitious in carrying out his work. Only 25 years old and with a degree from Lucknow University, he had come three years earlier to *Dainik Jagran* as a trainee. He started by covering educational issues but had soon advanced to the political bureau. On his beat were the Bahujan Samaj Party (which he had to give up after the incident), the Janata Dal and a number of minor low-caste parties. True, it was the least prestigious assignment in the political bureau—and the government had not yet accredited him—but nevertheless this was an important step in a journalistic career. In addition to this, he also covered Muslim affairs and the University. He was one of those reporters who often had a byline attached to his articles, which meant that he produced stories that were considered exclusive. Quite often his articles were also placed on the front page. This reporter could definitely be described as a young, 'hungry' news hunter who was not afraid of problems that might arise after publishing a story—a 'bloodhound' maybe. For the paper it was probably comfortable to have, in a staff predominantly consisting of Brahmin journalists, a Muslim reporter who did not hesitate to take on politically sensitive subjects, which were often about caste or religion. It need hardly be said that the resident editor Vinod Shukla was very satisfied with him.

So, it was no surprise that it was this particular journalist who had written the article under debate. He himself neither bragged about it nor showed any regret. He did not think he had made a mistake; he had simply quoted what one politician had said about another during an interview, and he had done what he could to give Mayawati a chance to comment on the article before it was printed. Otherwise, the reporter did not show much interest in matters of principle about journalistic professionalism and ethics. He was just doing his job as well as he could. And his notion about what could be 'good news' was probably derived from his socialisation into norms and values that in practice guided work in the editorial office, rather than from an independent professional ideology. The signals he received from the newspaper management were ambivalent. On the one hand, his story was excused as a journalistic mistake; on the other hand he was never reprimanded and the incident did not become an obstacle in his career.

The people

The journalists working on *Dainik Jagran* and the other Hindi-language newspapers in Lucknow did not interpret their professional role in any way that contrasted sharply with their critics in the 'national' elite press. As the incident of the article about 'the illicit daughter' illustrates, the journalists on *Dainik Jagran* did not try to defend the publication from a position outside the norms to which the critics referred. To an outside audience most of them would readily admit that there was an ethical and professional problem involved in this case. Among themselves, they still claimed that the facts had been correct. Anyway, they did not accept the view that this article was representative of the journalism that they generally practised. They tried to uphold the same professional standards as the 'national' press. Comparing themselves with the English-language newspapers in Lucknow, many journalists agreed that these were still more professional, with more qualified staff who wrote better stories. But they were not lagging very much behind, and in some respects they even beat the English-language papers. The trump card that all Hindi journalists referred to was their 'closeness to the people'. On one occasion when I talked to Vinod Shukla about the criticism of *Dainik Jagran*, and especially about the accusations that it was biased in favour of Hindu fundamentalism, he explained:

> Let us say that we sometimes have exaggerated things. But our journalists are out there when things happen. They are moved by the feelings of the mob, and that is reflected in what they write. It is because we are involved in people's feelings that we are accused of being biased.

This argument has two dimensions. The first is obvious. The English-language newspapers may boast about how professional, serious and credible they are; how essential their role is as 'watchdogs' in a democratic society. But they cannot possibly claim to play an important role in broad democratic participation, simply because the overwhelming majority of Indian people do not read English. The vernacular press can readily assert that it is they who have "the key role in forming the political awakening among the newly literate in our Indian democracy", as one Hindi editor put it to me. The second dimension of the argument that the Hindi-language press is 'closer to the people' has to do with the fact that English is not only a language that few people understand, but also that those who do know English are mainly the elite in society. Naturally, English-language newspapers are produced for readers with education and at least some influence and wealth. No one working with the English-language press would deny that. During several interviews I had with English-language journalists and editors we talked about the role of journalism in a democracy like India. When I asked how they 'served the people' with journalism that only the most educated in their society could read, the answer usually came back promptly and as a matter of course: the English-language press was more important than the vernacular press because it had more credibility and influence. People with education and power read English-language newspapers. As one senior journalist on a well-reputed newspaper explained to me:

> When we take up an issue, a social problem for example, it will be noticed by people who are in a position to do something about it, thus we serve the people better than the vernacular press.

Strangely enough, journalists of both Hindi and English-language newspapers basically seemed to agree on this bifurcation of the democratic role of the press. Journalists of the two languages did, of course, often claim in a general way that the newspaper published in their respective languages was the 'best' and more 'important' than the newspaper in the other language. But when they explained why, they emphasised different sides of the bifurcation. To say that the Hindi press was more influential and credible than the English press would clearly be a statement contrary to the dominant view among all journalists. And, certainly, no English-language journalist would claim that his paper was 'closer to the people' than any of the Hindi-language competitors.

Publicness and creativity

Does the practical work of a craft generate a particular consciousness that is shared by practitioners regardless of time and place? Some studies concerned with occupations claim precisely this, usually studies carried out in the 1970s from the perspective of a 'sociology of knowledge' (Bensman and Lilienfeld, 1973; Hughes, 1971; Salaman, 1974). In a volume concerned with specific 'habits of mind' shared by practitioners in the same occupation, Bensman and Lilienfeld described what characterised 'the journalist attitude'. This attitude they saw as formed by the three circumstances in the 'nature' of the occupation. The most important was 'time', the periodicity of publishing that is an objective factor beyond control; the journalists have to adjust their work to a given 'deadline'. The second circumstance was the relation to the public. Bensman and Lilienfeld claimed that the journalist has to do his work always with the reader in mind. He must be able to see what has news value, what may interest the reader; the journalist has to be synchronised with the public. As the third circumstance in the 'nature' of the occupation they saw the creative aspect of the occupation: the journalist has to offer a new perspective towards the well-known, he must find structure and connections behind all that is taken for granted. In this aspect, the journalist is much like an artist.

It is easy to raise objections to descriptions like this of an occupational 'nature' that would determine universal attitudes. And, the characteristics that Bensman and Lilienfeld ascribed to the journalist seem rather idealistic as well. The attitude to the public may not always be that well synchronised, the ability to provide new perspectives not very prominent and the daily deadline not absolutely constraining. Nevertheless, I believe, it is possible to identify universal circumstances of the occupation that certainly should be part of the picture if one tries to describe a professional 'attitude' or an occupational culture in a specific milieu. I would say that the newspaper journalists in Lucknow share with many colleagues globally a few such circumstances. The rhythm of publishing might be one; few journalists have the privilege of working on a story as long as they would like to, neglecting the daily deadline. This constraint is most acutely felt, however, by reporters working on hard news beats; a sudden political development, a bold crime or a catastrophe of some kind cannot wait for a later edition. But there are also plenty of stories in a newspaper that can be planned well in advance of the date of printing. Thus, to work against the clock is not a necessary condition of each and every journalist, at least not every day. The reasons why I refer to Bensman and Lilienfeld's somewhat obscure treatise on 'the journalist attitude' (this work is not widely cited in later studies in the sociology of news production) are the other two circumstances of journalism that they mentioned: the relation to the public and the creative aspect. Even though there are objections to their formulations, I think that they touch on some essential conditions of the journalistic occupation.

First, a journalist works in the public arena. What a reporter does on his beat during a workday might often appear ordinary, trivial or arbitrary—talking to people here and there about issues of limited significance, it seems. But something happens when that workday is over and the information is compiled: a piece of writing goes to press, printed in the small hours. It starts to circulate as a story on a page in the newspaper. The fruit of a day's work can be scrutinised by a vast number of people; in principle, it is available to anybody in the region of publication. A 'good' story has the potential of becoming 'public knowledge', a topic that people are talking about widely. To my mind, this is something profound. It is hardly possible for any journalist to neglect this aspect of the job. The journalist may have a distorted image of his readers and may not have 'the common man' primarily in mind when writing (perhaps producing stories to please the editor or impress his colleagues). But nobody can write as if only a select number of people are supposed to read the story; it can reach anyone within the region of publication (and occasionally even further).[14] A journalist always has to be aware that his work becomes instantly public.

Secondly, journalism is a creative occupation. Not only if it is successful in the sense that Bensman and Lilienfeld had in mind, as analysing and explaining society. More basically, journalism is a creative business because what one reads in the newspaper is not 'the reality' transcribed into text. It is a matter of constructing character: journalists select events from the reality and shape them into news stories. This was a major theme in several studies of journalism in the late 1970s, hinted at in the titles of important works like *Manufacturing the News, Deciding What's News*, *Putting Reality Together* and *Making News.*[15] That the mass media are constructing their own reality is not a very controversial opinion today, it is commonly held not only by scholars but also by media critics in general. Nevertheless, it might be an irritating view for journalists who honestly claim that they are trying their best to describe and report real events in an objective way. They are not flattered when their work is described as a business of 'manufacturing', 'constructing' or 'making' news. However, in emphasising the creativity of journalism, one does not have to judge the profession as such. The journalist is producing news in consonance with occupational paradigms on what has news value, following established norms for how to get it and present it. In this endeavour, a journalist might be an 'intellectual', critically investigating and reflecting on phenomena in society (Gouldner, 1979), or a mere 'knowledge worker' (Hannerz, 1992: 143), handling pieces of information in a routine uncomplicated way. But, the making of a newspaper is never a matter of holding up a mirror to society, because the images unfolded are acts of creation.

In what way did the Lucknow journalists experience these basic conditions of the occupation? Was there anything in their 'consciousness' or 'attitude' that seemed directly connected with these conditions? I believe there was. To start with, they were very much aware of the fact that they were working in public. They knew that they had a 'voice' that was louder than that of other people. They had the power to direct public attention to virtually any issue. This gave them an authority that was quite easily perceived. When they met and talked to people on the beat, the condition that everything said could end up in the paper was always prevalent. Journalists embody publicity. They may be feared, loathed or respected, but they can hardly be ignored. In the case of Lucknow, I would say that the journalists were most often respected. Even people with considerable social status (*bare log*), such as politicians and senior bureaucrats, treated them seriously. Few journalists had any complaints about the respect they enjoyed, they were mostly satisfied with their social status (which may not be the case for journalists everywhere). They were clear about where that respect came from: they did not have much formal power, special knowledge or financial means—but they did have control over a public voice. That gave them self-confidence.

If a great part of a journalist's occupational identity and social status comes from the fact that he has a piece of text in the newspaper every day, it is no wonder that a lot of emotions are involved in reading one's own stories in print. The Lucknow journalists are probably no different from colleagues all over the world in the excitement with which they open the newspaper each morning to find out how their own stories have come out. Not that they expect that the content of a story might have changed since they left the manuscript with the night editor (sub-editors of *Dainik Jagran* do not work much on the stories, apart from minor corrections). But it certainly makes a difference to see a story in print, exactly in the way it will appear before thousands of readers. And, although the story is well known, there is a lot to look for. Where does the story appear, on the front page or inside? Is it placed high or low on the page? What headline has it been given? What is the size of the headline? In how many columns is the story edited (the more, the better)? How does it work with the picture (if any)? Not least, did it get a byline with the name of the reporter? Without doubt, there are many details a reporter could object to, in the way a story has been edited. At times someone could be very dissatisfied and angry with the sub-editors. However, the overwhelming impression was that the journalists were generally pleased just to open the newspaper and see their stories in print. Of course, it was especially satisfactory to get four columns with a byline on the front page, but simply to be in the newspaper seemed to be a regular source of inspiration. Certainly, the journalists liked to be published. They felt dissatisfied on days when they had nothing in the newspaper, which occasionally happened.

They also enjoyed knowing that others had read or noticed their stories. Beat reporters were quite often reminded about articles they had written. People they met dropped a comment on something they had read and had some opinion about. Or they plainly tried to flatter the reporter—often successfully. Some bureaucrats were skilled at this. An instant way to get on good terms with a reporter was to show him some of his stories in the file of newspaper clippings that some public department kept. Even senior journalists appreciated a comment on their writings and never seemed to get blasé. This was a lesson that I soon learnt myself. The best way to establish a good relationship with a journalist was to pay attention to his articles. Many reporters did not have much to say about practical aspects of their job or did not seem particularly interested in journalism in general, but few missed an opportunity to talk about articles they had written. In the recorded interviews I conducted, the journalists were often happy to dwell at length on one of my requests: could you please mention a few stories that you have been particularly satisfied with. At the same time, a common complaint was that they got too little response on their stories, from readers as well as from editors and colleagues. A local reporter told me one day that he was very disappointed and had lost all enthusiasm for his work. This was in late February, and for several days he had extensively covered the celebration of *Id* among Muslim communities in the town. Even though he was a Hindu himself, he felt that he had done a good job and treated this event, which was so important for Muslims, with great respect. But no one seemed to be grateful for all the articles he had written; not even once had he been invited to participate in the celebrations in the house of a Muslim.

Whatever ideas he had about journalism, however he legitimated its practice, a strong motivation in the reporter's work and an emotionally loaded aspect of his job was its publicness: to be published and to be read. In the sociology of news, this observation belongs to an area of studies that has received little attention. Usually, journalists have been studied in relation to news organisations, colleagues, sources or (more rarely) ideas and symbols of cultural significance; the relation with the public has not been given much importance (cf. Schudson, 1991: 151–52). One reason for this is that mass media studies have often found that journalists have only vague images of their audience, or seem to lack all interest in how their products are consumed. According to Herbert Gans, the reporters and editors at news weeklies and network television programmes that he studied "had little knowledge about the actual audience and rejected feedback from it" (1979: 230; cited in Schudson, 1991: 152). Philip Schlesinger, in his study of radio news at the BBC, writes about 'the missing link', referring to "a structural lacuna between the producers and consumers of news" (1978: 106). I would not argue that the Lucknow journalists had a clear picture of their readers (except that the English-language journalists assumed, on good grounds, that only the English-speaking upper strata in society read them). Sometimes I tried to get a journalist to describe 'the typical reader' of his stories—without success, as the usual claim was that 'all kinds of people' read a newspaper.[16] I think, the Lucknow journalists conformed to what has been said about news producers in other places: primarily they had superiors, colleagues, sources and themselves in mind when writing their stories. This, however, should not be interpreted as if it was without significance for the journalist that he was widely read. The journalist is not like any other white-collar worker; publicness makes all the difference. I believe that this concerns not only journalists in Lucknow. Just as 'fame' has an attraction of its own for producers of popular culture, without bothering all that much about exactly who they reach, so 'publicness' has a diffuse but irresistible attraction for journalists. Perhaps, it is even a constitutive feature of 'the public' that it is faceless.

Having influence and being present

A journalist could be pleased with stories he had written for different reasons. If someone had made a big 'scoop' it was, of course, mentioned as a highlight of his career. What counted as real scoops were primarily political developments that the reporter had been the first one to disclose. Resignations of ministers, split-ups of political parties or political alliances that were coming up between parties were examples of stories that several journalists proudly explained they had been the first to break. Ideally, a really good scoop should also involve some smart or ingenious performance on the part of the reporter. Gyanendra, a senior journalist, recalled how (years back) he had been able to break a story about a major reorganisation of the State Cabinet by clever use of well-placed sources. Before anything had leaked out on this event an operator at the telephone company, who could overhear interstate calls, had given him a tip-off about something big going on in the highest echelons of state politics. Pretending to know more than he did, Gyanendra fooled one of the ministers into disclosing that it was about changes in the cabinet. And, he got the story confirmed by a typist in the Chief Minister's office who complained about being exhausted typing out resignation letters from ministers all day.

But it was not only the scoops that the journalists mentioned when they narrated stories that they had been very pleased with. Some reporters prided themselves on having done stories on human or social issues that they found important. Particularly if they had been privileged to work on ambitious projects taking several days and maybe involving longer travels—that is to say, stories outside the usual beat routines. One reporter mentioned as the best work he had done a series of articles on Hindu refugees from Kashmir in which he had described their miserable situation in refugee camps in Punjab. He had been released from his normal duties for a week in order to do the story. Another journalist, who was new in town, told how he had felt lonely far from his native place. This feeling gave him the idea of writing about others missing their homes, and he did a number of stories on people in Lucknow who had come from Pakistan after the partition of India in 1947, and never been able to return. What satisfied him, he said, was to write about the destinies and feelings of people who were seldom heard of in the newspapers.

The last two examples of stories that journalists were proud of obviously relate to the professional idea that journalism was first and foremost in 'the service of the people'. While scoops were undoubtedly something to boast about, they were not necessarily understood as being very important for 'society'; being the first to break a story was rather a kind of trophy for the reporter, raising his status among his colleagues as well as his popularity with the newspaper management. But stories about social issues, reflecting hardships among 'ordinary people', were often mentioned as something journalists *should* do, but seldom did, because of lack of time and reluctance on the part of the newspaper management. This kind of story was considered as 'good journalism' in a more idealised way than the scoop or other sensational writing. The same was true for a more common category of stories, namely, articles about problems in the public services or mismanagement in the bureaucracy. Being a watchdog on how society works was clearly part of the role that the journalists ascribed to themselves. On the other hand, this was more or less routine work for many journalists, particularly for local reporters who penetrated different departments of the government bureaucracy on their daily beats and exposed things that were working badly. In this respect, the political reporters, on more prestigious beats, were to a lesser extent engaged in scrutinising the government. When the journalists mentioned particular stories that they had been satisfied with in this genre, it was often cases where their coverage had had an impact on how things worked. These stories were often not particularly sensational. Usually, they concerned details or well-defined issues rather than more fundamental principles of government work. One example was the story one journalist wrote about how the authorities mismanaged malaria prevention in the state (Chapter Four). Another journalist pointed to several stories he had written some years back relating to problems with clean water supply in Lucknow. One issue he had given attention to was that a main sewage pipe from the city was feeding its content into the Gomati river, very close to the place where drinking water was taken for one-third of the city's population. The journalist claimed that his writings were a main reason for the government to implement a far-reaching project (the Gomati Action Plan) in which the sewage was cleaned up and the pipes diverted to a place downstream from where the water was taken.

Another aspect of the occupation that made the journalists convinced of their central location in society was the fact that they knew better than most people about what was going on in town. Each journalist, of course, only covered a fragment of everything that was happening, but he was certainly aware also of important events that his colleagues were covering. In a big city like Lucknow things happen all the time that affect citizens, but few people know about them in advance. When the main roads are blocked and people are stuck in the traffic jam on their way to work, when all shops in an area are closed on a normal market day, or when some famous person is visiting the town—such events often just seem to happen without much notice. Most ordinary citizens are taken by surprise and know nothing about the reasons or the circumstances. But, the journalists are always well informed. One day, for example, during my stay in Lucknow, one of the most important politicians in the country, BJP president Atal Bihari Vajpayee, who later became Prime Minister of India, visited the city and held a public meeting in the residential area where I lived. I knew nothing about it when I left my house in the morning for another day of fieldwork among the journalists, nor were my neighbours aware of the fact that such a prominent person was about to pay a visit in their neighbourhood. When I reached the editorial office, Brijesh, one of the political reporters, came with the news that Vajpayee was coming to town today for an unannounced visit in his constituency; he was elected to the *Lok Sabha* (central parliament) from Lucknow. Brijesh did not yet know exactly when he was coming or where he was going to make an appearance, but he would certainly be the first to know from his sources. So, by four o'clock in the afternoon, we took the scooter to the state guest house where visiting politicians and bureaucrats always stay. Together with journalists from other newspapers and state politicians from the BJP we were waiting when Vajpayee suddenly arrived from the airport with a group of white Ambassador cars with howling sirens. When they left again, after an hour or so, to take Vajpayee to the place where he would make his appearance, Brijesh and I, together with a few other journalists, were invited to follow in one of the cars. To my surprise we ended at the crossroads from where I had left for town in the morning. Now, there was a stage erected, and a crowd of people was assembling from nearby lanes. If I had not been in touch with journalists, I would probably have missed the event altogether.

To be present when things happen and to witness important events is part of the journalist's job. (This privilege is, of course, connected with the circumstance that it is the business of journalism to select and 'construct' those events that count as news.) 'I was there' is a prominent concept of the journalistic experience. When the journalists narrated 'good stories' that they had done during their careers, they often intertwined their accounts with important events they had been present to cover. Sometimes they did not claim exceptional qualities for the stories they had written but rather emphasised that they had 'been there' to report on a historical event. Senior journalists who had been in the occupation since the 1970s always reminisced about what it was like to work during the emergency, and those who had been witness to the dreadful events in the wake of the murder of Indira Gandhi never failed to narrate their experiences.

The most important event that had taken place in Uttar Pradesh during the recent time was, of course, the Ayodhya conflict. Since that controversy had been a source of news for a long time, many of the journalists in Lucknow had been involved in covering it at some stage. Most journalists who had 'been there' seemed to view Ayodhya as a crucial event in their careers. They all described it as a terrible experience, as many of them had been caught in the middle of riots, or been badly beaten by *kar sevaks.*[17] Ayodhya was also extraordinary in the sense that journalists were not only observers of the events. It soon became clear that they had played a major part in what happened. The coverage of the conflict in the papers instantly became important material in the way things evolved. The journalists had not only 'been there', but were even inscribed in these historical events. Most commentators, however, have described the role of journalism in a negative way: the coverage in the newspapers fuelled the controversy and made the conflict worse. So, for the journalists who had been there, it was an ambivalent experience. All the journalists I talked to denied that they had consciously sided with the *kar sevaks,* but few denied that their coverage had sometimes made things worse. Some of them had actually seen how photocopies of articles in their own papers had been distributed among people in order to stir up feelings. As one journalist, now regretting his role, explained to me:

> This whole Ayodhya problem has happened before my eyes. I have covered every incident since 1982 [when the previously locked mosque was opened up]. At that time we [the journalists of his age]were 20 years younger and were just after the stories. We were not aware of what could happen. We did not think that this genie would come out of the bottle due to our effort. That the RSS and the BJP would exploit our stories and create a divide between Hindus and Muslims that would culminate in nation-wide violence. If we had understood this at that time, then perhaps the BJP would not have been where it is today [that is, a very influential political party]. We should not have played on Ayodhya so much.

However, even though Ayodhya had been a shameful event for individual reporters, and Lucknow journalists collectively to some extent took over the blame, it nevertheless confirmed their opinion that the work of a journalist matters. It underscored the notion that a journalist was at the centre of events, that he was present at crucial points of history and that his stories excerted influence.

Notes

1. *Dainik Jagran*, Lucknow edition, 14 March 1996.
2. I recognised the stories from my Hindi-for-beginners' book as well.
3. Some important studies of the sociology and history of professions are Burrage and Torstendahl, 1990; Freidson, 1994; Hughes, 1971; Larson, 1977.
4. Journalists are rarely 'free' in relation to the media organisations that they depend on in order to practise their occupations (Becker et al., 1979; Katz, 1989); they do not have distinct clients and are able to act highly selectively towards persons and events they take on and they do not take full moral responsibility for the negative consequences of their stories (Kepplinger and Kösher, 1990). Furthermore, there are usually no licences or formal qualifications needed in order to practise the occupation.
5. 'Mayavati ki baarah baras ki ek larki bhi hai: bhaskar'. *Dainik Jagran*, Lucknow edition, 8 December 1995.
6. There are, of course, numerous other examples of journalism that have provoked strong reactions; for example, certain newspapers' (among them *Dainik Jagran*'s) coverage of events during conflicts

between religious communities. In these cases the infringements have, however, often been so flagrant that they have met with united condemnation. In comparison, the case of 'Mayawati's daughter' was a minor issue. It was on the agenda for a few months, then faded away—but it stirred up a discussion in which several different voices and arguments were heard.

7. Several writers in the Lucknow-based magazine *Patrakar Sadan*, for example, expressed this view. The incident was thoroughly discussed in the January/February 1996 issue.
8. Rather, as far as I understood, *Dainik Jagran* had tried without success to get in contact with her.
9. 'Patrakaaro ke samaksh barta sankat' (Increasing danger facing journalists). *Dainik Jagran*, all editions, 22 December 1995.
10. Neither Narendra Mohan nor Vikram Rao referred to an already existing 'code of conduct' that the Press Council had published in different versions since 1984 and which explicitly mentioned 'caution against defamatory writing'. It stated: "Newspapers should not publish anything which is manifestly defamatory or libellous against any individual or organisation unless after due care and checking, they have sufficient reason to believe that it is true and its publication will be for the public good." In the version of these norms of conduct published the year after the incident mentioned, an addition had been made: "Truth is no defence for publishing derogatory, scurrilous and defamatory material against a private citizen where no public interest is involved" (Press Council of India, 1996: 2).
11. However, after some time peace was negotiated between the Chief Minister and *Dainik Jagran*. Critics asked how this had come about so suddenly (*Vidura*, 1995:12–14).
12. *Dainik Jagran,* Lucknow edition, 22 January 1996
13. The resident editor referred to one specific incident of reporting, during the long-running Ayodhya conflict, when *Dainik Jagran* obviously had grossly exaggerated the casualty figures.
14. Also stories in the English-language press in India may be spread widely by mouth, or by being picked up in the vernacular press.
15. Fishman, 1980; Gans, 1979; Schlesinger, 1978; Tuchman, 1978.
16. One has to ask in the advertisement departments to get a more elaborate depiction of readers. See Chapter Three.
17. Those volunteers who took part in the movement aiming at demolishing the Babri Masjid mosque in order to construct a temple.

Seven

Global Modernity Spelt in Hindi

While I was working on completing this book in mid-2002, the chronic conflict between India and Pakistan concerning the Kashmir issue was escalating towards threatening dimensions, including the possibility of war on a grand scale with the use of the nuclear capabilities of the two states. I followed the disturbing developments through Indian newspapers and magazines that are easily accessible via editions on the Internet. Admittedly, the news reports that I consulted were primarily published by the English-language press, which includes dailies such as the *Times of India*, the *Hindu* and the *Indian Express* and the news magazines like *Frontline*, *India Today* and *Outlook*. Even though several Hindi-language dailies and magazines are available on the Internet, this was not where I looked to get the latest updates on the conflict. In a rather unreflecting way I stuck to the English elite press on this 'serious' matter, taking it for granted that they would have the best access to prime sources for all relevant information.

On 18th June, I became aware of my own bias. It was through the news magazine *Outlook*, which published an 'exclusive interview' with the Indian Prime Minister Atal Bihari Vajpayee, in which he dwelt at length on the Indian stance in the current situation. The interview, however, was not the work of *Outlook*'s own staff. It was lifted, and roughly translated in great haste, from a Hindi original published the day before. In *Outlook*, the story was published under the headline 'The *Dainik Jagran* Interview'.

Of course, this should not have come as a surprise to me: if the present Prime Minister of India favoured one newspaper for an 'exclusive interview', it was quite likely that it would be a vernacular daily. I had met Vajpayee when he was still leader of the opposition, at the state guest house in Lucknow. On that occasion there had been a dozen reporters present for a kind of informal press gathering with the BJP leader. Journalists from local dailies, both Hindi and English-language, as well as correspondents from the national media, had been present. And, after some relaxed small talk with the collected newspeople, I had noticed how Vajpayee escaped into an adjoining room for a confidential talk with only one of the journalists: the *Dainik Jagran* reporter.

It was nevertheless significant that an Indian Prime Minister, on the threshold of a possible war, gave his views on the situation exclusively to *Dainik Jagran*—and not to any of the prestigious English-language newspapers.[1] It was also notable that an English-language publication had to pick up the story from a vernacular daily. According to a stereotyped image prevalent among many supporters of the elite press, the opposite circumstance would be the standard procedure: the vernacular newspapers were full of local, trivial stuff, plus some of yesterday's news, stolen and badly translated from an English daily. I heard this repeatedly during my fieldwork, both as a fact stated by journalists working in English (more so in New Delhi than in Lucknow, however) and as an image that was disputed in the editorial offices of the Hindi newspapers. Now, we are breaking the news and they have to follow, the latter claimed.

Even though the focus of this study has been the Hindi press of Lucknow, I have throughout the book referred also to the English-language newspapers of the region. In some senses, journalism in the two languages makes up a rather strictly divided medium, almost parallel and with few junctures. Analysing how the Hindi and English-language newspapers covered the Ayodhya movement, Rajagopal (2001: 151–211) has described the news media in the two languages as a 'split public': they handled this event quite differently. I have claimed that this division is particularly clear if one looks at journalism as an occupational career and at the social background of journalists. Simultaneously, I have argued that the press in English and Hindi constitute each other. They operate as contrasting images within the same social field of cultural production (Bourdieu, 1993). Their respective positions in this field are not stable but constantly disputed and reconstituted. My point is not that the English-language press has been demoted to a secondary position in the social field of Indian journalism—which would surely be to overstate the case. But the superiority of the English-speaking elite and its dominance in the public sphere are no longer self-evident. Some political reporters of English dailies in Lucknow have admitted that they have sometimes had difficulties in getting news from the politicians. They felt that they could be neglected in a way that their colleagues of the Hindi press would never be. The Hindi journalists were not only 'closer to the people', occasionally they also appeared to be closer to the power.

'The *Dainik Jagran* interview' that I came across on my computer screen while seeking information on the Kashmir conflict, also relates to a question that I have pointed to several times in the preceding chapters, but not discussed thoroughly. In the introductory chapter I stated that this would be a study of cultural production in a universally well-known form; and in the ethnographic chapters, where I have tried to describe the particularities of Lucknow journalism, there have often been references to parallels elsewhere. I certainly hope that I have not portrayed the Hindi reporter as a strange variety of the familiar mass media profession. But, more precisely, the question is: in which way are these journalists participating in a globally diffused cultural practice? And, more broadly, how should they be understood in the context of globalisation?

The mass media are often thought of in a rather self-evident way when it comes to the processes of cultural globalisation. The flow of news, information, images, ideas and knowledge over long distances and across borders is, of course, greatly dependent on the various forms of mass media. It is through communication technologies that people are able to imagine events far away without leaving their own local place: things that in earlier periods of history were largely bounded and kept apart by time and space have been linked together. If we conceptualise a global interconnectedness, a world integrated by a network of communications interfering in common people's daily lives, media technologies are the crucial instruments (Appadurai, 1996; Castells, 1996; Hannerz, 1996; Held et al., 1999; Tomlinson, 1999; Uimonen, 2001).

It is evident that *Dainik Jagran* also had a role in the global network of news, both in the receiving and in the supplying sense. Every day readers in Lucknow were getting some news in their paper that had reached the editorial office via international news agencies. And, if the *Dainik Jagran* staff came up with some really exclusive story, there was a chance that their work would be distributed to a distant audience (picked up, probably, by the English-language press or by the Indian correspondents of international media organisations). '*The Dainik Jagran* Interview' published in *Outlook* magazine might have been interesting for at least some news agencies outside India, and in relation to the Ayodhya events, for example, *Dainik Jagran* photographers were proud to tell that their work had been published in newspapers across the world.

In the globalisation debate, the 'sceptic' who essentially sees globalisation as a myth (Held et al., 1999: 2–10) would, however, easily find a case in point in the pages of *Dainik Jagran*. To the extent that the growth of Hindi and other vernacular newspapers is a significant recent development of the Indian mass media, a deepening of worldwide interconnectedness is hardly the first thing that comes to mind. Concerned with local places, a region and the nation-state, this press looks more like the opposite of globalisation. After all, the flow of news originating from outside India is rather lean; the international section in *Dainik Jagran* was less than half a page daily. And it was only the most exceptional events that would make the Lucknow reporters actors in the global news network; on their daily beats they rarely came across subjects that would be dispersed outside the region. The Hindi journalists were indeed working with a mass medium that technically knew no borders; the practical work, however, was closely tied to the knowledge and experiences of a local context. In practice, face-to-face relations were a more prominent feature of the profession than were the global connections. And, in light of the fact that the regional/vernacular newspapers have broken an earlier dominance of a more 'cosmopolitan' (Hannerz, 1996) English-language elite press in the public sphere, India in a sense has become less globalised.[2]

The latter conclusion, though, is too rushed. It builds on a parallel, but partial, understanding of the mass media and cultural globalisation in which the common denominator is the flow of information, images, etc. over distances. The understanding of the media as an instrument for transporting information from one place to another should, however, be combined with another aspect: mediated information *passes through* a medium. Technologies of the mass media are not only facilitating a flow of information but are also shaping the content of this flow (cf. Tomlinson, 1999: 154). Thus, while one of the global dimensions of the mass media is that we sometimes share the same images across the world—we enjoy the same soap operas, music videos, sporting events and read similar reports about the same wars and elections—another dimension is that we get completely different images but in similar forms. It is with regard to the latter that I find it most relevant to comprehend the Hindi press in terms of globalisation: the medium that gives shape to everyday reading in *Dainik Jagran* has a form that is quite common world-wide. As Peter Golding observed already two decades ago: "The most striking feature of comparative analyses of news is the similarity of products available around the world" (1979: 304).

To elaborate on this point it is helpful to think along the lines of a framework that Appadurai has provided. He has looked at the relationship between five dimensions of global cultural flows that he has termed 'ethnoscapes', 'mediascapes', 'technoscapes', 'financescapes' and 'ideoscapes' (1996: 33–43). The most obvious dimension to consider would, of course, be the mediascape, which refers to the global distribution of imaginaries (and to the distribution throughout the world of electronic capabilities to produce and disseminate these imaginaries). But, corresponding to my argument above, I would, however, emphasise two other scapes.

One is 'technoscape', and in this dimension *Dainik Jagran* was definitely dependent on a globally dispersed technology for cultural production and distribution. As I have shown in Chapter Two, the state of the vernacular press in India owes much to new technology—the offset press, computer editing and electronic communication—that has recently become available. But the technoscape dimension is, of course, not confined to inventions of the last few decades. The newspaper, as a technical form of cultural production, has not been reinvented anew in each new place on earth where it has appeared. Again, it came to India with British colonialism, together with other institutions of modernity (the bureaucracy, railroads and the education system, for example). The technoscape dimension of globalisation is different from the mediascape in some culturally significant senses. Technology might be in some degree invisible even though it is pervasively present, and as a global mode of cultural production it might easily be disguised in indigenous forms. In the mediascape dimension the global flow is often obvious: a foreign news story has come from far away and tells about something that first and foremost concerns 'other people'. But, the newsreader in Lucknow probably does not pick up his morning paper each day with the reflection in mind that this reading is possible thanks to technology developed somewhere else—and that other people in numerous places around the world are getting *their* local news in a very similar way.

The other dimension of global flows of culture that I find relevant in the context of the Lucknow journalists has to do with ideas. Not primarily the ideas that are printed in the newspaper but ideas about *what* should be printed and *why*. I am convinced that a Lucknow journalist could very well have a fruitful conversation on occupational matters with someone else in the profession from practically any place in the world. They would most probably share a sense of the crucial role of journalism in their respective societies: as representing the people, scrutinising power, investigating misconduct and facilitating public opinion by disseminating important information. Ideas about the occupational role of the journalist seem to be diffused globally together with the great words of an 'enlightened' world-view, such as 'democracy', 'equality' or 'human rights'. This is a dimension that Appadurai has termed the global 'ideoscapes' (ibid.).

It is a central point that the technology and the ideas of journalism are intertwined; they come in a package, so to speak (cf. Golding, 1979). Combining the 'technoscape' and the 'ideoscape' dimensions we may talk about journalism as a globally practised model of cultural production. John W. Meyer and his associates (1997) have argued that the societies of the contemporary world, organised as nation-states, are surprisingly similar in many ways. Despite the variations in history, resources and local practice, a number of rationalised and consensual models structure social life almost everywhere. Journalism is clearly one of these institutionalised models that are apprehended as necessary in modern society, and that have been copied worldwide. Just as every state needs a parliament, schools, courts of law and a police force, so a contemporary society is almost unthinkable without its mass media. Furthermore, journalism is a global model that is extensively concerned with these other global models: with the state and its political and administrative apparatus, in particular. The Lucknow journalists are in this sense doubly imbedded in a world culture. Their practice can hardly be understood in a local context alone.

Trying to relate the Lucknow journalists to a macro-anthropological perspective, Hannerz's discussion around two coexisting major metacultures that are shaping the present-day globalisation of modernity will take us further (1996: 50–55). One is a metaculture of similarity, the other an emphasis on diversity and difference. Neither of these have much to do with the instant flow of global imaginaries that we mostly conceptualise with the mass media. The metaculture of similarity is precisely the diffusion of social practice, particularly at the level of institutions and organisations according to worldwide models, that Meyer has in mind. Hannerz draws on an article of Strang and Meyer (1993) in which they argue that 'theorisation'—as a self-conscious development and specification of abstract categories and the formation of patterned relationships—encourages the diffusion of similar practice. Thus people who are working with vernacular dailies in northern India are not trying to reshape the newspaper in a unique and locally adapted form, or to transform their occupation fully in accordance with indigenous traditions; in general, they are convinced that most things that work elsewhere will also work here. When the Hindi dailies during the 1990s started to carry a women's page, assign a reporter to the environment and publish the stock market prices, or make an Internet edition, it is quite unlikely that it was because of their readers' demand; they clearly conformed to a global model.[3]

The other metaculture has to do with a tendency that "[p]eople everywhere are showing a new level of self-consciousness about culture" (Hannerz, 1996: 52). They are emphasising their difference from others. Ways of living which were previously continuing in an unreflected manner are given new meaning and adjusted to new conditions. The world appears to be made up of a diversity of cultures, in a metaculture of difference. Local and regional newspapers in vernacular languages have increased the density of representation of the society close by. The Hindi newspapers in Lucknow write extensively about people, places and events that would be of absolutely no interest to most people in the world. Nevertheless, this is a feature of cultural globalisation: a higher awareness of local particularities. It is an example of the tendency that "global modernity is often reproduced as local diversity" (Sahlins, 1993: 2).

It is not surprising that the Hindi press is often understood in its relationship to the Hindu nationalist movement in India. The metaculture of difference often comes in a political form, in movements of cultural revival and with claims of collective rights. The *Hindutva* movement in India is a typical example of this kind of cultural revival within the horizon of a global modernity. Their claims of a unique Hindu identity are often asserted in universalistic terms (Hansen, 1999: 232). A press in a vernacular language that sees as one of its main objectives to be 'close to the people' and with its principal antagonists in a more cosmopolitan medium, may be an asset for a movement of cultural revival. Furthermore, Hindu nationalism and the movement of promoting the Hindi language have a common history (King, 1994). I have acknowledged that it is not without foundation to see a link between the contemporary Hindi press and *Hindutva*. If one searches for proprietors, editors and reporters with sympathies with BJP, or for stories with a bias in favour of Hindu nationalism, they will not be hard to find. That is, however, an exercise I have not pursued in this study, and on the whole my ethnography lacks cases with a transparent connection between *Hindutva* and the occupational practice of the Lucknow journalists. Moreover, I was not struck by the dominance of journalists with *Hindutva* sympathies at the editorial offices; rather the opposite. Even though *Dainik Jagran*, for example, had a reputation as a newspaper with loyalties to the BJP (and this was recognised by most of its journalists), there were surprisingly many journalists employed who were outspokenly against the political ideology of this party. I would argue that if the regional Hindi press has an influence on contemporary Indian politics, it is not primarily as a mouthpiece of a particular ideology, but rather as a particular form of imagining society. And this form might work well in consonance with a cultural revivalist movement.

At the same time, I am not convinced that the most significant impact of these newspapers is to cherish an awareness of cultural difference in a radical and confrontational sense. It is still important that all this local news is coupled with news of national and international concern—and with imaginaries of global modernity. The latter might come in relatively small amounts, but 'the global' certainly makes up the horizon even for a Hindi daily. Rethinking his earlier discussion of the newspaper (in *Imagined Communities*) Benedict Anderson has concluded that "[i]t would be *contra naturam* for a newspaper to confine its reports to events within the political realm in which it is published" (1998: 33). As one important base of the formation of collective subjectivities in the modern world, the newspaper is an example of what Anderson calls 'unbound seriality', it is open to the world in a standardised vocabulary that "radically overrides any formal division in the newspaper between local and foreign news" (ibid.). The newspaper reports on politicians, citizens, workers and bureaucrats; these are categories of people that are found all over the world. The Lucknow newspapers may be devoting most interest to events in their own region of circulation, but they certainly take for granted that these *kinds* of events exist elsewhere, and occasionally they also report from faraway places. There is no fundamental difference in the ways people are conceptualised around the world. In this sense, the Hindi press reports on local particularities, but within a discourse of "the world as one whole and the people within it as a single generic humankind" (Held et al., 1999: 369).

One late afternoon at the end of my fieldwork, I was sitting in the political bureau room at *Dainik Jagran*'s office. Most of the reporters had returned from their beats and were busy filing their copies. Everybody was quiet, concentrating on the work. The only sound came from the air-conditioner, or when someone occasionally turned a sheet of paper that had been filled with letters. Suddenly, Girish stopped writing, looked up from the table and broke the silence with a question addressed to no one in particular: "globalisation—what is that in Hindi?"

Notes

1. I use this example merely to illustrate my argument about the generally increased importance of the vernacular press. The fact that the Prime Minister gave an exclusive interview to *Dainik Jagran* could, of course, also be interpreted simply as a favour to a politically loyal newspaper.
2. Another recent development of the Indian mass media that obscures globalisation is the language- and region- specific television channels that during the latter part of the 1990s have largely displaced pan-Indian networks (Sonwalkar, 2001). Furthermore, cable-distributed television in India has a local dimension through cable-operators supplying rather small neighbourhoods with channels that are sometimes also locally produced (Mishra, 1999).
3. How this diffusion of models works in practice is a subject that falls outside the scope of this study. It is also something that probably needs a more multi-sited field approach. For example, several of the Lucknow newspapers had consulted a mass media specialist from Mumbai when they had reorganised their work or in connection with the introduction of new technologies. Another route of diffusion is most likely through the examples of successful south Indian newspapers.

References

Abu-Lughod, Lila. 1993. Finding a place for Islam: Egyptian television serials and the national interest. *Public Culture* 5: 493–513.

Ahmed, Akbar S. 1992. Bombay films: The cinema as metaphor for Indian society and politics. *Modern Asian Studies* 26(2): 289–320.

An Atlas of India. 1990. New Delhi: Oxford University Press.

Anderson, Benedict. 1991. *Imagined Communities: Reflections on the Origin and Spread of Nationalism*. London: Verso.

——. 1998. *The Spectre of Comparisons: Nationalism, Southeast Asia and the World*. London and New York: Verso.

Appadurai, Arjun. 1988. Putting hierarchy in its place. *Cultural Anthropology* 3: 36–49.

——. 1996. *Modernity at Large: Cultural Dimensions of Globalization*. Minneapolis: University of Minnesota Press.

Appadurai, Arjun and Carol A. Breckenridge. 1995. Public modernity in India. In *Consuming Modernity: Public Culture in a South Asian World*. ed. Carol Breckenridge. Minneapolis: University of Minnesota Press.

Bathla, Sonia. 1998. *Women, Democracy and the Media: Cultural and Political Representations in the Indian Press*. New Delhi: Sage.

Becker, Lee B., Idowa A. Sobowale and Robin E. Cobbey. 1979. Reporters and their professional and organizational commitment. *Journalism Quarterly* (Winter): 753–63.

Bensman, Joseph and Robert Lilienfeld. 1973. *Craft and Consciousness*. New York: John Wiley and Sons.

Béteille, André. 1994. The family and the reproduction of inequality. In *Family, Kinship and Marriage in India*, edited by Patricia Uberoi. Delhi: Oxford University Press.

Bird, Elisabeth (ed). 2010. *The Anthropology of News and Journalism: Global Perspectives.* Bloomington and Indianapolis: Indiana University Press.

Bourdieu, Pierre. 1990. *The Logic of Practice*. Stanford, CA: Stanford University Press.

——. 1993. *The Field of Cultural Production: Essays on Art and Literature*. Cambridge: Polity Press.

Boyer, Dominic and Ulf Hannerz (eds). 2006. Introduction: Worlds of Journalism. Special issue of *Ethnography*, 7(1): 5-16.

Brass, Paul. 1994. *The Politics of India Since Independence*. Cambridge: Cambridge University Press.

Brosius, Christiane and Melissa Butcher (eds.). 1999. *Image Journeys: Audio-visual Media and Cultural Change in India*. New Delhi: Sage.

Burrage, Michael and Rolf Torstendahl. 1990. *Professions in Theory and History: Rethinking the Study of Professions*. London: Sage.

Carey, James. 1986. Why and how? The dark continent of American journalism. In *Reading the News*, edited by Robert Karl Manoff and Michael Schudson. New York: Pantheon Books.

——. 1989. *Communication as Culture: Essays on Media and Society*. Boston, MA: Unwin Hyman.

Carroll, Lucy. 1973. Kayashta samachar: From a caste to a national newspaper. *The Indian Economic and Social History Review* 10: 280–92.

Castells, Manuel. 1996. *The Rise of the Network Society, The Information Age: Economy, Society and Culture*. Volume 1. Oxford: Blackwell Publisher.

Chatterjee, Partha. 1994. *The Nation and its Fragments: Colonial and Postcolonial Histories*. Delhi: Oxford University Press.

Cohn, Berhard. 1997. *Colonialism and its Forms of Knowledge: The British in India*. Delhi: Oxford University Press.

Curran, James and Myung-Jin Park. 2000. *De-Westernizing Media Studies*. London and New York: Routledge.

Dickey, Sara. 1993. *Cinema and the Urban Poor in South India*. Cambridge and New Delhi: Cambridge University Press.

——.1995. Consuming Utopia. In *Consuming Modernity: Public Culture in a South Asian World*. ed. Carol Breckenridge. Minneapolis: University of Minnesota Press.

——.1997. Anthropology and its contribution to studies of mass media. *International Social Science Journal* 49(3): 413–27.

Dirks, Nicholas B. 2001. *Castes of Mind: Colonialism and the Making of Modern India*. Princeton, NJ and Oxford: Princeton University Press.

Dornfeld, Barry. 1998. *Producing Public Television, Producing Public Culture*. Princeton, NJ: Princeton University Press.

Elliott, Philip. 1979. Media organizations and occupations: An overview. In *Mass Communication and Society,* edited by James Curran, Michael Gurevitch and Jane Woollacott. Beverly Hills, CA: Sage.

Engineer, Asghar Ali. 1991. Press on Ayodhya 'kar seva'. *Economic and Political Weekly*, May 18, 1263–6.

Ericson, Richard V., Patricia M. Baranek and Janet B.L. Chan. 1989. *Negotiating Control: A Study of News Sources*. Milton Keynes: Open University Press.

Escobar, Arthuro. 2002. Culture sits in laces: Reflections on globalism and subaltern strategies of localization. *Political Geography* 20: 139–174

Farmer, Victoria L. 1996. Mass media, images, mobilization and communalism. In *Making India Hindu: Religion, Community and the Politics of Democracy in India*, edited by David Ludden. Delhi: Oxford University Press.

Fernandes, Leela. 2000. Nationalizing 'the global': Media images, cultural politics and the middle class in India. *Media, Culture and Society* 22: 611–28.

Fisher, Michael H. 1997. Awadh and the English East India Company. In *Memories of a City*, ed. Violette Graff. Delhi: Oxford University Press.

Fishman, M. 1980. *Manufacturing the News*. Austin, TX: University of Texas Press.

Foster, Robert. 1991. Making national cultures in the global ecumene. *Annual Review of Anthropology* 20: 235–60.

Fraser, Nancy. 1993. Rethinking the public sphere: Contribution to the critique of actually existing democracy. In *Habermas and the Public Sphere*, edited by Craig Calhoun. Cambridge, MA and London: MIT Press.

Freidson, Eliot. 1994. *Professionalism Reborn*. Cambridge: Polity Press.

Fuglesang, Minou. 1994. *Veils and Videos: Female Youth Culture on the Kenyan Coast*. Stockholm Studies in Social Anthropology 32. Stockholm: Almqvist and Wiksell International.

Gans, H.J. 1979. *Deciding What's News*. New York: Pantheon.

Giddens, Anthony. 1990. *The Consequences of Modernity*. Stanford, CA: Stanford University Press.

Ginsburg, Fay. 1991. Indigenous media: Faustian contract or global village. *Cultural Anthropology* 6(1): 92–112.

——. 1993. Aboriginal media and the Australian imaginary. *Public Culture* 5: 557–78.

——. 1994. Culture/media: A (mild) polemic. *Anthropology Today* 10(2): 5–15.

Ginsburg, Fay, Lila Abu-Lughod and Brian Larkin (eds.). 2002. *Media Worlds: Anthropology on New Terrain*. Berkeley, CA and London: University of California Press.

Golding, Peter. 1979. Media professionalism in the Third World: The transfer of an ideology. In *Mass Communication and Society*, edited by James Curran, Michael Gurevitch and Jane Woollacott. Beverly Hills, CA: Sage.

Gouldner, Alwin W. 1979. *The Future of Intellectuals and the Rise of the New Class*. London: Macmillan.

Gupta, Akhil. 1995. Blurred boundaries: The discourse of corruption, the culture of politics and the imagined state. *American Ethnologist* 22(2): 375–402.

Habermas, Jürgen. 1989 [1962]. *The Structural Transformation of the Public Sphere: An Inquiry into a Category of Bourgeois Society*. Cambridge: Polity Press.

Hachten, William A. 1993. *The Growth of Media in the Third World*. Ames, IO: Iowa State University Press.

Hannerz, Ulf. 1992. *Cultural Complexity*. New York: Columbia University Press.

——. 1995. Trouble in the global village. *Antropologiska Studier* 52–53: 5–19.

——. 1996. *Transnational Connections: Culture, People, Places*. London and New York: Routledge.

——. 1998a. Other transnationals: Perspectives gained from studying sideways. *Paideuma* 44: 109–23

——. 1998b. Of correspondents and collages. *Anthropological Journal on European Cultures* 7: 91–109.

——. 1998c. Reporting from Jerusalem. *Cultural Anthropology* 13(4): 548–74.

——. 2001. Dateline Tokyo: Telling the world about Japan. In *Asian Media Productions*, edited by Brian Moeran. London: Curzon.

——. 2002. Among the foreign correspondents: Reflections on anthropological styles and audiences. *Ethnos* 67(1): 57–74.

——. 2004. *Foreign News: Exploring the World of Foreign Correspondents*. Chicago and London: University of Chicago Press.

Hansen, Thomas Blom. 1999. *The Saffron Wave: Democracy and Hindu Nationalism in Modern India*. Delhi: Oxford University Press.

——. 2000. Predicaments of secularism: Muslim identities and politics in Mumbai. *Journal of the Royal Anthropological Institute* 6(2): 255–74.

——. 2001. *Wages of Violence: Naming and Identity in Postcolonial Bombay*. Princeton, NJ and Oxford: Princeton University Press.

Hansen, Thomas Blom and Finn Stepputat (eds.). 2001. *States of Imagination: Ethnographic Explorations of the Postcolonial State*. Durham, NC and London: Duke University Press.

Hardtmann, Eva-Maria. 2002. In touch with politics: Three individuals in the midst of the Dalit movement. In *Contesting 'Good Governance': Crosscultural Perspectives on Representation, Accountability and Public Space*, edited by Eva Poluha and Mona Rosendahl. London and New York: Routledge/Curzon.

Hasan, Zoya. 1998. *Quest for Power: Oppositional Movements and Post-Congress Politics in Uttar Pradesh*. Delhi: Oxford University Press.

Held, David, Anthony McGrew, David Goldblatt and Jonathan Perraton. 1999. *Global Transformations: Politics, Economy and Culture*. Cambridge: Polity Press.

Holy, Ladislav and Milan Stucklik. 1983. *Actions, Norms and Representations: Foundations of Anthropological Inquiry*. Cambridge: Cambridge University Press.

Hughes, Everett. 1971. *The Sociological Eye: Selected Papers*. Chicago: Aldine Atherton.

Inden, Ronald. 1999. Transnational class, erotic arcadia and commercial utopia in Hindi films. In *Image Journeys: Audio-visual Media and Cultural Change in India*, eds. Christiane Brosius and Melissa Butcher. New Delhi: Sage Publications.

India 1999: A Reference Annual. 1999. New Delhi: Publications Division, Ministry of Information and Broadcasting.

Israel, Milton. 1994. *Communication and Power: Propaganda and the Press in the Indian Nationalist Struggle, 1920–1947*. Cambridge: Cambridge University Press.

Jeffrey, Robin. 1993. Indian-language newspapers and why they grow. *Economic and Political Weekly* 27: 2004–11.

——.1997a. Indian-language newspapers 1, Malayalam: 'The day-to-day social life of the people ...'. *Economic and Political Weekly* 32: 18–21.

——. 1997b. Indian-language newspapers 2, Hindi: 'Taking the Punjab Kesri line'. *Economic and Political Weekly* 32: 77–83.

——. 1997c. Indian-language newspapers 3, Bengali: 'Professional, somewhat conservative' and Calcuttan. *Economic and Political Weekly* 32: 141–4.

——. 1997d. Indian-language newspapers 4, Telugu: 'Ingredients of growth and failure'. *Economic and Political Weekly* 32: 192–5.

——. 2009[2000]. *India's Newspaper Revolution: Capitalism, Politics and the Indian-Language Press 1977–99*. New Delhi: Oxford University Press.

Johnson, Kirk. 2001. Media and social change: The modernizing influences of television in rural India. *Media, Culture and Society* 23: 147–69.

Joshi, Prabash. 1996. Ek nayii bhumikaa pratiikshaa mein hai (A new role is awaiting). *Vidura* 33(4): 45–7.

Kang, Bhavdeep. 2001. Of writes and wrongs. *Outlook Magazine,* 3 December.

Kaniss, Phyllis. 1991. *Making Local News*. Chicago and London: University of Chicago Press.

Katz, Elihu. 1989. Journalists as scientists: Notes toward an occupational classification. *American Behavioral Scientist* 33(2): 238–46.

Kepplinger, Hans Mathias and Renate Köcher. 1990. Professionalism in the media world? *European Journal of Communication* 5: 285–311.

Khilnani, Sunil. 1997. *The Idea of India*. London: Hamish Hamilton.

King, Christoffer R. 1994. *One Language, Two Scripts: The Hindi Movement in Nineteenth Century North India*. Bombay: Oxford University Press.

Kinsley, David. 1987. *Hindu Goddesses: Visions of the Divine Feminine in the Hindu Religious Tradition*. New Delhi: Archives Publishers.

Köcher, Renate. 1986. Bloodhounds or missionaries: Role definitions of German and British journalists. *European Journal of Communication* 1: 43–64.

Kumar, Anup. 2011. *The Making of a Small State: Populist Social Mobilization and the Hindi Press in the Uttarakhand Movement*. New Delhi: Orient Blackswan.

Larson, Magali Sarfatti. 1977. *The Rise of Professionalism: A Sociological Analysis*. Berkeley, CA: University of California Press.

Lelyveld, David. 1993. The fate of Hindustani: Colonial knowledge and the project of a national language. In *Orientalism and the Postcolonial Predicament*, edited by Carol Breckenridge and Peter van der Veer. Philadelphia, PA: University of Pennsylvania Press.

——. 1995. Upon the subdominant: Administering music on All-India Radio. In In *Consuming Modernity: Public Culture in a South Asian World*. ed. Carol Breckenridge. Minneapolis: University of Minnesota Press.

Lindquist, Johan. 2001. *The Anxieties of Mobility: Development, Migration and Tourism in the Indonesian Borderlands*. Stockholm: Department of Social Anthropology, Stockholm University.

Madan, T.N. 1987. Secularism in its place. *Journal of Asian Studies* 46: 747–59.

Malkki, Liisa H. 1997. News and culture: Transitory phenomena and the fieldwork tradition. In *Anthropological Locations*, edited by Akhil Gupta and James Ferguson. Berkeley, CA: University of California Press.

Mankekar, D.R. 1978. *The Press vs the Government*. New Delhi: Clarion Books.

Mankekar, Purnima. 1999. *Screening Culture, Viewing Politics: An Ethnography of Television, Womanhood and Nation in Postcolonial India*. Durham, NC and London: Duke University Press.

Manoff, Robert Karl and Michael Schudson. 1986. Reading the news. In *Reading the News*, edited by Manoff and Schudson. New York: Pantheon Books.

Manuel, Peter. 1993. *Cassette Culture: Popular Music and Technology in North India*. Chicago and London: University of Chicago Press.

Marcus, George E. 1995. Ethnography in/of the world system: The emergence of multi-sited ethnography. *Annual Review of Anthropology* 24: 95–117.

McLuhan, Marshall. 1994. *Understanding Media: The Extensions of Man*. Cambridge, MA and London: MIT Press.

Meyer, John W., John Boli, George M. Thomas and Francisco O. Ramirez. 1997. World society and the nation-state. *American Journal of Sociology* 103: 144–81.

Mishra, Samina. 1999. Dish is life: Cable operators and the neighbourhood. In *Image Journeys: Audio-visual Media and Cultural Change in India*, eds. Christiane Brosius and Melissa Butcher. New Delhi: Sage Publications.

Mitra, Ananda. 1993. *Television and Popular Culture in India: A Study of the Mahabharat*. New Delhi: Sage.

Molund, Stefan. 1988. *First We are People …: The Koris of Kanpur between Caste and Class*. Stockholm Studies in Social Anthropology 20. Stockholm: Almqvist and Wiksell International.

Munshi, Shoma. 1998. Wife/mother/daughter-in-law: Multiple avatars of homemaker in 1990s Indian advertising. *Media, Culture and Society* 20: 573–91.

Nader, Laura. 1972. Up the anthropologist—perspectives gained from studying up. In *Reinventing Anthropology*, edited by Dell Hymes. New York: Pantheon.

Naim, C.M. and Carla Petievich. 1997. Urdu in Lucknow/Lucknow in Urdu. In *Memories of a City*, ed. Violette Graff. Delhi: Oxford University Press.

Nandy, Ashis. 1988. The politics of secularism and the recovery of religious intolerance. *Alternatives* 8: 177–94.

——. 1998. Introduction: Indian popular cinema as a slum's eye view of politics. In *The Secret Politics of Our Desire: Innocence, Culpability and the Indian Popular Cinema*, edited by Ashis Nandy. Delhi: Oxford University Press.

Nandy, Ashis, Shikha Trivedi, Shail Mayaram and Achyot Yagnik. 1995. *Creating a Nationality*. Delhi: Oxford University Press.

Narain, Kirti. 1998. *Press, Politics and Society: Uttar Pradesh, 1885–1914*. New Delhi: Manohar.

Natarajan, S. 1962. *A History of the Press in India*. Bombay and London: Asia Publishing House.

Navlakha, Suren. 1989. *Elite and Social Change: A Study of Elite Formation in India*. New Delhi, Newbury Park and London: Sage.

Neyazi, Taberez Ahmed. 2010. Cultural imperialism or vernacular modernity? Hindi newspapers in a globalizing India. *Media Culture and Society*, 32(6): 907–24.

——. 2011. Politics after vernacularization: Hindi media and Indian democracy. *Economic and Political Weekly*, XLVI(10): 75-81.

Ninan, Sevanti. 1995. *Through the Magic Window: Television and Change in India*. New Delhi: Penguin Books.

——. 2007. *Headlines from the Heartland: Reinventing the Hindi Public Sphere*. New Delhi: Sage.

Nireekshak. 2000. Media watch: Unnecessary controversy. *Economic and Political Weekly*, 25 November.

Ochs, Elinor and Lisa Capps. 1996. Narrating the self. *Annual Review of Anthropology* 25: 19–43.

Pande, Mrinal. 1996. Ek rahin hindii ek rahin patrakaaritaa (Hindi is one thing, journalism another). *Vidura* 33(4): 48–50.

Pandey, Gyanendra. 1990. *The Construction of Communalism in Colonial North India*. Delhi: Oxford University Press.

Pandian, M.S.S. 1992. *The Image Trap: M.G. Ramachandran in Film and Politics*. New Delhi: Sage.

Pant-Joshi, Kusum. 1991. The choice of a capital: Lucknow under the British. In *The City in Indian History*, edited by Indu Banga. New Delhi: Manohar.

Parry, J.P. 1989. The Brahmanical tradition and the technology of the intellect. In *Literacy and Society*, edited by Karen Schousboe and Mogens Trolle Larson. Copenhagen: Akademisk Forlag.

Parthasarathy, Rangaswami. 1995. *Journalism in India: From the Earliest Times to the Present Day*. New Delhi: Sterling Publishers.

Pedelty, Mark. 1995. *War Stories*. New York: Routledge.

Pemble, John. 1977. *The Raj, the Indian Mutiny and the Kingdom of Oudh, 1801–1859*. Delhi: Oxford University Press.

Peters, John Durham. 1997. Seeing bifocally: Media, place, culture. In *Culture, Power, Place: Explorations in Critical Anthropology*, eds. Akhil Gupta and James Ferguson. Durham, NC and London: Duke University Press.

Prasad, Madhava M. 1998. *Ideology of the Hindi Film: A Historical Construction*. Delhi: Oxford University Press.

Press Council of India. 1996. *Norms of Journalistic Conduct*. New Delhi: Press Council of India.

——. 1997. *18th Annual Report*. New Delhi: Press Council of India.

——. 1998. Report of the Committee Constituted by the Press Council of India to Conduct a Comprehensive Study on All India Basis with Regard to All Kind of Favours Extended to Journalists by various Authorities (1985–1995). File No. 17/13/95–PCI.

Radcliff, Sara A. 2001. Imagining the state as a space: Territoriality and the formation of the state in Equador. In *States of Imagination: Ethnographic Explorations of the Postcolonial State*, edited by Thomas Blom Hansen and Finn Stepputat. Durham, NC and London: Duke University Press.

Rajagopal, Arvind. 1993. The rise of national programming: The case of Indian television. *Media, Culture and Society* 15(1): 91–110.

——. 2001. *Politics after Television: Hindu Nationalism and the Reshaping of the Public Sphere in India*. Cambridge: Cambridge University Press.

—— (ed). 2009. *The Indian Public Sphere: Readings in Media History*. New Delhi: Oxford University Press.

Rao, K. Vikram. 1996. Patrakaar dekhen, sunen magar jaanchen, phir likhen. (Journalists may watch and listen, but before writing they should investigate.) *Patrakaar Sadan*, January/February: 13–16.

Rao, Ursula. 2010. *News as Culture: Journalistic Practices and the Remaking of Indian Leadership Traditions*. New York and Oxford: Berghahn.

Rau, Chalapathi. 1968. *The Press in India*. Bombay: Allied Publishers.

Reeves, Peter. 1997. Lucknow politics: 1920–47. In *Memories of a City*, ed. Violette Graff. Delhi: Oxford University Press.

Robinson, Frances. 1997. The re-emergence of Lucknow as a major political centre. In *Memories of a City*, ed. Violette Graff. Delhi: Oxford University Press.

Rudolph, Lloyd I. 1992. The media and cultural politics. *Economic and Political Weekly*, July 11,1489–96.

Sahlins, Marshall. 1993. Goodbye to Tristes Tropes: Ethnography in the context of modern world history. *Journal of Modern History* 65: 1–25.

Salaman, Graem. 1974. *Community and Occupation*. Cambridge: Cambridge University Press.

Sardar, Ziauddin. 1998. Dilip Kumar made me do it. In *The Secret Politics of Our Desire: Innocence, Culpability and the Indian Popular Cinema*, edited by Ashis Nandy. Delhi: Oxford University Press.

Schlesinger, Philip. 1978. *Putting 'Reality' Together*. London: Constable.

Schudson, Michael. 1995. *The Power of News*. Cambridge, MA and London: Harvard University Press.

——. 1991. The sociology of news production revisited. In *Mass Media and Society,* edited by James Curran and Michael Gurevitch. London: Edward Arnold.

——. 2002. The news media as political institutions. *Annual Review of Political Science* 5: 249–69.

Sheth, D.L. 1995. The great language debate: Politics of metropolitan versus vernacular India. In *Crisis and Change in Contemporary India*, edited by Upendra Baxi and Bhiku Parekh. New Delhi: Sage.

Shils, Edward. 1961. *The Intellectual between Tradition and Modernity: The Indian Situation*. The Hague: Mouton.

Sigal, Leon V. 1986. Who? Sources make the news. In *Reading the News*, edited by Robert Karl Manoff and Michael Schudson. New York: Pantheon Books.

Singhal, Arvind and Everett M. Rogers. 1989. *India's Information Revolution*. New Delhi: Sage.

Soloski, John. 1989. News reporting and professionalism: Some constraints on the reporter of the news. *Media Culture and Society* 11: 207–28.

Sonwalkar, Prasun. 2001. India: Makings of little cultural/media imperialism? *Gazette* 63(6): 505–19.

Spitulnik, Debra. 1992. Radio time sharing and the negotiating of linguistic pluralism in Zambia. *Pragmatics* 2(3): 335–54.

——. 1993. Anthropology and mass media. *Annual Review of Anthropology* 22: 293–315.

——. 1995. 'Making money': Corporate culture and the commoditization in Zambian broadcasting. In *Money and Moral Economics in Africa*, edited by J.L. Comaroff and J. Comaroff. Chicago: Chicago University Press.

Srikandat, Sivaram. 1991. Cultural values depicted in Indian television advertising. *Gazette* 48: 165–76.

Srivatsan, R. 1991. Looking at film hoardings: Labour, gender and everyday life in India. *Public Culture* 4(1): 1–22.

Ståhlberg, Per. 2002. The illicit daughter: Hindi-language newspapers and the regionalisation of the public sphere in India. In *Contesting 'Good' Governance: Crosscultural Perspectives on Representation, Accountability and Public Space*, edited by Eva Poluha and Mona Rosendahl. London and New York: Routledge/Curzon.

Strang, David and John W. Meyer. 1993. Institutional conditions for diffusion. *Theory and Society* 22: 487–511.

Sullivan, Nancy. 1993. Film and television production in Papua New Guinea: How media become the message. *Public Culture* 5: 533–55.

Taylor, Charles. 2002. Modern social imaginaries. *Public Culture* 14(1): 91–124.

Thomas, Rosie. 1996. Melodrama and the Negotiation of Morality in Mainstream Hindi Film. In *Consuming Modernity: Public Culture in a South Asian World*. ed. Carol Breckenridge. Minneapolis: University of Minnesota Press.

Thompson, John B. 1995. *The Media and Modernity: A Social Theory of the Media*. Cambridge: Polity Press.

Tomlinson, John. 1999. *Globalization and Culture*. Chicago: University of Chicago Press.

Tuchman, Gaye. 1978. *Making News*. New York: Free Press.

Turner, Terence. 1992. Defiant images: The Kayapo appropriation of video. *Anthropology Today* 8(6): 5–16.

Uimonen, Paula. 2001. *Transnational.Dynamics@Development.Net: Internet, Modernization and Globalisation*. Stockholm Studies in Social Anthropology 49. Stockholm: Almqvist and Wiksell International.

Upadhyaya, Prakash Chandra. 1992. The politics of Indian secularism. *Modern Asian Studies* 26(4): 815–53.

Valicha, Kishore. 1988. *The Moving Image: A Study of Indian Cinema*. Bombay: Orient Longman.

van der Veer, Peter. 1994. *Religious Nationalism: Hindus and Muslims in India*. Delhi: Oxford University Press.

Varadarajan, Siddharth. 1999. The Ink Link: Media, communalism and the evasion of politics. In *The Concerned Indian's Guide to Communalism*, edited by K.N. Panikkar. New Delhi: Viking.

Varma, Pavan K. 1998. *The Great Indian Middle Class*. New Delhi: Penguin Books.

Varshney, Ashutosh. 2002. *Ethnic Conflict and Civic Life: Hindus and Muslims in India*. New Haven, CT and London: Yale University Press.

Vidura. 1992. Who is afraid of Hindi journalism? 29(2): 4–19.

——. 1995. Editors Guild Report: Halla bol and the Press, 32(1): 12–14.

——. 1996. Editors Notebook: Two edged news technology, 33(4): 1.

Weaver, David H. and Cleveland Wilhoit. 1991. *The American Journalist: A Portrait of U.S. Newspeople and their Work*. Bloomington, IN: Indiana University Press.

Weiner, Myron. 1965. India: Two political cultures. In *Political Culture and Political Development*, edited by Lucian W. Pye and Sidney Verba. Princeton, New Jersey: Princeton University Press.

Wilkinson-Weber, Claire M. 1999. *Embroidering Lives: Women's Work and Skill in the Lucknow Embroidery Industry*. Albany, NY: State University of New York Press.

Wood, Mike. 1999. Rimbunan Hijau versus the World Bank and Australian miners: Print media representations of forestry policy conflict in Papua New Guinea. *Australian Journal of Anthropology* 10(2): 175–90.

Yadava, J.S. 1991. Press system in India. *Media Asia* 18(3).

Index